MW00781785

*Acts and The Movement of God* is a cc
move, and his desire is for the entire w
understands this and, using Acts, shows us that it is God's plan for his people
to be his messengers, whether that be in our own backyards or halfway across
the world. This book gives the means and methods for sharing God's love, and
it will ignite a passion within readers to see God move with power to the ends
of the earth.

DAVE FERGUSON, lead visionary, NewThing; author, *B.L.E.S.S.*

A great way to describe what God is doing in movements is, "It's like the Book of
Acts is happening again in our day." That's why I'm so thankful Steve has written
this book detailing the movement of God in Acts and drawing out the timeless
truths it contains.

CHRIS GALANOS, author, *From Megachurch to Multiplication*; pastor,
Experience Life

Steve Addison has given us another powerful book on movements. In *Acts and
the Movement of God*, he masterfully unpacks what the Holy Spirit did in the
book of Acts over a period of about forty years, following the resurrection of
Christ. Addison boldly challenges us to embrace God's holy disruption from
our ways of doing the church to that of God's. I encourage you to study this
book, reflect on the best practices gathered from around the world, apply the
principles, and help build God's movement through intentional multiplication of
disciples and churches.

BEKELE SHANKO, leader, Global Church Movements, Cru; president,
GACX—a global alliance for church multiplication

Steve Addison's work offers us a lens to consider contemporary practice. Will
the millennial mission movement be found faithful? We will see. Carefully
weighing the practices of our generation is a stewardship. Addison leads in this
direction.

NATHAN SHANK, affinity global strategist, South Asian Peoples, IMB; author,
*The 4-Fields Manual*

Every disciple maker's most important textbook is the book of Acts. As you
study Acts, Addison's insights, inspiring stories, and commentary will propel you
forward in fulfilling the mission of God—to multiply thousands of new disciples
in your area. This is recommended study material for everyone pursuing disciple
making movements!

C. ANDERSON, founder, DMMs Frontier Missions

Steve Addison does an incredible job of providing a clear, biblical, and experiential look at Acts and the movement of God. I'll be recommending this book to our workers around the world who are pursuing movements of disciples and churches.

SCOTT CHEATHAM, president, e3 Partners

The book of Acts describes the unfinished story of the church that keeps rapidly emerging in unfamiliar places, as the gospel movement continues its journey. I am delighted to recommend *Acts and the Movement of God*. This book will be around for a long time, helping generations understand the message of Acts in their world.

VICTOR JOHN, CPM strategist, catalyst and facilitator; coauthor, *Bhojpuri Breakthrough: A Movement that Keeps Multiplying*

# ACTS

## AND THE

## MOVEMENT

# GOD

OF

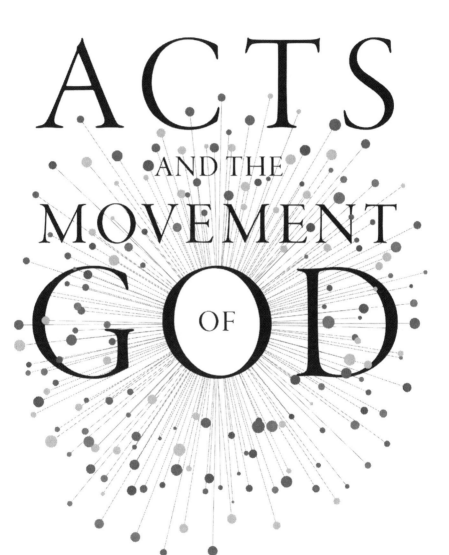

# ALSO BY STEVE ADDISON

*Movements That Change the World: Five Keys to Spreading the Gospel (2009)*

*What Jesus Started: Joining the Movement, Changing the World (2012)*

*Pioneering Movements: Leadership That Multiplies Disciples and Churches (2015)*

*The Rise and Fall of Movements: A Roadmap for Leaders (2019)*

*Your Part in God's Story: 40 Days from Genesis to Revelation (2021)*

FROM JERUSALEM TO THE ENDS OF THE EARTH

# ACTS

## AND THE

## MOVEMENT

# GOD

OF

# STEVE

# ADDISON

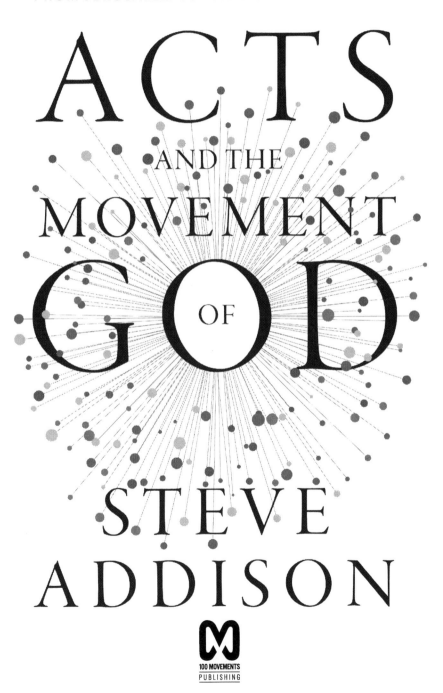

100 MOVEMENTS
PUBLISHING

ISBN 978-1-955142-33-5 (print)
ISBN 978-1-955142-34-2 (ebook)

Front cover design: Jeff Miller
Cover jacket and interior design: Revo Creative Ltd
Interior illustration: Peter Bergmeier

Maps on page 11 and page 71 taken from *What Jesus Started* by Steve Addison. Copyright (c) 2012 by Steve Addison. Used by permission of InterVarsity Press, P.O. Box 1400, Downers Grove, IL 60515, USA. www.ivpress.com

100 Movements Publishing
An imprint of Movement Leaders Collective
Cody, Wyoming

www.movementleaderscollective.com
www.catalysechange.org

*To Jeff and Angie*

*Then he opened their minds so they could understand the Scriptures.*
LUKE 24:45

# CONTENTS

*List of* Deeper *Sections*                                                      xi
*Acts Timeline*                                                                  xiii
*Foreword by Peyton Jones*                                                       xv
*Introduction*                                                                   xvii

1   The Mission of the Risen Lord (1:1–11)                                        1

2   Filling Jerusalem (1:12–5:42)                                                 7

3   Out of Jerusalem (6:1–12:25)                                                 59

4   The Movement Into Europe (13:1–15:34)                                       115

5   The Gospel Goes to the Greeks (15:35–18:17)                                 135

6   The Word Reaches Asia Minor (18:18–20:38)                                   159

7   Trials and Triumph (21:1–28:31)                                             187

*Appendices*                                                                    221
*Bibliography*                                                                   229
*Notes*                                                                          239
*Acknowledgments*                                                                271
*About the Author*                                                               273

# LIST OF *DEEPER* SECTIONS

*These sections take an in-depth look at important themes that arise across the whole of Acts.*

| | |
|---|---|
| The Father's Plan | 5 |
| Acts of the Risen Lord | 9 |
| The Movement of the Holy Spirit | 12 |
| The Message | 19 |
| The Church | 27 |
| Apostles | 31 |
| Prayer | 40 |
| Poverty and Riches | 43 |
| The Battle | 49 |
| Peter and the Shaping of a Movement Leader | 54 |
| The Word | 63 |
| Persecution | 68 |
| Baptism | 78 |
| Signs, Wonders, Word | 87 |
| Household Conversions | 93 |
| How the First Church Became a Movement | 111 |
| The Mission | 123 |
| Divine Disruption | 130 |
| The Gospel for Pagans | 151 |
| Movements and Money | 161 |
| The Difference Teams Make | 172 |
| Local Leaders | 184 |
| Prophets | 189 |
| Rulers and Authorities | 203 |
| Paul and the Shaping of a Movement Leader | 211 |

# ACTS TIMELINE[1]

| Date | Event | Reference |
|------|-------|-----------|
| *26/27* | *John the Baptist's ministry* | *Acts 1:5* |
| *27–30* | *Jesus' ministry* | *Acts 1:1* |
| *30* | *Crucifixion and resurrection of Jesus* | *Acts 1:1–11* |
| *30–41* | *Mission to Jerusalem* | *Acts 2–5* |
| *31/32* | *Death of Stephen* | *Acts 6–7* |
| | *Philip's mission to Samaria* | *Acts 8* |
| | *Disciples flee Jerusalem to Antioch* | *Acts 11:19–24* |
| | *Conversion and call of Saul–Paul near Damascus* | *Acts 9; Gal. 1* |
| *32/33* | *Mission of Paul in Arabia and Damascus* | *Acts 9:19–22; Gal. 1:17* |
| *34–42* | *Mission of Peter in Judea, Galilee, Samaria, and the coastal plain* | *Acts 9:32–43* |
| | *Mission of Paul in Syria and Cilicia* | *Acts 9:19–25, 30; Gal. 1:21–24* |
| *37* | *Mission of Peter in Joppa and Caesarea* | *Acts 10–11* |
| | *Conversion of Cornelius, a Roman centurion in Caesarea* | *Acts 10* |
| 41 | Persecution of the Jerusalem church by Herod Agrippa I | Acts 12:1–4 |
| | James the apostle executed by Agrippa I | Acts 12:17 |
| | Peter and the apostles leave Jerusalem for new fields | Acts 12:17 |
| | James and the elders lead the church in Jerusalem | Acts 12:17; 21:18 |
| *42–44* | Paul and Barnabas active in Syrian Antioch | Acts 11:25–26 |
| *44* | *Church in Antioch provides famine relief for Jerusalem Christians* | *Acts 11:27–30; 12:25* |
| *45–47* | *Mission of Paul and Barnabas to Cyprus and southern Galatia* | *Acts 13–14* |
| *48* | *Council in Jerusalem* | *Acts 15* |
| *49* | *Mission of Barnabas and John Mark on Cyprus* | *Acts 15:39* |
| *49–52* | *Mission of Paul in Macedonia and Achaia* | *Acts 16–18* |

| Date | Event | Reference |
|------|-------|-----------|
| 49 | Disturbances in Rome over "Chrestus." Jews expelled | Acts 18:2 |
| 50–51 | Paul's mission to Corinth | Acts 18 |
| 52–55 | Paul's mission to Ephesus | Acts 19 |
| | Paul visits Corinth and returns to Ephesus<br>Paul travels from Ephesus to Troas<br>Paul stays in Macedonia over the winter | Acts 20:1–4 |
| 56 | Mission of Paul in Illyricum (?) | Rom. 15:19 |
| | Paul visits Achaia/Corinth | Acts 20:1–6 |
| 57–59 | Paul arrested in Jerusalem, imprisonment in Caesarea | Acts 21–26 |
| 60–62 | Paul a prisoner in Rome | Acts 28:11–31 |
| 62 | Paul executed (?) | |
| 62–67 | Paul released, continued his mission, re–arrested and executed in Rome around the same time as Peter (?) | |

# FOREWORD

Steve Addison has established himself as the foremost movement scholar in the church today. Steve is not just a theorist, writing dry, dusty, theological treatises; he is also a practitioner, and because of this, his books are a living, vibrant chronicle of how God moves.

In *Church Plantology: The Art and Science of Planting Churches*, I proposed three overlapping circles, focused on timeless principles of planting practiced by the apostles that still apply to planters today; principles for planting anywhere, with anyone, during any time. Those three overlapping circles consisted of 1) the pages of Acts, 2) church history, and 3) global missional practice. I constantly found myself reaching for Steve's books because all three are in his purview of study.

Of all Steve's books, *Acts and the Movement of God* is the one I am most excited to hit the shelves. Not only is it the book I will find myself giving away more than any other, but it has also been the greatest delight to read. That's because it goes straight to the source of all missionary endeavors; the Scriptures themselves. Steve brings his acumen to the book of Acts in a way that I've come to appreciate as a missiologist practitioner. Unlike so many authors, when Steve writes about Acts, it is as if there is no demarcation between what has gone before and what God continues to do in the world; and that is because there truly isn't any.

In reading this book, you will come away with three principles. First, as you are brought into the strange and unfamiliar world of the first century, you will come to see that the challenges they faced are not unlike our own. Steve asserts at the outset that "to ignore the lessons of Acts is an act of pride." If the church in Acts faced similar challenges to us today, is it possible that their solutions could be ours too? Could we not reach back into the past for something to guide us in our present and future? Keep reading, and Steve will convince you that the answer is obviously a resounding yes.

Second, you will be bolstered in the knowledge that what God did then can happen today ... because it already is. In his approach to the book of Acts, Steve brings the knowledge of how movements work all over the world today. Acts was written by a missionary, to a missionary church. Because Steve is an active practitioner in missionary movements throughout the world, his insight into people, and how they react to the gospel, permeates this book and flavors his exposition of Acts. In this book, Steve is walking with one foot in the past and one in the present; and in both worlds, he seems at home.

Lastly, you will be reminded that we are not left alone to carry out the mission of God; it is God who is on a mission, and we are invited to play a part in what he is doing. That knowledge will energize us all and provide the opportunity to transform us from theorists to practitioners; from a fear of the unknown to a faith born out of experience. It is with this hope that Steve Addison has written this book for you. I am sure that the God of the printed page wants to reveal himself to you as the God who also writes living epistles in our lives as we trust him today, just as the apostles did yesterday. With that kind of faith, new movements will continue to break out all over the world.

# INTRODUCTION

*Anyone who listens to the word but does not do what it says is like someone who looks at his face in a mirror and, after looking at himself, goes away and immediately forgets what he looks like.*

JAMES 1:23-24

When I was young, there were a few hundred known believers in the Hindu kingdom of Nepal. Now there are over one million.[1]

Iran fell to the Islamic revolution in 1979, and yet now the number of believers in that nation is approaching one million.[2]

A decade ago, researcher Justin Long thought there were around a hundred multiplying movements of disciples and churches around the world.[3] By 2017, he'd documented six hundred movements. By 2020, he was tracking 1,369 movements, with at least seventy-seven million disciples in 4.8 million churches; that's 1 percent of the world's population.

There are multiplying movements in China, in India, in the nations of Sub-Saharan Africa, in Latin America, in the United States prison system, and among hi-tech professionals in world cities. And in 1,400 years, we've never seen so many movements in the Muslim world.[4]

Yet despite our history and resources, these movements are the exception in the Western world.

It doesn't have to be that way.

It's time to gaze into the mirror of Acts and allow God to disrupt and inspire us.

## *Exploring an Unfamiliar World*

When we enter the book of Acts, we enter an unfamiliar world, a world in which the good news about Jesus' life, death, and victory is advancing in the power of the Holy Spirit.

God's people are united around the teaching of the apostles in joyful prayer and worship. Their love for one another overflows in generosity. They gather in public places and from house to house. Every day, God adds to their number those being saved. They are fearless in persecution and bold in proclamation. Signs and wonders accompany the spread of God's Word. Troubles abound—false disciples, violent opposition, internal disputes, limited resources, imprisonment, and danger. Yet the Word continues to advance from Jerusalem to the ends of the earth, and in its wake, communities of disciples emerge in every place.

New Testament scholar Eckhard Schnabel writes, "Acts relates what Jesus continues to do and teach, now not only in Galilee and in Jerusalem, but in the whole world, through the witness of his disciples."[5]

The book of Acts calls us back to the beginning. Luke provides a picture of the movement of God—not just how it *was* but how it's meant to be *today*. The world may have changed since Luke's time, but God hasn't; Jesus promised that the movement of God will continue until his Word reaches every people and every place.

Although we may think there is a sharp distinction between Luke's day and ours, Schnabel argues that Luke "was convinced that what God was doing through Jesus Christ and through the power of the Spirit, Christians in all churches should experience and be involved in."[6] We tame Acts by rejecting its relevance, believing our context to be so different that the lessons of Acts no longer apply. It's time to tear down the wall we've built between Luke's age and ours. What God was doing through the power of the Holy Spirit is relevant for every generation of disciples. That's why Luke wrote Acts.

When Luke tells the stories of people like Peter, Philip, Stephen, Barnabas, Paul, Lydia, and Priscilla, he expects us to learn from their example. We are to look for principles, not rigid rules. The repeated patterns we can see in Acts point the way to how God works today.[7]

Acts contains only a few incidental details about church structures and organization. Luke's focus is on God's action: how Jesus defines the core missionary task; how God provides the power to overcome unbelief and opposition; how he disturbs his people when they settle down; how he ensures the messengers get to where they need to be at just the right time.

In Acts, there is one gospel message, adapted for different audiences. Yet the response is always the same: repentance and faith, expressed in baptism for the forgiveness of sins; and the gift of the Spirit.[8] New disciples are added to the community of God's people. The gospel goes out into unreached fields, disciples are made, and new churches formed; leaders are identified; and churches are strengthened and multiplied from Jerusalem to the ends of the earth. This is the repeated pattern of Acts. Luke is showing us what the movement of God looks like, what it does, and how it achieves its God-given mission. Throughout history, movements rise and fall depending on their alignment with the life and mission of Jesus—which begins in the Gospels and continues in Acts. We too must align ourselves with the life and mission of Jesus.

To ignore the lessons of Acts is an act of pride. Not to look back is to measure ourselves by ourselves rather than look into the mirror of God's Word. The mirror of Acts shows us how God fulfills his mission in the world and how we are to play our part. We need to be disturbed about the gap between what we read in Acts and our current experience. Despair is a virtue if it drives us to the sufficiency of God. He wants to inspire us to believe that what he did in Acts, he can do today. And around the world, it's already happening.

I'm thinking of Don, who is at the center of a movement of God in the Texas prison system, which began among prisoners in maximum security. Hundreds of prisoner-led discipleship groups have been formed and are spreading from prison to prison. These groups are the body of Christ in the prisons; they just can't call them churches because it's against the regulations.

There is Jeff, a pastor in Canada who has trained teams from his church to go into their suburban community, offering prayer and the gospel, followed by discipleship around the Scriptures. New disciples are being baptized and added to the church, and new churches are popping up in homes and in a local bar.

I'm thinking of my friends Kumar and Lipok in India who are training, coaching, and mobilizing disciples across their nation of 1.3 billion.

I have in mind Oggie, an apostle to the world's one billion Latinos, on both sides of the Mexican border, with refugees and immigrants baptizing new disciples in water barrels, teaching them to form new churches wherever they go.

There's Amid, a Muslim background believer from Afghanistan. He found Christ as a refugee in Greece where he now makes disciples and forms churches among Pakistanis, Afghans, Iranians, and Syrians as they move through Greece on their way into Europe. As they go, they take the gospel with them. When they settle, they know how to make disciples and form simple churches modeled on Acts 2:36–47.

I'm thinking of Cindy, whose online training and coaching has launched and multiplied workers across South Asia and Africa, all of whom are planting churches.

Then there's George, who retrained his band of evangelists across twenty-one African nations as catalysts for church-planting movements.

I have in mind a young American couple who started off making disciples in Long Beach, California and have now launched into a Muslim nation somewhere in Central Asia.

Acts was written for desperate people, for people who want to play their part in God's mission. Like Paul on the road to Damascus, let God unravel you and remake you. Let him shatter your confidence in your gifts, your knowledge, and your experience, and hear his call afresh. Like Paul, he is sending you to open eyes that are blind, to turn people from darkness to light, and to shift them from the power of Satan to God, so they can receive forgiveness of sins and a place among his people.[9]

Scripture is full of the stories of men and women whom God has disrupted and remade so they could play their part in his mission. It's how he works.

Acts is the model, the example to which every new generation of disciples must return for renewal, inspiration, and direction.[10] As we read Acts, we must ask the following questions: What did Jesus do? What did he train his disciples to do? What does the risen Lord and the Holy Spirit continue to do through God's people in Acts? Finally, what does that look like today?

Acts calls every new generation back to the beginning—to a movement born in obscurity without power, wealth, or influence, devoted to prayer and the spread of God's Word, bold in the face of opposition, generous in love, experiencing God's powerful presence, captivated by his saving love in Jesus, on the move from Jerusalem to the ends of the earth.

God wants to disrupt us and bring us back to the life and mission of Jesus.

## Is This Book for You?

I'm writing for two groups of people who need to return to the movement of God in Acts.

The first group includes those who may be looking from the outside, wondering if these movements around the world are a legitimate work of God that could happen in their context. The place to start is in Acts. Let the patterns and teaching of Scripture shape your understanding and form the foundation for your engagement.

The second group are those who are already pursuing multiplying movements around the world—cross-cultural workers and national leaders on the frontline. Not everything that multiplies is good, so how can you recognize a movement of God and play your part to ensure its health and faithfulness to God? Allow Acts to be your yardstick. Let God's Word determine your thinking and actions.

This is a book for people who want to rediscover the reality of the movement of God in Acts as the foundation for pursuing the movement of God today. Acts reveals that the risen Lord is on a mission to get his Word from where you are to the ends of the earth—every people, every place. As the Word goes out in the power of the Spirit, it leaves in its wake disciples and churches to the glory of God. Is that what you long for? Then you've come to the right place.

### A Roadmap Through Acts

We'll be going on a journey through Acts, chapter by chapter, story by story, to discover God's purposes and what it means to be a movement that multiplies disciples and churches. As you read, you'll find *Deeper* sections, which take an in-depth look at important themes that arise across the whole of Acts. You'll also find *Movements Today* sections, which give examples from around the world of the lessons from Acts lived out today. I can vouch for each story I tell, but for good reasons I can't always identify the exact location or names of the people involved.

Read this book with Acts open beside you. For those who want to capture and apply the learning, there's a 4-Fields Discovery Worksheet with instructions in the appendix (see pages 221–23). To lock in the learning, you can form a group to share your insights and action steps.

There are many excellent academic commentaries on the book of Acts. You'll find them in the notes. This book is different. It's an attempt to bridge the gap between our understanding of Acts and our engagement in reaching a lost world.

Acts is both a serious work of history *and* the living Word of God. It tells the story of salvation through Jesus Christ, the crucified, risen, and exalted Lord. It describes how the Spirit came upon his disciples, granting them power to be his witnesses from Jerusalem to the ends of the earth. Acts shows how God works through ordinary people, sustaining them in troubles and conquering every obstacle and enemy.

What if Luke isn't just telling us, "This is how it was," but he's also saying, "This is how it can be"?

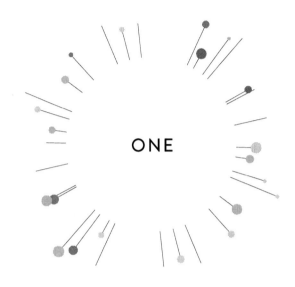

ONE

# THE MISSION OF
# THE RISEN LORD

(1:1–11)

# YOU WILL BE MY WITNESSES (1:1–11)

Luke wrote a second book because the story of Jesus was not finished. The story that began with Jesus' life, death, and resurrection continues. Luke's Gospel is about what Jesus *began* to do and teach.[1] Acts is about what the risen Lord *continues* to do through his disciples in the power of the Holy Spirit. He is not just the God who acted in history. He is not just the God of the early church. He is the God of today, the One who rose from the dead and is living and active among his people and continues to lead the way.

When Jesus rose from the dead, he encountered a band of disciples who were defeated and disillusioned. They had given up everything to follow him. They believed he was the Messiah. Yet at his arrest they fled in fear, and they watched him die alone.

Jesus had forty days to turn these failed followers into a missionary movement that would go to the ends of the earth. He began by providing convincing proofs of his resurrection. If Jesus had not risen bodily from the grave and planted his feet on solid ground, his death would have had no power, there would be no forgiveness of sins, and our reconciliation with God would not be possible. Jesus would have been just another messianic pretender.

Over forty days, Jesus taught them that God had broken into history to establish his rule over the whole world. He took his disciples through the whole of the Old Testament, explaining how the Messiah must suffer and rise again and how repentance for the forgiveness of sins would be preached in his name to all nations, beginning at Jerusalem.[2]

The kingdom came in the life, death, and resurrection of Jesus—and it's still available to all who repent and believe in the good news of salvation in Christ. We can experience the kingdom now, yet we await its fullness in a restored creation.[3] The encounters Jesus had with people demonstrated the presence of the kingdom. He healed Peter's mother-in-law. He brought peace to a deranged man oppressed by demons. He forgave the sins of the woman who wept tears of joy at his feet. He brought salvation to the house of Zacchaeus and set him free from the love of money. He promised paradise to a criminal hanging on a cross.

In Acts, the spread of God's rule takes place as the Word goes out in the power of the Holy Spirit, and new communities of disciples are formed from Jerusalem to the ends of the earth.

As he sends his disciples to the ends of the earth, Jesus promises to pour out his Spirit upon them. To be baptized in the Holy Spirit is to be immersed, overwhelmed, and flooded with the presence of God. The Spirit is both the foretaste of the kingdom and how the kingdom comes, as Jesus' disciples bear witness to him throughout the world.

The Spirit is the true sign of conversion and inspires the new believers to declare the wonders of God in the languages of the world, filling them so they can proclaim the gospel boldly in the face of violent opposition. Despite persecution, the disciples are filled with joy and the Holy Spirit. The Spirit opens and closes doors for the messengers as they go out— when the Spirit is poured out in Samaria, thousands turn and put their faith in Christ. The Spirit removes the obstacles to the Gentile mission. The apostles choose leaders who are filled with the Holy Spirit, and he appoints leaders over the churches. Stephen, the first martyr, dies filled with the Holy Spirit, and it is the Spirit that enables Saul to see again. The church is built up and strengthened by the Holy Spirit, and he speaks to believers through visions and dreams.[4]

The Spirit has one unifying goal in all his activity—he comes to bear witness to the Lord Jesus. Without the Spirit, there would be no missionary movement.

The prophets linked the pouring out of the Spirit with the restoration of Israel.[5] The disciples want to know if this is the time for the restoration of the kingdom to Israel. They want the certainty of a timeline. Will God now overthrow the Roman oppressors and set up his kingdom over Israel? Yet the Father will determine when and how the kingdom comes in its fullness. What should matter to his disciples is the task he has given them. Jesus' answer turns their attention away from dates and timelines to their mission to be his witnesses throughout the world.

As the prophets predicted, the Spirit will be poured out, and Israel will be restored, but not as an earthly kingdom. The twelve apostles are the nucleus of the restored people of God, who will fulfill Israel's calling as a light to the nations, proclaiming salvation to the ends of the earth.[6]

When the gospel of the kingdom has been proclaimed throughout the whole world, the end will come, and Jesus will return to judge the world and establish the kingdom of God in its fullness.[7] This is God's mission, and Jesus still calls every disciple to play their part.

Meanwhile, when the Spirit comes, the Word will go out, and thousands of disciples will be added to the community. But they are not to settle in Jerusalem and wait for the world to come to them. Their call is the same as ours. They are to go. Their destination is the ends of the earth. Jesus' words are a command in the form of a promise, "You *will* receive power. ... You *will* be my witnesses ... to the ends of the earth."[8] The mission is to proclaim the good news of Jesus in cities and towns in every region of the earth.[9]

As eyewitnesses, the Twelve know the events of Jesus' life and ministry; they know his teaching. Their witness is unique. Our role today is to bear witness to what the apostles have seen and heard from Jesus.

Jesus' disciples are "to reach people wherever they live with the news about the offer of salvation, whether they are Jews, or Samaritans, or Gentiles."[10] As far as there are people, that's how far Jesus' disciples are to go. We are called to go to the ends of the inhabited world—every place and every people.[11] That's why Acts is structured around geographic divisions: Jerusalem (Acts 1–7), Judea and Samaria (Acts 8–12), the ends of the earth (Acts 13–28). The plan was not gradually developed by the disciples but was gradually revealed and extended by God.[12]

Acts finishes in Rome, but Rome is not the ends of the earth. Rome is a new starting point from where the gospel is proclaimed until it reaches every place and every people group.[13] The task remains unfinished. Luke writes because every new generation, including our own, must take up the challenge until the task is complete.

When Jesus finishes what he needs to say, a cloud descends, and he is caught up into the glory of God's presence.[14] He will return in the same way. He is gone, yet he is with his people. From his position at the Father's right hand, he will send the Holy Spirit who still leads and energizes this missionary movement today.

The mission began with Jesus' command, it is sustained by his presence, and it will end when he returns to judge the world. The challenge the angels gave the first disciples remains for us today: Stop looking up to heaven; you have work to do on earth![15]

By the time Jesus was finished, these men and women were grounded in his Word, dependent on the Holy Spirit, and committed to the core missionary task. Jesus turned shattered disciples into a movement of God. He did it for them, and he can do it for us. His mission begins and ends, not with our knowledge and resources but by returning to the life and ministry of Jesus. That's what we're trusting him to do as we allow the book of Acts to disrupt us.

# DEEPER: THE FATHER'S PLAN

*If it is from God, you will not be able to stop these men;*
*you will only find yourselves fighting against God.*

ACTS 5:39

Acts is not just a book about the early church. Acts is a book about God and how he brings salvation.[16] Luke writes so that we can see what God is doing and align ourselves with his purposes.

The Father's plan is centered on his Son, whose obedience to death brought forgiveness of sins and a restored relationship with the Father. Now risen and enthroned, the Lord Jesus rules through the Spirit, who empowers the disciples to proclaim this salvation to all. As the Word spreads, the Spirit forms those who repent and believe into the new people of God who are witnesses to the ends of the earth.[17]

God is the chief character, and his Word is the driving force propelling the story forward.[18] Angels appear, prophets speak, prison doors open, houses shake, thousands believe, persecutors fall to the ground, the Scriptures are fulfilled—God directs the mission.

Luke places Acts in the widest possible context. It looks back to the life and ministry of Jesus; his death, resurrection, and exaltation, as well as his future role as universal Judge. Acts looks back to the call of Abraham and the unfolding story of Israel. The plan of God stretches back to creation and stretches forward to the final judgment and to the end of history.[19] Then and now, God acts in history to bring salvation to people who are far from him.

The risen Lord makes God's plan clear to his disciples—repentance for the forgiveness of sins will be proclaimed in Jesus' name to all nations.[20]

God fulfills his promise to send the Spirit at Pentecost to breathe life into the restored people of God who will become a light to the nations. God ensures the gospel goes beyond Jerusalem and Judea to Samaria and then to the world. He works through Peter, Stephen, Philip, through the unnamed disciples who flee persecution, and through Paul and Barnabas. God gets Paul to Rome safely through riots, murder plots, beatings, prison, endless legal proceedings, and wild storms at sea. Although human beings can oppose God's will, God can make their disobedience serve his purposes.

At the very center of this mission is the witness to the life, death, and victory of Jesus, calling everyone to turn and believe in him and leading to the formation of communities of disciples in every place. Every obstacle will be overcome, not by the believer's might and intelligence but by God who intervenes on their behalf.

God moves powerfully, filling his servants with boldness, sending angels to rescue them from prison, striking down evil rulers, healing the sick, and freeing the demonized. As Jesus faced rejection and suffering, so do his followers. The messengers experience both the cross and the resurrection power of Jesus. Their experience will be ours.

From creation to the final judgment, God is working out his plan. He fulfills his promises. He directs the life and mission of Jesus and his disciples, as his Word goes out from Jerusalem to the ends of the earth.[21] Then the end will come, and Jesus will return to judge the world and establish God's rule over all things.

It's his mission, and he will fulfill it his way. So often his power is revealed in our weakness. When we least expect it, he brings the breakthrough. All he wants from us is faith expressed in obedience.

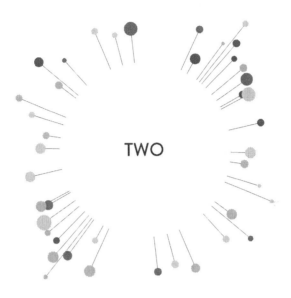

TWO

# FILLING JERUSALEM

(1:12–5:42)

# LET ANOTHER TAKE HIS PLACE (1:12–26)

Jesus' disciples return to Jerusalem. Among them are the women who had come with Jesus from Galilee, some of whom had been with him from the beginning.[1] Jesus' mother is also there, as well as his brothers who previously thought he was mad.[2] The risen Lord had appeared to his brother James who may have converted his three younger brothers.[3] Despite the group's diversity, it was Jesus who brought them together.

They meet on the top floor of a large house, probably in the wealthier district of Jerusalem.[4] Peter stands up among the believers. He is not the Peter we encountered in the Gospels. He is not the Peter who stood between Jesus and his calling to suffer and die in Jerusalem. And he is not the Peter who boasted of his willingness to die for Jesus and then denied him three times. This is a Peter who has been transformed by the risen Christ, prepared for this moment by Jesus who has opened his mind to understand God's purposes in the Scriptures.[5]

Before the Spirit comes and the mission begins, the Twelve must be reconstituted. Peter explains how the Scriptures were fulfilled by Judas's treachery and why Judas must be replaced.[6] Judas had forfeited his place in the Twelve, not by his death but by his betrayal. As Israel had twelve patriarchs over twelve tribes, now the twelve apostles will become the core of the new Israel, made of those who have responded to the gospel with repentance and faith.[7] They are the faithful remnant who will take the gospel to the nations.

Because the witness of the Twelve is the unique foundation for this new movement, the one who takes Judas' place must have been with Jesus from the beginning—he must bear witness to Jesus' ministry and teaching and to his death, resurrection, and ascension.[8] There is no other Jesus than the one revealed in the books of the Old and the New Testaments. We know him because of the apostles' witness, and we know him experientially through the Holy Spirit. These two ways of knowing are the basis of our witness and must align.

Assured that the Lord Jesus who chose the original twelve apostles was present, they cast lots according to the Old Testament pattern, a method to discern God's will that was not repeated once the Spirit came.[9] With the appointment of Matthias, the Twelve are restored.

As the disciples wait for God to fulfill his promise, they pray constantly.[10] Prayer is evident in almost every decisive moment in the advance of this new movement.[11] They have been with Jesus, and he has prepared them for this time. Unlike the Sadducees, who control the temple and the priesthood and who have the ear of Rome, these disciples have nothing but their faith in the promises of God. New movements are only formed when we are aware of our own weakness and our dependence on God. Perhaps that's why, throughout history, the breakthroughs in the renewal and expansion of the movement of God always occur on the fringe, never at the center of power.[12]

# DEEPER: ACTS OF THE RISEN LORD

*In my former book, Theophilus, I wrote about all that Jesus began to do and to teach*

ACTS 1:1

Following his death and resurrection, Jesus ascended to the right hand of the Father from where he lives and rules as King. That does not mean he is now absent from the world. He is powerfully present through the Holy Spirit whom he has poured out on his people.

The book of Acts tells the story of the continuing mission of the risen Lord.[13] All who respond to him with repentance and faith are added to God's people.[14] Because Jesus' reign is universal, the gospel must go to all—every people group and every place.

The living and reigning Lord directs this movement,[15] whether it's restoring and instructing his fallen disciples, sending the Holy Spirit, or appointing witnesses. The living and reigning Lord is present with his people. As Stephen faces death, Jesus appears to him as the Son of Man, standing at the right hand of God. He appears to Paul, bringing salvation, a missionary commission, and later standing with him in persecution and prison.[16] And when Paul and Barnabas appoint elders, they commend them to the Lord who will protect and lead them.[17]

The risen Lord is present with his people, just as Yahweh was present with Israel.[18] When the early church grows in number, it is the Lord who adds those being saved.[19] When they are persecuted, he is persecuted.[20] When they don't know how to defend themselves, he provides words and wisdom that no adversaries can resist or contradict.[21]

The Jesus of Acts is the Jesus who is present with us today, as we seek to step out to obey his command to make disciples.

# SUDDENLY, A SOUND ... (2:1–13)

**AD 30**

Everything is ready. The Twelve are restored. The disciples are together, united in prayer. They have Jesus' mandate to take the gospel to the world. There's just one more thing . . .

It is early in the morning on the fiftieth day since Passover; the day of Pentecost, a harvest festival that has come to be linked with the giving of the Mosaic law and the renewing of the covenant between God and his people.[22] It is one of the three great pilgrimage festivals of Judaism, and Jerusalem is packed with people. All work has stopped.

There are 120 men and women gathered in the upper room when the Holy Spirit comes with a sound like the blowing of a violent wind from heaven. Tongues of fire rest on each person. God shows his awesome presence among them through wind and fire. The disciples, filled with the Holy Spirit, begin declaring the wonders of God in languages they have never learned nor needed. Right from the outset, the Spirit empowers God's people to cross the boundaries of culture, language, and race with the message of salvation.[23] As this new movement begins, God has the whole world in his sights.

As Acts unfolds, God scatters his people in ever-widening circles of cross-cultural engagement. The Spirit is the architect of each breakthrough, and tongues are a sign of what God has done. Later, the Samaritans, the Gentiles, and the disciples of John praise God in unknown languages, just as the Jews did at Pentecost. For Luke, the experience of speaking in tongues is a reminder of the Spirit's work to take the gospel to every place, every people, and every language.

These strange signs of the Spirit are God's way of disrupting his people—his ways are not their ways—and realigning them with his purposes.[24] The words of the prophets have been fulfilled: The age of the Spirit has begun, and the Spirit is on the move. Previously, God dwelled in the temple in Jerusalem, but now the glory of God dwells in common houses, among ordinary people, all of whom are empowered as witnesses.

The sound of worship in many languages draws a crowd, and soon the worshippers spill out onto the streets. At some point, they move to the vast temple courts that could accommodate up to seventy-five thousand people.[25]

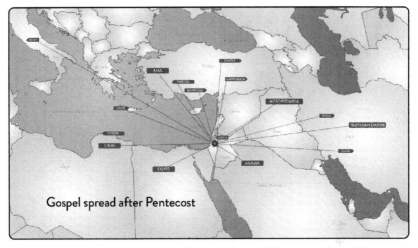

Gospel spread after Pentecost

*At Pentecost, there were Parthians, Medes, and Elamites; residents of Mesopotamia, Judea and Cappadocia, Pontus and Asia, Phrygia and Pamphylia, Egypt and the parts of Libya near Cyrene; visitors from Rome (both Jews and converts to Judaism); Cretans and Arabs (Acts 2:9-11).*

The crowd includes Jews living outside of Israel from the diaspora or dispersion. They are the descendants of those who, over the centuries, had been exiled by the powers of Assyria, Babylon, Persia, Greece, and Rome.[26] Some were pilgrims visiting Jerusalem for the feast. Others lived permanently in Jerusalem. Together they represent the whole Jewish world. They are amazed to hear these Galileans, who normally spoke a dialect of Aramaic, speaking in their local languages.[27]

God is gathering and restoring his people through his Messiah Jesus. The prophets spoke of the day when the Spirit would come, a new covenant would be made between God and Israel, and the light of God's glory would go to the nations.[28]

The Spirit comes upon them so they can proclaim the mighty works of God and extend Israel's salvation to the whole world. God intends to form one people from every tribe and language under the rule of his Son.[29]

The movement of God cannot be copied, bottled, or franchised. It cannot be explained by natural causes. There is only one foundation of this movement of God: the life, death, and victory of Jesus; and the energizing power of the Spirit propelling God's people out from Jerusalem to the ends of the earth.

What would happen if the Spirit came in power today, as he did at Pentecost? I imagine we might try and camp in that upper room if we could, day and night soaking in God's presence. No doubt, before long, someone would set up a live video feed so the world could watch. Soon pilgrims would start arriving to visit this scene of revival, only to find the upper room empty and that the Spirit has left the building.

For when the Spirit came in power at Pentecost, God's people were propelled onto the streets to proclaim the message of salvation, and as a result, three thousand disciples were baptized and added to the community of God's people. Pentecost didn't end with a spiritual experience contained in the upper room. The fruit of Pentecost was disciples and churches to the glory of God, throughout Jerusalem and the nations. Without the coming of the Holy Spirit, there would be no worldwide mission.[30]

If you want to see a movement of God, live in these first two chapters of Acts. Make them your home. Form a group and start working through Acts, a section at a time, with the 4-Fields Discovery Worksheet in the appendix (see page 221). With God's grace, let the Word and the Spirit lead you to obey what you learn. Our traditions, our strategies, and our best thinking must be laid aside to learn from what God did in Jerusalem that day and receive what his Spirit is calling us to do today.

# DEEPER: THE MOVEMENT OF THE HOLY SPIRIT

*In the last days ... I will pour out my Spirit on all people.*

ACTS 2:17

Acts is not about a bygone era. Jesus continues to reign; his mission continues; and he is still looking for willing disciples who will spread the word, empowered by the Holy Spirit.[31]

There are two opposite errors regarding the work of the Holy Spirit today. One is to confine the work of the Spirit to the pages of Scripture and banish him from contemporary experience. The other is to pursue personal experiences of the Holy Spirit as the destination. Luke wrote Acts to remind every generation that the Spirit is given to bear witness to Jesus throughout the world. The one who empowers is also the one who unsettles God's people, ensuring they remain on the move. We are in as desperate need today for the power of the Holy

Spirit as that first generation of disciples. How are we to recognize a true work of the Holy Spirit? When the Spirit moves in power, we'll see the life and ministry of Jesus lived out by disciples in communities, spreading from Jerusalem to the ends of the earth.

The Spirit serves the expansion of the Word.[32] Luke says it is the Word, not the Spirit, that grows, and the outcome is communities of disciples.[33] And so, on the day of Pentecost, the outpouring of the Spirit reaches its climax in the proclamation of the Word to the nations and the formation of the church in Jerusalem.[34]

Out of the nations of the world, the Holy Spirit creates the people of God—Jews, Samaritans, Ethiopians, Romans, Syrians, Greeks, Galatians, Lycaonians, Macedonians, Achaians, and Asians—united in their faith in Jesus as Savior and King.[35] This work of the Spirit is at the heart of God's mission.

The Spirit breathes life into this movement of God, directing, intervening, propelling, correcting. There are apostles, prophets, evangelists, teachers, and elders, all gifted by the Spirit, but they don't direct the movement; the Spirit does, and he uses whomever he chooses.

As the movement expands, it is the Spirit who forms new disciples into churches and strengthens the life of the churches, enabling them to live in the fear of the Lord, encouraged and increasing in numbers.[36] When Ananias and Sapphira deceive the community, it is the Holy Spirit who protects the purity of God's people.[37] When the mission to the nations languishes, the Spirit uses persecution to get Philip to Samaria.[38] When the Samaritans believe, the Spirit confirms their place among the people of God.[39] It is the Spirit who brings Peter to the house of Cornelius; and as Peter preaches, the Spirit falls upon Gentiles, demonstrating acceptance by God through faith in Christ alone.[40] The Spirit is given to the Samaritans and the Gentiles, just as it was to the Jews at Pentecost. The Samaritans and Gentiles will also now bear witness to Jesus throughout the world.[41] When the barrier between Jewish and Gentile disciples must be removed, it is the Spirit who guides the Jerusalem Council.[42] The Spirit appoints both leaders within the churches and leaders who multiply churches in new fields.[43]

It is the Spirit who blocks Paul and his missionary band from pushing further into Asia Minor, and it is the Spirit who then flings open the door into Europe.[44] After his final mission as a free man, Paul is compelled by the Holy Spirit to go to Jerusalem, which brings about his arrival in Rome, where he will bear witness to the emperor.[45] The book of Acts ends with Paul in chains, awaiting trial in Rome. The missionary is bound, but the Word still goes out in the power of the Spirit. The mission will continue, despite what happens to Paul. The story is not finished, and so the Holy Spirit continues to work, as a new generation of disciples accept the challenge of taking the gospel to the ends of the earth.

Without the work of the Spirit, there would be no proclamation, no conversions, no churches, no power to release Satan's captives, and no missionary movement.[46]

## MOVEMENTS TODAY: BEHIND BARS IN RIO

Sociologist Andrew Johnson wanted to understand the impact of Pentecostalism in Brazil's prison system. So he went behind bars to find out.

He recalls how at exactly 6 a.m., the war cry of the *Comando Vermelho* (Red Command, Brazil's oldest criminal gang) rose from the cells of Rio prison.[47] A lone voice was answered by four hundred inmates living in gang-controlled cells:

"Comando Vermelho!"

"Comando Vermelho!"

"Comando Vermelho!"

"Comando Vermelho!"

"Comando Vermelho!"

But earlier that morning, another war cry had sounded—by the Heroes for Christ at the close of their worship.

"By what are we saved?" the leader cried.

"By the blood of Christ!" thirty inmates responded.

"If he is your Shepherd ..." called out the leader.

"We lack nothing!" replied the members.

Johnson found movements of multiplying disciples and churches flourishing inside Rio de Janeiro's gang-controlled prisons. The prison system is an extension of Rio de Janeiro's impoverished *favelas*, where the drug gangs rule, and the police dare not enter. On the inside, it is the gangs, not the prison officials who rule. Yet, where the gangs are strongest is where the churches are thriving. Faith in Christ has enabled desperate men in appalling conditions to reject death and embrace life. The churches have adapted to this harsh environment by taking on the structure and function of the prison gangs. Prisoners run the prison churches. Members are easy to identify: They dress differently, they quit drugs, and spend time studying the Bible.

The relationship between the churches and the narco-gangs is characterized by respect. The churches treat gang members as people worthy of redemption but do not condone their activities. The gangs tell their members to treat the church members and pastors well and to acknowledge their authority in the community.

The local leader preaches, sings, prays, fasts, suffers, and praises alongside the other disciples. Inmates not only set the vision for the future of the churches, but they also negotiate with gang and prison officials and make themselves available to meet the spiritual and sometimes physical and emotional needs of inmates twenty-four hours a day.

If the Pentecostals practice what they preach, they are safe from prison violence and are allowed to occupy space in the prison.

Rio's most stigmatized residents have built churches where they experience joy, brotherhood, and dignity in one of the city's most apparently God-forsaken places.

The living Word of God and the power of the Holy Spirit are the one driving force in every genuine movement of God. Together, the Word and the Spirit witness to the life, death, and victory of Jesus through his disciples, in every place and among every people group throughout the world.

If God's light can shine through convicted criminals in a Rio prison, it can shine anywhere in this lost world.

# PETER STANDS UP (2:14–36)

Peter stands in the temple courts where Jesus had taught. Peter who had heard the mob cry, "Crucify him!" Peter who had denied his Lord to a servant girl and hidden behind locked doors. Now this same Peter stands before thousands to bear witness to his Lord.

Peter's message is an example of prophesying in the power of the Spirit. His message is steeped in the Scriptures, and although he is not a qualified religious teacher, it's evident this Galilean fisherman has been shaped and taught by Jesus.[48]

Peter explains that these are the days of which the prophet Joel spoke. These "last days" began with the coming of Jesus and will end when he returns.[49] Through Jesus, the age of salvation has dawned. The Spirit of the new age has broken in to bring life to the old. The Spirit-filled people of God will see wonders in the heavens and signs on the earth. They will prophesy, and God will speak to them in dreams and visions.[50]

In the Old Testament, the Holy Spirit came upon individuals to bring God's Word to his people. But now all of God's people can proclaim his Word. The risen Lord will enable them to be his witnesses to the ends of the earth.[51]

And this promise is for the whole human race: Jews and Gentiles, people from every nation, women and men, rich and poor, young and old. To prophesy is to bear witness to Jesus in the power of the Spirit. In Acts, this includes proclaiming the Word, speaking in tongues, dreams and visions, predictions of danger and guidance in the mission.[52] This work of the Spirit through every disciple will not cease until Jesus returns.

In "the last days," there will be signs on earth and signs in the heavens. The glorious day of the Lord will occur when he judges the nations. As in the times of the prophets, the fate of Israel hangs in the balance, for the nation has rejected its only hope of salvation.[53] What's true for Israel is true for the world today. The whole of Scripture affirms the coming of the final day of judgment. Now is the time to call upon the name of the Lord and be saved.

Peter tells of how Jews and Gentiles conspired to kill Jesus. He was handed over to evil men. Yet Jesus' death was God's will, and now God has enthroned the One they crucified as Lord. Peter urges everyone to break with their corrupt generation and surrender to Jesus and his cause.[54]

Notice the tone of Peter's message. He is a man called and trained by Jesus, transformed through his failure and restoration; changed by Jesus' instruction and the presence of the Holy Spirit. There is no gap between Peter's lived experience and the message he proclaims. That's a sign of a movement on the rise. The messengers embody a life with God, and that's the reality they share with others. When a movement drifts into decline, there is a reluctance to proclaim and live by its core message, for fear of rejection.

Peter overcame such fear by turning back to God in his darkest moment and allowing God to remake him. His bold message at Pentecost does not depend on natural talent and courage but on the power of God. This is true today. God will achieve his purposes, and he will use broken and failed people who return to him as Peter did. When we cast ourselves on him in humility, God reshapes us as he works through us for his glory.

## MOVEMENTS TODAY: BORN IN A BARN

On an April night in 1906, a group including cooks, janitors, laborers, railroad porters, and washerwomen met for prayer in a poor neighborhood of Los Angeles.[55] When the Spirit fell, they erupted into worship, and some began speaking in tongues. Soon the house in which they met could not contain the crowds that gathered night after night. They secured a broken-down building on Azusa Street, a former Methodist church converted into stables. They cleared out the rubbish and swept the dirt floor clean. Two large wooden crates served as a pulpit.[56]

Their leader was William Seymour, the son of former slaves who had worked as a farm laborer, janitor, waiter, and holiness preacher. Inspired by reports of the Welsh revival, he believed the end times outpouring of the Spirit was coming.

Thousands came from around the United States and soon from around the world. They were made up of every race, nationality, and social class. Meetings were held morning, afternoon, and night. Eight hundred people crammed inside, while four to five hundred stood outside. For the next three years, the meetings continued without a break.[57]

There was no central coordination, and Seymour rarely preached. He stood at the pulpit with his head bowed in a crate, crying out to God for the holiness and power of the Spirit.

As Blacks, Latinos, Asians, and whites knelt beside each other for prayer, one observer commented that, the "color line" had been washed away by the blood of Christ.[58] Seymour taught that tongues is one sign of the baptism of the Spirit, but the real evidence of the Spirit is love.[59]

From the start, this was a missionary movement. Seymour taught that the power of the Spirit was given so that the gospel would go to the ends of the earth. Within weeks, missionaries left for Scandinavia, India, and China. Through the gift of tongues, they expected to be able to speak all the languages of the world and take the gospel to the ends of the earth.[60]

The missionaries were "mostly poor, untrained and unprepared for what awaited them."[61] Their experience of the Holy Spirit energized their mission. They arrived without funding, expecting the Spirit to provide and guide. Some returned home when they discovered they could not speak any local languages. Some died on the field. Many gave the rest of their lives to the work.[62]

Within two years, they had brought the gospel to parts of Asia, South America, the Middle East, and Africa. Their sacrifices were rewarded: In the twentieth century, the Pentecostal-charismatic movement became the fastest growing, and most globally diverse expression of worldwide Christianity.[63]

There are now 650 million Pentecostal-charismatics around the world. Most live in Africa, Asia, and Latin America—all of which are home to the world's youngest and fastest-growing populations. If there is a "typical" Pentecostal, it is a young person living in a Nigerian village or a Brazilian *favela*.

Pentecostal or not, Christians of the global South have a high view of Scripture and a supernatural worldview. They believe that what they read in the Gospels is happening in their midst. They believe that the world of the apostles is a present reality. They are more interested in saving lost people and planting churches than radical politics and social change.[64] Yet research shows they are making life better for themselves and their communities.[65]

Not every disciple making movement is Pentecostal, but every disciple making movement has a high view of Scripture, a confidence in the power of the Holy Spirit, and an unswerving focus on the core missionary task of making disciples.

# DEEPER: THE MESSAGE

*Salvation is found in no one else, for there is no other name under heaven given to mankind by which we must be saved.*

ACTS 4:12

At Pentecost we have the first of Peter's recorded messages.[66] The contexts vary, and none of the messages are the same, yet we can identify six themes:

1. The kingdom has come; the promised age of salvation has dawned.
2. As prophesied, this has taken place through the ministry, death, and resurrection of Jesus.
3. Through the resurrection, Jesus has been exalted at the right hand of God, as Messianic head of the new Israel.
4. The Holy Spirit has been poured out by the risen Lord upon his people.
5. The age of salvation will end when Christ returns to judge the world.
6. Therefore, repent, be baptized, and receive forgiveness of sins and the gift of the Holy Spirit and be added to the community of God's people.[67]

We know where these themes originated. After his resurrection, Jesus had spent forty days opening Peter and the disciples' minds to understand the Scriptures. It was this teaching that was passed on and became the basis for the disciples' preaching throughout Acts.

Peter built his case based upon the authority of the Hebrew Scriptures. When Paul preached before pagans, he did not quote the Hebrew Scriptures directly, yet he still spoke about the God of Israel, the one true and living God, before he spoke about Jesus as Lord and Savior.[68]

Whatever their approach, the good news remained the same: "The good news ... is always the good news of Jesus, the crucified and risen Messiah and Savior, who died and rose from the dead so that sinners can have forgiveness of their sins, find salvation, receive God's Spirit, and be granted eternal life."[69]

The gospel knows no barriers of culture, geography, and ethnicity.[70] It goes out in temple courts, from house to house, in the synagogue and the marketplace, the jail and the workshop, and on board a sinking ship. And it is for everyone, including the elite and powerful of the Roman world and the barbarians on the island of Malta. The gospel is for a jailer and his prisoners; for a demonized slave girl and a wealthy businesswoman; for God-fearing Jews and idol-worshipping pagans.

Acts shows us what God is up to, revealing how to identify a movement of God. Today we must keep our ear to the ground, listening for the stories, asking where God's living Word is overcoming barriers to reach new people groups. It may be down at a suburban skatepark, or in a Brazilian prison, or among Iranians in Tehran, or immigrants on the Mexico-United States border, or in the villages of Communist controlled Laos. Where is the gospel getting out? Where are people turning and following Christ? Where are disciples being formed and new churches planted? We can't control when and where the break-throughs come, but God is always at work through his people.

Only one recorded message in Acts is delivered to believers; all the rest are evangelistic. Sometimes Paul engaged in conversation; other times it was discussion, debate, or teaching. No matter the method, the message remained constant.[71]

Movements that spread are characterized by the free, open, uninhibited communication of the gospel from person to person. It is as true today as it was at the beginning.

Jesus trained his disciples in what to say by making sure they understood why the Messiah had to suffer and rise from the dead and why repentance for the forgiveness of sins must be preached to all nations.[72] This is a simple test of any Jesus movement—do new disciples know how to pass on the gospel message to those who are far from God in their world?[73] Do they know what to say, just as Jesus' disciples knew what to say? If they don't, who will train them?

# WHAT SHOULD WE DO? (2:37–41)

When the crowd ask, "What should we do?" Peter tells them they must call on the name of the Lord. They must turn to God and be baptized in the name of Jesus Christ for the forgiveness of sins, and they will receive the Holy Spirit.[74]

This is the message of repentance that both John the Baptist and Jesus preached. However, the focus of the proclamation shifts: After Jesus' death and resurrection, Jesus becomes the center of the message, and the Holy Spirit is promised to everyone who believes.[75] The message pivots from the kingdom to the King, from the reign of God to the One who reigns.[76]

In Peter's response, we can identify four elements of true conversion:

*1. Repentance (and Faith).* There can be no salvation without the forgiveness of sins and no forgiveness without repentance. They must turn to God and confess the sin of rejecting the Lord's Messiah. They must accept Jesus as the risen and exalted Lord.[77]

*2. Immersion.* They must demonstrate their repentance and call on Jesus' name by being immersed (baptized) in water as a sign of cleansing from sin.[78]

*3. Forgiveness.* Their release from sin is made possible by his death, resurrection, and exaltation to God's right hand. Salvation is found in no other name under heaven.[79]

*4. The Holy Spirit.* The forgiveness of sins opens the way for the gift of the Holy Spirit—God's transforming presence.

Peter doesn't mention faith, but elsewhere in Acts, faith is a key element of salvation. Luke doesn't list every aspect of conversion each time. Faith is assumed here, just as repentance is assumed when Luke only mentions faith. Likewise, immersion in water is always assumed, even when it's not mentioned.[80]

This promise of salvation is for Israel, for Jews who are in distant lands, and for future generations. It will soon become clear that salvation is also for the nations of the world.

Jesus promised that when the Spirit came, they would do greater works than he had done. Now, in one day, Jesus gained more disciples than in his entire ministry.[81] Three thousand responded in a city of over a hundred thousand residents and pilgrims.[82] Together with the 120 they formed a remnant, called out of Israel, who are the nucleus of the new people of God.[83]

A mere profession of faith was not enough. When Luke counts, he only records disciples who have turned, believed, been baptized, and added to the community.[84] This movement does not confuse crowds with disciples. Jesus loved the crowds: he taught them, he healed them, and he wept over them; but he knew their faith was fickle. Jesus condemned the masses who witnessed his miracles but refused to repent and believe in him.[85] Jesus called disciples out of the crowds to follow him and learn how to make disciples.[86]

Movements don't just win converts; they make disciples who together learn to obey Christ. Success is not measured by the size of the crowds gathered. In an age obsessed with celebrity and consumerism, it's easy to fall into a trap of ministries that please and entertain crowds; but disciples are not formed this way. Instead, movements look for evidence of disciples who have repented and believed, who have been baptized and added to the community, who are showing signs of following Jesus, and learning to disciple others.

# THEY DEVOTED THEMSELVES (2:42–47)

In a movement, discipleship and church formation are two sides of the same inseparable work of God. God is not just saving individuals; he is gathering a people. He does not add them to the community without saving them, and he does not save them without adding them to the community.[87]

Luke provides a concise summary of the life of the first church. This is one of several summaries that describe the church in Jerusalem as a pattern that God intends for every church.[88]

Luke tells us they devoted themselves to four essentials, and a fifth characteristic flowed from these four:[89]

***1. The Apostles' Teaching.*** The disciples were *devoted* to the Word of God entrusted to the apostles—they not only heard but were also willing to obey what they learned. The Twelve are the authoritative witnesses to Jesus' mission, teaching, death, and resurrection. Luke uses "the Word" to describe their message about Jesus.[90] It is the dynamic Word of God that brings salvation and adds disciples to the life of the church. It is this gospel of salvation through Jesus Christ that creates the church. Eventually, the New Testament became the divinely inspired source of apostolic teaching.

***2. Fellowship.*** Salvation meant joining the community of God's people. They shared one heart and soul. They were one because they all accepted Jesus as Messiah and Savior, and they all received the same Holy Spirit. They grew together as they learned, worshipped, and shared meals in homes and as they gave sacrificially to ensure no one was in need.[91]

***3. Breaking of Bread.*** Meals together had been a characteristic of Jesus' ministry. Aware of his continuing presence, they broke bread together in private homes and on the temple mount and shared the Lord's Supper. They remembered Jesus' death and looked forward to his return as he'd taught them.[92]

***4. Prayer.*** This movement was born in prayer and worship. In homes and on the temple mount, they continued to praise and petition God with glad and sincere hearts. They prayed and sang with joy because the Lord was present. Prayer expressed their utter dependence on God as the movement advanced; they prayed when selecting leaders; they prayed for healing; they prayed when they were persecuted; leaders devoted themselves to prayer; and they prayed for new believers to receive the Holy Spirit.[93] As they prayed, they experienced the presence and power of the Spirit in tangible ways. They were filled with awe. Signs and wonders accompanied the spread of the Word.

**5. *Multiplication of Disciples.*** These four essentials describe the life of the church, and the fruit of that life was that every day God added to their number those who were saved. The disciples spread the Word from house to house and in public spaces. Soon the Word was spilling over to the surrounding towns and villages, to Judea and Samaria, just as Jesus had predicted.

Through his Spirit, God created the life of this community. God was present in the message of the gospel. He was present as the believers shared the Lord's Supper. His presence brought generosity. He was present through his Spirit, working miracles and freeing those under the power of Satan. He was present as his people prayed. His presence was the key to their life together and the reason that disciples were added every day. His presence will propel them out from Jerusalem to the ends of the earth.

Note the simplicity in Luke's description of the life of the first church. The essentials are there, with no extras. If the church in Jerusalem was to become a multiplying movement, ordinary disciples must be able to reproduce that life wherever they go. Jesus had trained the Twelve; they in turn were able to train others in a simple, reproducing pattern of discipleship and church life.

Later in Acts, we find disciples in Syria, North Africa, Cyprus, and Rome. Most likely, these churches were started by Jewish converts who returned home from Pentecost with the good news and a simple but powerful pattern of discipleship in community. As the movement spread out from Jerusalem, churches were planted in the cities and villages of Judea, Galilee, and Samaria.[94]

Jesus turned a fearful and fractured band of disciples into a missionary movement. The first church became one of the churches in a multiplying movement of disciples, crossing ethnic, cultural, and religious barriers.

Today, there are movements of disciples and churches in the Himalayan villages of Nepal and among hi-tech workers in London. There are movements in the prison systems of the United States, Zambia,

Columbia, and Brazil. There are movements among Afghan refugees moving up through Greece into Europe. Like the first church in Jerusalem, they all have simple but powerful patterns of making disciples in communities that can multiply.

Movements of disciples and churches all start the same way—with a few individuals who place their confidence in the power of God through his Word and the Spirit and are obedient to Christ's command to go and make disciples of every people group and in every place.

## MOVEMENTS TODAY: HEALTHY CHURCH CIRCLES

Picture a room of twenty to thirty leaders comprising farmers, schoolteachers, and small business owners from low- to mid-Hindu caste backgrounds in northern India. They are volunteers—the fruit of Indian workers who went from village to village, proclaiming the gospel and discipling new believers using a simple method of 3-Thirds discipleship.[95] Over six to nine months, they identified and appointed leaders who showed the characteristics of 1 Timothy 3.

Now gathered, these leaders read the description of the first church in Acts 2 and identify the functions of a healthy church.[96] A symbol represents each function: a heart for loving relationships; clasped hands for prayer; the Indian rupee for giving; an open book for the Word; bread and a cup for the Lord's Supper, and so on. Symbols are drawn inside the circle if the function they represent is practiced by local believers and are placed outside the circle if the function is either not being practiced or if it is being performed by someone outside of the local community.

Based on what's outside the circle, the church planter and the local leader determine next steps for teaching and strengthening each church.

They ask questions such as: Is the church regularly celebrating the Lord's Supper? Are the disciples learning to love one another? Are they giving generously to the work and to those in need? Are the new disciples baptized, and does the new church know it has the authority to baptize? Have godly leaders been appointed? Is the Word going out from this new church?

If the church has started any new churches, a line is drawn from the first church circle and a new circle is drawn.

# The Church Circle
## Acts 2:36–47

Those who repent and believe are added to the church.

Disciples are baptized and have the authority to baptize.

Prayer: Corporate and individual prayer.

Disciples are trained to share the gospel.

Love for one another expressed in deeds.

Worship: Corporate and individual worship.

Regular celebration of the Lord's Supper.

Giving to those in need and for the spread of the gospel.

Learning obedience to God's Word.

Recognized local leaders.

A dotted line circle indicates a group. A solid circle indicates the group identifies as a church.

The Church Circle is a tool that enables any community of disciples to identify the functions of a healthy church from Acts 2, assess their level of health, and take steps to improve.

From the villages of northern India to the suburbs of Los Angeles, it is proving to be a powerful method for strengthening the churches in a multiplying movement based on the patterns of the first church in Jerusalem.

# DEEPER: THE CHURCH

*Then the church throughout Judea, Galilee and Samaria enjoyed*
*a time of peace and was strengthened. Living in the fear of the*
*Lord and encouraged by the Holy Spirit, it increased in numbers.*

ACTS 9:31

In one sense, the church began its existence when Jesus came into Galilee and called his first disciples to follow him and to learn how to fish for others. The call to follow Jesus was a simultaneous call to both join and form communities of his disciples.

Jesus called his disciples and taught them what it meant to follow him together. He taught them to obey his commands. He taught them to live a life of love, forgiveness, generosity, and servanthood. He taught them to proclaim the good news of God's reign and to make disciples. He taught them to pray and expect God to answer. He taught them not to fear persecution. He taught them to baptize new disciples and to celebrate the Lord's Supper together. Most of all, he taught them who he was—Messiah, Lord, and Savior of the world. The identity of the people of God was formed from the life and mission of Jesus—"Jesus is the Church modelled."[97]

At the core of the new church community were twelve apostles. Their authority was derived from their faithfulness to the good news and their willingness to bear witness to Jesus throughout the world. The identity of the church is therefore found in its faithfulness to the apostolic witness; the willingness to live and proclaim it in the power of the Spirit. In that sense every true disciple and every true church is "apostolic."

Luke gives us a clear picture of the life of the first church as God's intention for all churches.[98] He shows us how the church should function. They are devoted to the apostles' teaching, to each other, and to prayer. They gather publicly and from house to house, sharing meals, experiencing the power of the Spirit. They meet the needs of the poor within the community.

As the gospel went out, churches were established in Jerusalem, and the regions of Judea, Galilee, and Samaria; in the cities of Lydda, Joppa, Damascus, Caesarea, Tyre, Sidon, Tarsus, Antioch, Salamis, Paphos, Pisidian Antioch, Iconium, Lystra, Derbe, Perge, Philippi, Thessalonica, Berea, Athens, Corinth, and Ephesus; and the regions of Achaia and Asia Minor; in Troas, Miletus, Puteoli, and Rome. The churches came into existence through the pioneering ministry of the Twelve, as well as through Philip, Barnabas, Paul, and other coworkers and unnamed disciples.[99]

Luke uses the word "church" for any local congregation, but he also refers to the one church spread across Judea, Galilee, and Samaria, made up of many churches.[100] In the same way, the churches in Jerusalem, Damascus, Antioch, Corinth, Ephesus, and Rome were made up of many local churches in the city and surrounding regions— which is why, when Paul wrote to the church in Rome, he could identify up to five churches meeting in various homes.[101]

Wherever the gospel finds faith, churches are formed ... all the way from Jerusalem to the ends of the earth. In Acts, the core missionary task is about taking the gospel to every people and every place, forming new disciples into churches to the glory of God.

For the last hundred years or so, Westerners have been debating and redefining the nature of God's mission in the world.[102] Since the 1920s, "mission" has increasingly been framed in political, economic, and social terms, with the restructuring and transformation of society as the goal. But this is not the pattern of mission in the New Testament, including Acts. Not even Jerusalem is transformed but must await the judgment of God in history.[103] As the Word goes out, cities are divided and in turmoil, yet the fruit of the gospel is always disciples in community: churches in the pattern of the first church in Jerusalem.

# IN THE NAME OF JESUS—WALK! (3:1-26)

Luke has shown us the life and witness of the church in Jerusalem; now he reveals the threats the movement faces, internally and externally.

Peter and John are doing what they normally did: going up to the temple to pray, open to who they might meet along the way. It is midafternoon, and the busiest time of the day, when the burnt offering was sacrificed.[104] Thousands would visit the temple court every day, and it was therefore a natural place for beggars, who relied on the generosity of worshippers.

Peter and John pass a man who had been lame from birth. He'd probably sat at this gate for much of his life, so the two apostles must have passed him many times before. They have no money to give him, but instead they offer healing in Jesus' name. They act in Jesus' name for "Jesus has the power that only God the Creator can exercise."[105]

His healing is immediate. Though the muscles of the man's feet were once wasted away, he can now stand, jump, and walk as he praises God. When the people see this, they come running.

Peter tells those gathered in Solomon's Colonnade that wonder and amazement are not saving faith. He is quick to deny that their power or godliness healed this man. Instead, he points to the presence and power of the risen Jesus.[106] He explains to his listeners how Jesus' death fulfilled the prophecies of the Messiah as the Suffering Servant of the Lord who will bring salvation to Israel and to the nations.[107] God reversed the judgment on people, Jesus is exalted, and this healing is a foretaste of the restoration of all things.

Peter tells the crowds that forgiveness of sins is only available through Jesus and calls them to repent—to turn away from their disobedience, confess their wrongdoing, and give up their sin. They must embrace a new way of life, characterized by faith and obedience to God.[108] Their sins will be wiped out, and they will receive the Holy Spirit.

Peter not only offers an invitation, but he also delivers a warning: The only way to remain as God's covenant people and enjoy the blessings of salvation is to turn and believe in Jesus.

The miracle was not an end in itself. It bore witness to the living Lord Jesus and opened the way for the gospel to be proclaimed and will soon result in thousands being added to the disciples.

Movements of God are made up of people who keep their eyes and ears open to where God is at work in their everyday lives, whether in their workplace, in their neighborhood, or at the school gates. A simple offer of prayer—whether for healing, for a grieving heart, or for a person calling out to God for guidance—opens hearts and minds to the gospel. God is especially gracious to answer the prayers of those who are seeking him.

## MOVEMENTS TODAY: CAN I PRAY FOR YOU?

All around the world, one of the simplest ways to engage someone in a conversation about Jesus is by asking, "Is there anything I can pray for you right now?" It's useful with people you know, as well as with people you've met for the first time.

Once, while in the English town of Basildon, I was out with my teammate Russell Godward, looking for people we could pray for and share the gospel with. One retired couple were open to prayer. We got chatting with them, and they told us that they had just come from the hospital, where the husband had received treatment for depression. After I shared briefly about my own background with depression, the man then opened his heart and told us how twelve months ago their daughter had succumbed to cancer, leaving behind a husband and young family. As I prayed for them, I felt God's heart for this couple. I shared the gospel. Although they weren't ready to take things further, as they drove away the husband's face was beaming. God had done something in his life through a simple offer of prayer.

If the Good Shepherd is our model of pastoral ministry, then, just as he went out looking for lost sheep, so should we. Find a partner, and discover how Jesus is already active in the lives of your friends, neighbors, and the strangers you meet.

Don't stop with prayer. If someone wants to know more, explain the gospel to them, and invite them to read the Bible with you. Ask three questions: When could we meet? Where could we meet? Who else do you know who would be interested?

Remember, your imperfect start in making disciples always beats someone's perfect but untried model.

# DEEPER: APOSTLES

*When Jesus had called the Twelve together, he gave them
power and authority . . . and he sent them out.*

LUKE 9:1–2

An apostle in the New Testament is someone sent with a commission to convey news. In the Jewish background, the concept refers to someone who represents another with full authority. An apostle adheres strictly to his commission and acts in the interest of the sender.[109]

After a night of prayer, Jesus chose twelve out of his wider band of disciples and called them apostles.[110] The Twelve were appointed to be with him and to learn how to make disciples—they were missionaries-in-training. As apostles, they were given power and authority to cast out demons, to heal the sick, and to preach the good news of the kingdom.[111]

Neither Scripture nor the early Christian writings indicate that apostleship was limited to the Twelve.[112] Luke applies the term apostle to Paul and Barnabas;[113] and in his letters, Paul applies the term to James, the brother of Jesus and to Paul's coworkers Silas, Timothy, Apollos, Andronicus and Junia, and Epaphroditus.[114] Paul distinguished the Twelve from "all the apostles"[115] and taught that apostleship is a spiritual gift for the church's common good and its ministry.[116]

The word "apostle" was applied to individuals in the New Testament in two main ways.[117]

## 1. The Twelve (and Paul)

The Twelve occupy a unique place in God's purposes as the nucleus of a missionary movement. Their number is closed, symbolizing the twelve tribes of the new Israel.

The Twelve are unique as the authoritative witnesses of the life, death, and resurrection of Jesus. They became guardians of the gospel, which has been preserved for us in the New Testament. Paul was rightly not a member of the Twelve. He had not been a witness to Jesus from the beginning.[118] Yet the risen Lord chose Paul, as an apostle and witness to the resurrection.

The uniqueness of the Twelve and Paul lay not in their function as missionary pioneers but in their calling as witnesses to the life, death, and resurrection of Jesus and as guardians of the gospel. There are no successors to the apostles in this sense.

Yet the church in a wider sense is *apostolic*, founded on the witness of the apostles, empowered by the Spirit, and sent into the world to continue the ministry of Jesus.[119]

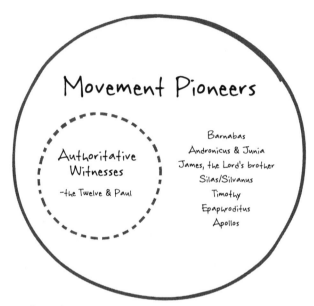

*All apostles are movement pioneers; some (the Twelve and Paul)*
*are also authoritative witnesses.*

## 2. A Wider Group of Movement Pioneers

In the New Testament, there is also a wider group of apostles who serve as pioneer missionaries, spreading the gospel, training disciples, and multiplying churches.[120] Alongside their unique role as authoritative witnesses, the Twelve and Paul also shared in this functional ministry of apostleship.

Jesus continues to call movement pioneers to lead his people into the fullness of what it means to be a missionary movement. These movement pioneers follow the example of Jesus and the disciples he trained.[121]

**They see multiplying movements of disciples and churches.** They are catalysts for movements of disciples and churches spreading to every place and every people group.

***They connect with people in unreached fields.*** They cross boundaries (geographic, linguistic, cultural, social, economic) to establish contact with people who are far from God. They seek out responsive people who have been prepared by God.

***They share the gospel.*** They communicate the truth about the nature of God and salvation through Christ calling everyone to repentance and faith expressed in baptism. They equip new disciples to spread the good news about Jesus throughout their community and region.

***They train disciples.*** They lead people to faith in Jesus Christ and teach them to obey all that Jesus has commanded.

***They gather communities.*** They form disciples into church communities with local leadership. They engage in loving one another, faithful witness, and the observance of the Lord's Supper.

***They multiply workers.*** They equip local church leaders to reach their region in depth. In partnership with the churches, they form apostolic teams that are launched into unreached fields.

For the first decade, the Twelve did not leave for the ends of the earth but remained based in Jerusalem. It was important for the Twelve to be in proximity, as they established the norm of apostolic teaching. Yet even in those early years Peter and John led the movement's spread throughout the city of Jerusalem and the whole of Judea, Samaria, and Galilee.

All that changed by AD 41 when we encounter James and the elders, not the apostles, leading the church in Jerusalem. At that time Peter, and most likely the other apostles, were forced out of Jerusalem by Herod's persecution.[122] The Twelve were no longer based in Jerusalem but left to pursue their wider missionary callings. The apostles understood themselves not as local pastor-elders but as movement pioneers. When the work in any location was established, they handed leadership over to others and left for unreached fields.[123]

This pattern of apostolic ministry is found throughout the book of Acts, with a particularly clear example of the process found in Paul and Barnabas's first missionary journey together.[124]

The ministry of an apostle is to pioneer and strengthen movements of multiplying disciples and churches as they break into unreached fields—a ministry that will not end until Christ returns. Their leadership empowers and releases those around them to lead. Jesus rarely ministered alone, but took others with him, including women, as he went from village to village.[125] In the same way, Paul rarely minis-tered alone. The New Testament identifies around one hundred men and women connected with Paul's pioneering and church strengthe-ning.[126] Both men and women serve as coworkers in the local churches and on his mobile missionary band.[127]

Acts provides examples of how movement pioneers functioned, but Luke has little interest in clarifying the structure of the early church.[128] He is more focused on the nature of God's mission, the content of the gospel, and the work of the Holy Spirit in gifting not just apostles but prophets, evangelists, teachers, elders, and all of God's people to serve in the spread of the gospel.

Today, many are reluctant to apply the term "apostle" or "apostolic" to any individual because of a valid concern to protect the unique role of the Twelve and Paul. Instead, we tend to use the words "missionary" and "mission," words that are equivalent in meaning to "apostle" or "apostolic." However, in doing so we have lost not just the title but also the function of apostolic leadership.

Our primary model of church leadership is a settled pastor-teacher overseeing a congregation of believers. Although this is a legitimate leadership role in the local church, it should not come at the expense of movement pioneers. Paul's apostolic ministry meant that while he was at Ephesus, the gospel went out to a city of two hundred thousand; and through the disciples trained by Paul, the Word went out to the whole of Asia Minor, and churches were planted throughout the region.[129] Once Paul had strengthened the disciples and churches, and appointed local leaders, he and his team moved on to unreached fields.

Paul could function as a pastor-teacher, but he was not confined to that role. As an apostle, he saw whole cities and regions penetrated by the gospel. He set in motion movements of disciples and churches. Wherever there are disciple making movements, we will find apostolic leaders like Paul.

I'm wary of anyone who wants to put the title "apostle" on their business card. The title can be used as a shortcut to spiritual authority. Paul was called by the Lord Jesus to proclaim the gospel in unreached fields, make disciples, plant and strengthen churches, and multiply workers before seeking out new, unreached places. His life and ministry were shaped by the death and resurrection power of Jesus. These are the realities that matter more than any title. Until the gospel reaches the ends of the earth and Jesus returns, there will always be a need for apostles.

There are some good examples of movements making room for apostles to emerge today. They begin by training every disciple to be seed sowers. Those who do so effectively are trained to form new disciples into healthy churches. Those who can multiply churches receive coaching and further training. Those with apostolic gifts emerge from engagement in sharing the gospel, making disciples and multiplying churches. The critical transition to a movement occurs when there are streams of multi-generational new disciples and churches.[130]

# WE WON'T STOP (4:1–22)

Jesus told his disciples that they would be arrested, imprisoned, and persecuted. He told them not to worry when they stood before rulers because
he would provide the words and wisdom that none of their enemies
would be able to resist or contradict.[131] This promise is about to be tested.

Peter and John are still speaking when the priests and Sadducees
arrive with the captain of the temple guard. The two apostles have been
at the temple since 3 p.m. By now it is evening and too late to convene
the Sanhedrin—Israel's highest court—so Peter and John are placed in
overnight custody.

Meanwhile, many who heard the Word "believed"— Luke's shorthand
for "they repented, they were baptized, their sins were forgiven, they
received the Holy Spirit, and they were added to the community."[132] At
the very least, the total number of disciples in Jerusalem now rose to five
thousand.[133]

The Sanhedrin would have sat in a semi-circle with the two apostles
standing in the middle, just as Jesus had once stood before them.[134] The
rulers, elders, and teachers of the law represented the elite ruling families of
Jerusalem. Under the Romans they controlled the temple, the priesthood, and
the Sanhedrin. At their head was Annas, a former high priest and patriarch
of the most powerful clan in Jerusalem. He was the real power behind his
son-in-law Caiaphas, the reigning high priest who presided at Jesus' trial.[135]
These officials were dismayed that Jesus' execution had not squashed his
movement. They believed they alone had authority to teach the people.

Peter decides the best defense is to preach the gospel to his judges, so,
like an Old Testament prophet, he speaks God's Word in the power of the
Spirit. Peter bears witness to Jesus of Nazareth, the man they crucified,
yet God raised from the dead. He points to the lame man's healing as a
sign that, through Jesus' death and victory, the restoration of all things
has begun.[136]

God's purposes for Israel are fulfilled in Jesus Christ. Only he can
forgive sins and rescue from God's judgment. The high priest cannot save;
the temple and its sacrifices cannot save—only Jesus can.

Peter and John are ordinary men—amateurs, untrained in theology—
yet they speak with authority because they had been with Jesus, and he

had shaped their hearts and minds to become the leaders of the movement that will fulfill Israel's calling.

The authorities can't deny the miracle, but they object that the healing was performed in Jesus' name and that salvation was proclaimed in his name. They will allow the church in Jerusalem to heal the sick, but they must not speak in the name of Jesus—the very thing Peter and John refuse to do.

After further threats, they are released. The apostles have their first warning under Jewish law. They will not get off lightly if there is a second offense. The persecution will end if they are silent. Yet they must continue to speak.

The leaders of the nation are powerless to stop this new movement. For them and their rulership, this is the beginning of the end. Two unschooled fishermen, who had been trained by Jesus, are shown to be the true leaders of God's people.

God is not simply going to reform the leadership of Israel; he is replacing it. Because they refuse to listen to Jesus, they will be cut off from God's people.[137]

As the religious institution crumbles, God is forming his people out of the ruins. At their center are twelve ordinary men with Galilean accents and empty pockets. They can't boast of silver and gold, but in Jesus' name, they can heal a lame man and proclaim the good news that brings salvation.

The lesson still applies. God will abandon any religious institution that rejects the authority of his Word, resists the Holy Spirit, and is unfaithful to the core missionary task. There is no shortage of examples in the Western world of once-dynamic movements that are now in terminal decline.[138] What matters is not the institution and its history but the men and women who have put their faith in Jesus and given him their allegiance. God will do a new thing and fulfill his purposes through those who are faithful to him.

Within a generation, Roman armies will surround Jerusalem and take the city. The temple, the priesthood, and the sacrifices will end. Jesus' words of destruction and desolation will be fulfilled. Meanwhile, these disciples will take the message of repentance and the forgiveness of sins to the ends of the earth.[139]

# WHY DO THE NATIONS RAGE? (4:23–31)

After they are released, Peter and John seek out "their own"—a phrase that normally refers to family but here describes the family of faith.[140] The true household of God has been cast out of the temple and now gathers in a home. The apostles give a report, and then the room erupts with prayer.

Luke shows us how a persecuted movement prays.

*They place the threat in the context of the character and power of God revealed in Psalm 2.* God is the Sovereign Lord, the all-powerful Ruler and Creator. He rules over the world he has made. He rules over history. Why should they fear men?

*They know who they are.* David is their father, and they are the true Israel, the inheritors of God's promises. They find their identity in the Scriptures, seen through the lens of Jesus' life, death, and resurrection. David's words in the psalm are the words of God, inspired by the Holy Spirit.

*They note that powerful men can only do what God allows.* Herod and Pilate, who persecuted Jesus, are like the rulers who opposed God and his king in David's day. The rulers are persecuting his disciples, but God will still achieve his purposes. The disciples will not give these rulers a place only God occupies. "The One enthroned in heaven laughs!"[141]

*They place themselves in God's care.* Like Moses, like David, like the prophets, like Jesus, they are God's servants. The believers did not ask God for peace. Without telling God what to do, they asked him to take note of the threats made against them. God will take note, and he will bring these rulers to account—in his way and in his time.

*They ask for boldness—confidence, openness, freedom—as they keep speaking God's Word.* This boldness is not natural; it is a gift from God. Their bold proclamation is a sign of the Spirit who empowers all of God's people to prophesy. They ask God to confirm his Word through signs and wonders. They could have asked for miracles of judgment upon their oppressors; instead, they ask for miracles of mercy. They seek power in Jesus' name that will confirm the message about him.

These believers are praying themselves into both greater trouble and a greater harvest. God answers, and the house is shaken. As at Pentecost, they are all filled with the Holy Spirit, and *all* the believers speak the Word of God boldly.

This won't be the last time the movement is threatened. Messengers will be beaten, arrested, jailed, put on trial, and murdered. God will answer their prayer. The Word will grow, spread, and multiply, producing disciples and churches to the glory of God.

Peter and John did not go to the temple looking for trouble. They went ready to proclaim the good news about Jesus whenever and to whomever they could. They did not calculate the risk; they obeyed God and took the opportunity. They knew what to do because they had been with Jesus. They'd watched him, and he'd trained them and given them his authority. If persecution came, it came; but, regardless, they will follow Jesus and make disciples.

## MOVEMENTS TODAY: DAW'S STORY

For centuries, Christianity was the dominant faith of Western society. A generation ago, it lost its favored status and became just one of the many acceptable options in a pluralistic world. In the last decade, Western society has repudiated Christian faith and morality as harmful.[142] How should we respond? Not by hiding behind locked doors as the disciples once did. If Acts is our guide, our response should be the free and open communication of God's living Word, a willingness to suffer for his name, and a confidence in God for the outcome. Across the world, many believers are already living this way.

Husband and wife, Peter and Saeng, served as movement pioneers in a rural district in a small Asian nation under Communist rule.[143] Through his work as a development project leader, Peter met a village leader named Daw and led him to Christ.

Peter met secretly with Daw to share stories about Jesus and lead him through a journey of discovery from Genesis to Christ. The change in Daw's life was dramatic. He gave up drinking and stopped beating his wife. She too wanted to know Christ, which drew the attention of everyone in the village.

Peter modeled for Daw how to share the gospel, how to baptize, and how to begin a 3-Thirds Discipleship group.[144] Eleven families (166 people) believed and were baptized by Daw who became the leader of the new church.

As the movement spread from person to person and village to village, so did the government's opposition. The local governor arrested and imprisoned the seven elders of the church. Although they spent months in prison, their faith grew. One local leader was jailed four times, and during one of those imprisonments they beat him so severely that his skull was fractured.

Then the killings began. One believer was shot dead in front of his young daughter. Another was beheaded. Then, in 2004, Daw, his wife, and child were taken and never seen again.

Some churches struggled to survive the onslaught. Others continued to spread the gospel and plant new churches in unreached villages. By 2007, there were around five thousand believers in one hundred churches.

Peter and Saeng and their children sacrificed to see this movement of God; the new disciples paid an even greater price, giving up not only their own lives, but in one case, the life of their child. How pointless unless Jesus is our only hope of salvation. How foolish unless the risen Lord is with us when we suffer for his name.

The greatest defense of the gospel is that it is worth dying for.[145]

Most of us will not face violent persecution. But we all need help to overcome the fear of rejection. How? By taking a step of obedience. Offer to pray for someone in need, right there on the spot. Share a story from the life of Jesus and ask the person what they think. Learn a simple gospel outline. Invite someone to read the Bible with you, using a 3-Thirds approach. You might ask one hundred people and get ninety-nine knockbacks. That's the bad news. The good news is, if you ask one hundred people, someone might say yes.

# DEEPER: PRAYER

*After they prayed, the place where they were meeting*
*was shaken. And they were all filled with the Holy*
*Spirit and spoke the word of God boldly.*

ACTS 4:31

From the beginning of Luke to the end of Acts, the references to prayer mark turning points and new beginnings.[146]

In the opening scene of Luke's Gospel, the angel announced to Zechariah, "Your prayer has been heard."[147] In the Garden of

Gethsemane, Jesus' disciples slept while he prayed, but at Pentecost, as the disciples waited for the promised Spirit, prayer filled the upper room. They prayed because Jesus had restored them and commanded them to be his witnesses. They prayed, not to summon the Spirit but because the Spirit was coming, and when the Spirit came, the mission began.

Prayer is a distinguishing mark of the movement. In the first description of church life, Luke writes that they devoted themselves to the apostles' teaching and to fellowship, to the breaking of bread and to *prayer*. To be devoted means to be persistent without giving up.[148] The disciples met in one another's homes and in the temple courts; they gave thanks, they worshipped, and they prayed. This is a pattern that was repeated, not just in Jerusalem but wherever we find communities of disciples. They were a praying people.

This commitment to prayer is drawn from Jesus' example and teaching.[149] Jesus prayed at his baptism, and the Spirit descended upon him; as the disciples prayed, the Spirit fell at Pentecost. Jesus prayed all night before appointing the Twelve; the disciples prayed before choosing Matthias. Jesus prayed on the cross that his enemies would be forgiven; Stephen cried, "Lord do not hold this sin against them" as he was martyred.[150] As Jesus committed his spirit to the Father, so the first martyr called out to the Lord Jesus to receive his spirit.

The prayers the church offered were centered on Jesus.[151] He is the Savior, the Author of life, the One who grants repentance and forgiveness, the coming Judge. He sends the Holy Spirit. There is no salvation except through him. Salvation comes, and discipleship begins, by calling on his name.

Prayer is animated by the presence of the Spirit. The Spirit enables visions, dreams, prophetic words, unknown tongues, and wisdom. Through prayer, the lame walk; Tabitha was restored to life; Publius's father was healed, and the gospel spread to those who had eyes to see and ears to hear.[152]

Prayer was linked with the selection and commissioning of leaders.[153] When the apostles were overwhelmed with needs within the community, they appointed additional leaders so they could prioritize prayer and the spreading of the Word. Saul's confrontation with Jesus led to three days of prayer and fasting. The proud persecutor was transformed into a humble man of prayer.[154] When the Spirit set apart Paul and Barnabas for the work, the church at Antioch sent them off with prayer and fasting. At the completion of the work, Paul and Barnabas prayed and fasted before appointing elders to the new churches.[155]

The gospel brought persecution, and persecution fueled their prayer. After Peter and John were released from arrest, the disciples raised their voices together and prayed.[156] When Paul and Silas were beaten and thrown into prison, they prayed and sang to God at midnight, while the other prisoners listened.[157] They prayed because there is one true God who is the Creator and Lord of history and the Father of his people. They prayed because they were dependent on God for the progress of his mission. Only God can convince people of the truth of the gospel. Only God can confirm his Word in power. Only God can change the human heart. And so they prayed.

These were the prayers of a people on the move; a people who knew what their mission was and were pursuing it. When they prayed, the Spirit came, and the Word went out. Prayer is not a substitute for action but goes hand in hand with obedience to the core missionary task.

# ONE HEART, ONE MIND (4:32–37)

This is the second summary describing the life of the disciples. Luke is not just concerned with growth; he also wants to show the quality of communal life that the gospel brings.

The Spirit is at work, both through signs and wonders and in the miracle of sacrificial giving. In line with the Old Testament and the teaching of Jesus, they determine that among God's people, there should be no one in need.[158]

There is famine and political turmoil in the region, and life is hard.[159] Diaspora Jews often returned to Jerusalem to live out their later years, and many ended up as widows without local family support. The Galileans had left behind their occupations to live in Jerusalem. Some disciples would have faced the loss of income or family support due to their new faith.

Those in financial need are provided for, as wealthier members sell property and give the proceeds to the apostles to distribute. The sale of assets happens as needs arise and is not compulsory.[160]

Luke gives us this glimpse of church life, not just to satisfy our curiosity but because he is seeking to show the importance of discipleship lived in community. Salvation begins with the grace of God, but it is always expressed in community, and leads to love and generosity.

Luke often introduces his main characters before focusing on them. On this occasion it's Joseph. To distinguish him from the many other Josephs, the apostles call him Barnabas. He is from Cyprus where there was a large Jewish colony. Full of the Holy Spirit and faith,[161] Barnabas is a positive example of generosity and is in stark contrast with the tragic example of Ananias and Sapphira.

## DEEPER: POVERTY AND RICHES

*No one claimed that any of their possessions was*
*their own, but they shared everything they had.*

ACTS 4:32

Israel neglected her mission to be a light to the nations. As a result, she was under the domination of a Gentile empire, suffering under Satan's oppressive rule. Jesus proclaimed the coming of God's rule and the plundering of Satan's kingdom. This was good news to "the poor" who call upon God in their need.[162]

## Good News to the Poor

Following Isaiah 61, Jesus announced that he came to preach good news to the poor.[163] Who are the poor? He was referring to the whole of Israel, returned from exile, dispirited and longing for God's salvation.[164] The poor are not limited to the economically poor, or else how are we to understand the breadth of Jesus' ministry?[165] The poor are those who, in their need, cry out to God for deliverance. For Jesus, the poor are those who are regarded as outside the boundaries of God's people—prostitutes, the demon possessed, tax collectors, and Gentiles. Jesus came to release the prisoners, those who are captive and oppressed by Satan through illness, demonic control, and sin.[166] The word for *release* in the New Testament refers to the release from or forgiveness of sins.[167] The release from sin and the freedom to live a new life was at the center of Jesus' mission.

## True Discipleship

Jesus appeared as the suffering Servant of God, calling everyone to turn back to God and receive forgiveness for their sins. A true disciple must be willing to turn their back on wealth, family loyalties, and even life itself. Those who refuse to turn are "the rich" who are satisfied with their life in this age. Poverty is not an ideal to be sought after, but, if necessary, the disciple must be willing to renounce wealth to follow Jesus. Some, like the young nobleman, chose riches above the chance to be with Jesus in his missionary band.[168] Others chose discipleship expressed in sacrificial generosity toward those in need. Zacchaeus's restitution and generosity to the poor did not earn him his salvation but flowed from it.[169]

That same generosity was on display in the church in Jerusalem. The disciples in Jerusalem shared meals and opened their homes to one another, regardless of differences in wealth and social status. God's grace was so powerfully at work that there were no needy persons among them.[170] Some disciples continued to own property, and there were different social and economic levels represented within the church community.[171]

When Greek-speaking widows were overlooked in the distribution of food, it became a matter for the whole community. The matter was resolved in a way that did not impinge on the apostles' priority of prayer and getting the Word out to a lost world.

Later in Acts, generosity helped strengthen the bonds between the disciples of the Gentile mission and the church in Jerusalem. On two occasions, Paul collected funds from the churches of the Gentile mission and delivered them to the church in Jerusalem for the needs of the poor.[172]

## Money and the Spiritual Battle

Satan sought to destroy the Jesus movement from within—through greed in the case of Judas's betrayal, and through deception in the case of Ananias and Sapphira.[173] Amid a great move of God in Samaria, the newly converted Simon sought to buy the power of the Holy Spirit by offering Peter money; in Ephesus, an attack on the disciples is instigated by people whose trade was threatened by the gospel;[174] and Paul's long imprisonment in Caesarea was in part due to the governor's hope that Paul would offer him a bribe.[175]

This spiritual battle continues today. In recent times there has been a flood of high-profile church leaders who have chosen wealth, pleasure, and power over sacrificial service—with devastating consequences. We need to heed Peter's warning to Simon of Samaria who thought he could buy the gift of God with money—"May your money perish with you!"[176] In contrast, Paul worked with his hands to supply his needs and the needs of his coworkers when it was required.[177] John Wesley, who led a movement that shook the world, could say with Peter and John, "Silver or gold I do not have." Wesley lived his motto: Earn all you can; save all you can; give away all you can.[178]

## Good News for Everyone

Luke dedicated his Gospel and Acts to the well-born Theophilus and was happy to identify the prominent people who joined the movement. Some of them opened their homes and provided a place for the disciples to meet. Luke records the conversion of Cornelius the Roman Centurion; Sergius Paulus, the proconsul of Cyprus; some prominent women of Thessalonica and Beria; and Dionysius, a member of the Athenian Areopagus. Paul included among his friends some of the leading officials of the province of Asia Minor.[179] In Rome Paul bore witness both to the slaves in the emperor's household and before the emperor himself.

The gospel is for everyone: jailers and sailors, soldiers and businesswomen, widows and governors, kings and slaves.

## *Mission Drift*

Mission in Acts is the spread of God's Word throughout the world, resulting in disciples and churches among every people and every place. But Western Christianity has shifted the emphasis to the transformation of the world politically, economically, and socially. With this mindset, the church is viewed as an illegitimate center of God's mission and instead the world sets the agenda for the church.[180] The right ordering of society has become the center of God's mission.

In Acts, the message is clear: Discipleship should result in the elimination of poverty within the believing community. In addition, every disciple is bound to obey Christ's teaching in caring for those who are in need outside the Christian community. However, the restructuring of society is not part of the core missionary task God has given his people.

# GREAT FEAR SEIZES ALL WHO HEAR (5:1–11)

The movement has faced the external threat of persecution. Now it faces an internal threat from two of its own members, corrupted by Satan.

The property belonging to Ananias and Sapphira is theirs to keep and theirs to give away. They are not compelled to sell. They publicly declare all the proceeds of the sale to be available for the poor. Yet their motive is to position themselves as generous donors, worthy of respect and honor. In lying to the community, they lie to the Holy Spirit. They pretend to be insiders, but their actions deny God's holy presence with his people.[181]

Satan seeks a foothold within the church through this couple. The last time Luke mentioned Satan was when he entered Judas and sought to sift the disciples like wheat.[182] This couple act like Judas, who also betrayed Jesus for money.

Peter does not cause the deaths of Ananias and Sapphira—God does. Peter, led by the Spirit, speaks prophetically of what God is about to do. The same power that healed is now at work to judge. In the new Israel, judgment begins in the house of God.[183]

Twice Luke tells us that great fear fell on the whole church and the wider community. A revelation of the holiness and power of God is the point of the story.[184] God is present with his people and can act in judgment.[185] The same Spirit that gave the community its life also maintains its holiness and unity.[186]

When we avoid the warnings in this episode, we recast God in our own image.[187] The possibility of God's judgment on sinners on this side of eternity is found throughout the New Testament.[188] Paul knew of many among the Corinthians who were sick and some who had died because of their abuse of the Lord's Supper. Luke doesn't tell us how to know for sure when God's judgment occurs in this life, just that it happens. He pulls back the curtain to reveal how God works to discipline and warn those within the community who take the death of his Son for granted.

For the first time, Luke introduces the word "church," meaning an assembly or gathering. Why has Luke waited so long before using this word? He wanted to show us the reality of church before he gave it a name.

The word he uses refers to the assembly of free men eligible to vote in a Greek city—the *ecclesia*. But the most important background for understanding the term is found in the Greek version of the Hebrew Scriptures, where the word describes redeemed Israel, gathered before God.[189]

The disciples are the true people of God; they must not take their identity for granted.

## MOVEMENTS TODAY: WHEN A LEADER FALLS

Husband and wife Terry and Amy Ruff arrived in Ghana, trusting God for an indigenous movement of disciples and churches in the north of the country.[190] On their first day, God led them to Isaac, a local disciple with the same heart. They worked together for the next ten years, and through Isaac, a multiplying movement emerged, evidenced by thousands of baptisms and hundreds of new churches.

Then Satan struck back.

Isaac began an adulterous relationship. He claimed God had spoken to him in a dream and approved of the new relationship. When Terry challenged him, Isaac announced he would return to Islam and take his disciples and groups with him.

Terry told him, "Your dream doesn't trump the Word of God." Terry loved Isaac like a son, and so it broke his heart to know his discipline of Isaac could destroy their relationship and undermine the movement. However, he knew that not only was the movement in danger, but that Isaac was also in danger of God's discipline and must be warned.

God's grace won the day as Terry spoke the truth in love. Weeks later, Isaac returned and confessed, "I feel like a ram, caught in the thicket, deep in the bush, and I want to come back." Recognizing that Isaac was truly repentant, Terry and a local pastor from Isaac's tribe journeyed with Isaac for the next eighteen months and restored him.

Today the movement continues to advance in northern Ghana. Partly through Isaac's leadership, the movement has spread to Ivory Coast, Niger, Nigeria, and Zimbabwe.

We cannot understand the movement of God until we realize we are at war, and the battle is not just out there but is also within our own hearts. The battle is won in our surrender to the Father in the wilderness, before it is ever played out on the stage of history. Before Jesus proclaimed the gospel of the kingdom, he learned obedience. God uses every temptation and every attack of our enemy to take us deeper in loving surrender. That's where victories are won and lost.

## DEEPER: THE BATTLE

*God anointed Jesus of Nazareth with the Holy Spirit and power, and ... he went around doing good and healing all who were under the power of the devil.*

ACTS 10:38

Luke shows Satan to be the enemy of humanity, and the ruler of the kingdom of darkness opposed to God's reign.[191] He attacked and undermined every new stage in God's plan of salvation. He tempted Jesus to betray his Sonship and his mission. He sifted the disciples like wheat and inspired Judas to betray Jesus.[192]

Satan's purpose is to snatch away the Word of God so that people do not believe and are not saved.[193] This battle against Satan was won by Jesus' obedience to his Father's Word, dependence on the Holy Spirit, and faithfulness to his mission to lay down his life as a ransom for many.

After his defeat in the wilderness, Satan withdrew to wait for the "decisive moment" when Jesus was in Jerusalem, and it was then that Satan entered Judas the traitor.[194] Meanwhile, Jesus returned to Galilee in the power of the Holy Spirit to launch his assault on Satan's kingdom. As he healed the sick, cast out demons, and called everyone to repent and believe, Jesus was engaged in spiritual warfare—setting Satan's captives free.

Jesus enlisted his disciples in the battle and shared his power and authority over the Enemy.[195] Satan fell like lightning as Jesus' disciples cast out demons in his name. Such power over demons is a sign that the kingdom has come.[196]

Jesus described his approaching death as "the hour when darkness reigns."[197] When Satan entered Judas, he was seeking to destroy Jesus and expected the movement to die with him.[198] Though victory is won through the cross, the war still rages. The disciples' mandate is to turn people from the dominion of Satan to God.[199] As the Word goes out, the captives are set free, and they are united with all those who are made holy by faith in Christ.[200]

Satan tried to shake Peter's faith, in the hope that he would bring down Jesus' leading disciple. But Jesus prayed that Simon's faith would not fail and that he would turn back to God and strengthen his brothers.[201] And indeed, Peter did turn back and fulfilled the role Jesus gave him in strengthening his brothers as they awaited the coming of the Spirit and the launch of a missionary movement.

Satan fought back through persecution and attacks on the unity of God's people. The new movement was threatened from without and from within. But the Spirit filled and united the new community in Jerusalem in genuine love. However, one couple allowed Satan, rather than the Holy Spirit, to fill their hearts and undermine the purity of God's people.[202] Satan failed once again to undermine God's plan. Great fear seized the whole church and all who heard about these events. Yet more and more men and women believed in the Lord and were added to their number.[203]

When Satan stirs up the rulers of this world to destroy the movement, Jesus' disciples pray for the power of the Spirit and boldness to proclaim the Word.[204] The victory over Satan is tangibly demonstrated by the establishment of disciples and churches learning to obey Jesus.

Saul launched a violent persecution against the early church, but his attempts failed, as those he persecuted were scattered and subsequently preached the Word everywhere they went. Although Satan sought to use Saul in his attempts to destroy the church, Jesus was triumphant, capturing Saul and choosing him to open the eyes of Gentiles and Jews so that they would turn from darkness to light.[205]

In Cyprus, the proconsul Sergius Paulus, wanted to hear the Word of God, but Elymas, a false prophet and magician stood in his way.[206] Paul, filled with the Holy Spirit, denounced Elymas as a son of the devil and an enemy of all that is right. Elymas was blinded for a time and the proconsul believed the teaching about the Lord.

In Philippi, Paul cast out a demon from a fortunetelling slave girl—and all hell broke loose. Later, Paul and Silas were deep in the inner cell of the prison with their feet shackled. All they had left was their worship and unrelenting faith in God. God intervened, and the jailor and his household believed … Satan's prisoners were set free. Paul and Silas departed the city as free men, leaving behind a vibrant community of disciples who continued the battle.

Satan attacked each phase of God's plan, whether through individuals within or outside the movement.[207] He aims to destroy faith in God's Word, which alone brings salvation.[208] The key weapon in Jesus' arsenal was his surrender to the Father's will.

## MOVEMENTS TODAY: SO MUCH WAS AT STAKE!

I was interviewing Terry and Amy Ruff about the disciple making movement they've seen in northern Uganda.[209] After ten years, there are now multiple streams of new disciples and churches in the region, and the leaders they have trained are sparking movements in other African nations.

They shared the lessons they've learned, including the importance of a simple strategy, the training and coaching of local leaders, input from those who have already seen movements take place, and adapting their methods to the context. I turned off the recording and told them how their partnership in the ministry as a couple shone through their answers. "It hasn't always been that way," they said.

"Really," I said. "Do you mind if I keep recording and you tell me more?"

They described the spiritual battles they'd fought. There were the moral failures of two key local leaders. There was Amy's battle against life-threatening cancer. Their home in Ghana had been robbed five times, and on one occasion, Amy was held at knifepoint. The list went on. In every battle, they learned to trust God to work through their weakness.

"We couldn't give up," Terry kept repeating. "So much was at stake!"

In Acts, and for us today, Satan is always opposing the advance of the Word. Satan is defeated, yet the battle rages, and our calling is to turn people from the dominion of Satan to God.[210] The messengers may suffer, but they remain in God's care. We do not need to fear. Jesus showed the way. The battle is won through loving surrender and obedience to the Father's will revealed in his Word.

# YOU HAVE FILLED JERUSALEM! (5:12–42)

Earlier, the disciples responded to persecution by praying for signs and wonders accompanied by the bold proclamation of the gospel. Their prayers were answered as they gathered in large numbers on the east side of the temple mount in Solomon's Portico.

The new movement is highly regarded by the people, yet following the deaths of Ananias and Sapphira, some are afraid to join them. The power of the miracles is attractive, but the Holy Spirit also demands obedience. The people keep their distance with healthy respect until they are willing to surrender to that power and follow.[211]

Still, thousands are added to the community as they come to faith in Jesus. God's power is on display through signs and wonders, adding authority to the apostles' message. The Lord Jesus is continuing his ministry through his people.

The movement overflows from Jerusalem to the surrounding towns.[212] It is spreading beyond the center. The authorities cannot ignore this threat to their position.

The high priest and the Sadducees have all the apostles rounded up and jailed. In the middle of the night, God intervenes through an angel who releases them and tells them to go to the temple courts at dawn and proclaim this new life to the people. (Ironically, the Sadducees do not believe in angels.[213])

The apostles were not to flee Jerusalem or hide behind closed doors. They were to go to the one place where they can be found and do what they had been forbidden to do.[214] This rescue was not an escape but an opportunity to proclaim Christ. In Israel's most holy place, God was provoking a confrontation. The leadership of Israel has passed from the high priests to the Twelve, who proclaim Jesus as Messiah and Savior, in defiance of the Sanhedrin's ban.[215]

They arrest the apostles a second time and rebuke them for disobeying the order not to teach in "that name." (The high priest can't even bring himself to say the name "Jesus.") Despite the order, the apostles had filled Jerusalem with their teaching and were holding these religious leaders guilty of Jesus' death.

Peter and the apostles declare, "We must obey God rather than human beings!" This is not a defense but a restatement of their position.

Then Peter puts his accusers on trial, reminding them that they crucified Jesus, but the God of their ancestors raised him from the dead; he is at the right hand of God as Prince and Savior that he might bring Israel to repentance and forgiveness of sins.

God offers salvation to the officials who had Jesus crucified.

The leaders of the Sanhedrin are furious and want the apostles executed. Under Roman rule they do not have the authority to do so, but they will find a way, as they did with Jesus, and will do with Stephen.

Gamaliel, the leading Pharisee, and teacher of Saul, speaks up. The Sadducees listen to this Pharisee who has the support of the people.[216] Gamaliel reminds them of other rebellions, which came to nothing once the leader was dead. He argues if this movement is of human origin it will fail. If it is from God, they must not oppose it.

The Sanhedrin relent and have the apostles flogged. They would have been stripped to the waist and made to kneel to be lashed up to thirty-nine times on the back and chest with a three-stranded strap of calf hide.[217] It was a severe punishment that could result in a fatal loss of blood.

Again, the apostles are ordered not to speak in Jesus' name. They leave rejoicing that they are worthy to suffer disgrace for Christ. Earlier, the believers prayed for boldness rather than safety; God answers their prayer.[218]

The suffering of the apostles does not halt the advance of the movement. Every day they go to the temple and disobey the command not to speak in Jesus' name. They preach and teach and fellowship at Solomon's Portico and in homes. This is a movement of God, and Gamaliel was right: those who oppose it are fighting God. The Twelve have replaced the Sanhedrin as the true leaders of Israel, but the conflict will continue to escalate.

Jesus promised his disciples persecution. Throughout history and around the world today, wherever the gospel advances, there is pushback. Those of us who live in relative safety may wonder if we would have the courage to stand up in the face of threats and intimidation. But to think this way is to place our focus on the limits of our courage rather than the sufficiency of Christ. Jesus, who promised persecution, also promised his presence through the Holy Spirit. The Spirit sustained them and made them bold.

In the wealthy West, the gospel has been met with indifference; increasingly it is met with ridicule and hostility but rarely violence. Tolerance can be purchased at the price of our silence: We are not to talk about salvation through Jesus' name alone. I grew up going to a private school named after the missionary William Carey. There are two other elite schools in Melbourne also named after missionaries—Wesley and Xavier. Each of the three have arisen from different Christian traditions, but they all believed in salvation through Christ alone, and they all upheld the teaching of Scripture on human sexuality. Today, I doubt if these three missionaries would be welcome to speak at the schools that bear their names. We can be left alone if we agree to be silent about salvation through Christ alone and the call to obey him.

Meanwhile, in Iran, China, northern Nigeria, and North Korea, the gospel is spreading through the testimony of disciples who refuse to be silent.

# DEEPER: PETER AND THE SHAPING OF A MOVEMENT LEADER

*Go away from me, Lord; I am a sinful man!*
LUKE 5:8

Peter is a major figure throughout Luke's Gospel and the first half of Acts. Only Paul matches his contribution. Peter's life is a case study in how God shapes movement leaders over the whole course of their lives.

## 1. Calling

For Peter, the journey began when the carpenter from Nazareth burst into his fisherman's world and disrupted his existence.[219] The miraculous catch of fish that day revealed Jesus' power and authority in Peter's world. His response was to fall at Jesus' feet and confess not just his weakness but his sinfulness.

What qualified Peter as a disciple and leader in training was not his abilities or his experience or his godliness; he was qualified because he obeyed Jesus' call—to follow him and learn to fish for others. Natural abilities, spiritual giftedness, positional authority, and charisma are poor substitutes for the spiritual authority that comes from surrender and obedience to Christ. This is the first and most important lesson of movement leadership.

## 2. On the Road

There was no classroom to sit in or textbook to read. Peter had to follow Jesus and learn how to make disciples. That meant going on the road, learning to be like Jesus, and learning to do what Jesus did. This is how movement leaders are made.

Peter accompanied Jesus as they went from town to town, learning how to heal the sick, cast out demons, proclaim the kingdom, and call everyone to repent. Jesus taught Peter how to go into unreached communities and make disciples. How different this is to our training programs today. We prefer to make leaders in the classroom; Jesus trained Peter on the road.

Eventually Peter grasped that Jesus was the Messiah, the Son of the living God. Yet Peter could not accept that God would hand the Messiah over to suffer a shameful death. He played Satan's part in seeking to dissuade Jesus from going to the cross.

Peter would never grasp the reality of God's grace until he had faced the depth of his own sinfulness. Only then would he become a rock on which Jesus would build a movement.

## 3. Deep Change

Peter's transformation started when he denied his Lord three times. It was the same lesson he learned at the beginning of his calling, but now it had to go deeper … much deeper. Peter discovered he was still a sinful man who feared Jesus' presence. In his failure and shame, he was forgiven and restored by the risen Lord.

At Pentecost, the Spirit fell upon a man who had been called and trained by Jesus. A man who knew the reality of his sinful heart. A man who had turned back to be forgiven and restored. Between the resurrection and ascension, Jesus had walked him through the Scriptures, explaining why the Messiah had to suffer and rise again and why the gospel must go to the ends of the earth. And so, when the Spirit fell at Pentecost, Peter was ready to lead the movement. His preparation was years in the making. He had paid the price; he had learned the lessons. He was a God-shaped man being formed into the likeness of Jesus. No movement leader can avoid this task.

This transformation is apparent when he stood to proclaim the gospel to those who had crucified his Lord. Peter is no longer a captive to fear; he is ready to face arrest, prison, sham trials, and death.[220] The apostle who had led the way in denying Jesus now leads the way in bold proclamation.

Despite the attacks, the message went out every day in the temple and from house to house. They did not stop teaching and preaching Jesus as the Christ.[221]

Jerusalem became the source of an expanding movement of men and women, transformed like Peter. Under his leadership, they planted churches throughout Jerusalem, Judea, Galilee, and Samaria, and on the coastal plain to the west. As a movement pioneer, Peter prioritized prayer and the spread of God's Word.[222] He multiplied and strengthened disciples and the churches wherever he went. Yet God had more for Peter, and he will take the initiative to unsettle and redirect this movement leader.

### 4. Fresh Vision

Under Peter's leadership, thousands in Jerusalem joined the movement. The church had withstood the persecution, even thriving because of it. Surely now the Gentiles would be drawn into the light of Jerusalem as the Scriptures foretold?

It was more than ten years since the command to go to the nations was given. Those on the edges of Judaism—Samaritans and the Ethiopian eunuch—were being drawn in, but there was still no focused Gentile mission and no clarity on how to include Gentiles within a Jewish movement. So God intervened to open the door for the Gentiles.

Peter was away from headquarters in Jerusalem, moving further and further into Gentile territory. On the rooftop in Joppa, and later in Cornelius's house, the Lord disrupted Peter and transformed his understanding in the space of a few days. The Lord was still shaping and remaking Peter who would now lead others to embrace this fresh work of the Spirit.

### 5. Legacy

Movements thrive when the founding figures release authority and responsibility to others and affirm new streams of disciples and churches over which they have no direct control or relationship. Peter had to learn how to release authority and responsibility and embrace what God was doing in raising up new leaders beyond his sphere of influence:

**The Seven.** Peter led the way in the appointment of the seven men who oversaw the distribution of food to widows in the community.[223] It soon became clear that at least two of them would also play a pioneering role in the spread of the movement. Stephen's teaching and martyrdom prepared the way for the movement's expansion. Philip's mission to Samaria took the movement beyond the bounds of Judaism. Peter and John were the first apostles to embrace the new work and extend it into new Samaritan villages.

**Paul.** God raised up a movement leader without Peter's involvement who would surpass him in achievement. Paul pioneered a whole new stream of Gentile disciples and churches, sparking a major conflict among the Jewish believers. Peter and Paul clashed publicly in Antioch over Peter's inconsistency in welcoming the Gentiles.[224] Yet by the time of the Jerusalem Council, Peter led the way in winning the acceptance of Paul's mission to the Gentiles.[225]

**James and the elders.** At first, Peter led the church in Jerusalem but eventually handed the leadership over to James, the Lord's brother, and the elders. Then, around AD 41, pursued by Herod, Peter fled the city.[226] He returned to Jerusalem in AD 48, but by then James was in charge of the church and the proceedings at the Council.

Peter, the natural leader, released authority to others. He made room for leaders like Stephen and Philip and for James and the elders of Jerusalem. He embraced and welcomed the Gentile mission led by Paul and others. When his job was done in Jerusalem, he left to pioneer in new fields.

## 6. Finale

Luke doesn't tell us where Peter went after he fled Jerusalem.[227] Early traditions point to the northern regions of Asia Minor as one of Peter's mission fields. His first letter is addressed to the believers in the provinces of Pontus, Galatia, Cappadocia, Asia, and Bithynia.[228] These churches may have been the fruit of his missionary work. Peter could also have traveled to the larger Jewish communities of Antioch in Syria, Alexandria in Egypt, and Ephesus in Asia. There is a strong tradition that claims that by the mid-AD 60s, near the end of his life, Peter was in Rome, where he was arrested, tried, and crucified under Nero.

Jesus shaped Peter over the whole course of his life. Peter learned how to follow Jesus and make disciples. Through his greatest failure, he was transformed by the grace of God. Restored, Peter boldly led the movement that reached Jerusalem, and then he released others to lead the work. He kept pushing out beyond the center of Judaism, and God opened his heart to the Gentile mission. He embraced the initiatives and breakthroughs of others. Refusing to settle down, he kept pressing into unreached fields until his life was taken from him.

Two constants guided Peter: Jesus' command to follow; and Jesus' promise to teach him to fish for others. We should expect no less today. God wants us to share in the life and ministry of Jesus. He shapes us over the whole course of our lives, forming the life of Christ in us and equipping us to make disciples. We will be bewildered and confused unless we accept that our lives and ministries are in his hands. He's shaping who we are, and what we do, toward a unique contribution to his mission.[229]

THREE

# OUT OF
# JERUSALEM

(6:1–12:25)

# THE WORD OF GOD SPREADS (6:1–7)

### AD **31/32**

Luke has written candidly about the threats to the church in Jerusalem, both from within (Ananias and Sapphira) and from without (persecution). Now we learn of another internal threat which the new movement must resolve: conflict between language groups.

The church in Jerusalem is full of both Aramaic-speaking and Greek-speaking Jews. The Greek speakers, or Hellenists, who make up about one-tenth of Jerusalem's population, are primarily diaspora Jews born outside Israel who now attend Greek-speaking synagogues.

Many Greek-speaking women had returned to Jerusalem to end their days in the holy city, and when their husbands died, are left alone without financial support. Care for widows was a clear command from God, and up to this point in the story, Luke reports that all those in need were provided for.[1] However, as the number of disciples grows, the Greek-speaking widows are being overlooked.

The apostles ask the Greek-speaking disciples to choose men with a good reputation who are full of the Spirit and wisdom. All of those chosen have Greek names and are appointed by the Twelve to oversee the fair distribution of food.[2]

Luke tells us very little about the organizational structure of the movement; instead, his attention is on the movement's identity. Whereas an institution maintains rigid structures and often drifts or denies its identity, a movement shapes its form to the situation and remains true to its origins. This account tells us how they resolved an important conflict, remaining true to their identity as a movement.

The apostles:

- Listen to the widows' concerns.

- Acknowledge the issue and do not defend themselves.

- Involve the Greek-speaking believers in finding a solution.

- Set the criteria for leadership and empower the believers to identify the right individuals.

- Remain flexible and make a simple change to the organizational structure.[3]

- Use their position to transfer authority and responsibility to others.

- Publicly lay on hands and pray for the new leaders.

- Maintain their focus on prayer and the spread of the gospel.

Once again, there are no needy people among them, as God intends for every community of believers. And once again, the Word goes out, and the number of disciples grows. The apostles, as the leaders of an expanding missionary movement, devote themselves to prayer and the spread of the Word. Throughout Acts, prayer often preceded or followed breakthrough in the spread of the Word.[4]

Three times in the story of Acts, Luke records how the Word spread, grew, and multiplied.[5] On each occasion, the growth occurs after conflict was resolved or after persecution ceased.[6] Luke shows how the gospel advanced amid suffering, conflict, and persecution and how the advance led to new disciples and new churches.

On this occasion, many priests become "obedient to the faith," a term Luke uses to describe genuine discipleship. They aren't from the powerful, high priestly families, but from among the thousands of ordinary priests from all over Israel who work a trade and serve in the temple for two weeks of every year.[7] Movements don't start in the centers of power but on the fringes, with ordinary people who become obedient to the faith. That's what Jesus did and what he sent his disciples to do. Today, we can find them meeting in a downtown office or a refugee camp, at home in the suburbs or in a prison cell, in London or Beirut.

## MOVEMENTS TODAY: MAWLING

Grant is a friend who served as a movement catalyst in China for over ten years. Grant began his ministry assuming it was his role to be the evangelist, teacher, and church planter. His early efforts didn't meet with much success, so he decided to become a learner. He looked for evidence of God's activity in the field. When Grant visited some communities, the police would arrive to find out why he was there. So, for security reasons, he decided to play a background role and equip new converts to do the ministry. Soon, he discovered that this was not just good for security, but it was also good church-planting practice. The new believers could do a far better job than he could.

Grant became convinced that foreigners don't make the best church planters—local believers do. He discovered he could contribute by partnering with locals through coaching, problem solving, and training. He coached local leaders, equipping them to lead the movement of thousands of new disciples and hundreds of new churches. Most of the disciples never met Grant.

On one occasion, an unexpectedly large number of people showed up for two days of leadership training. They had only enough beds and food for half of the people! Grant gathered the leaders together and told them they needed to find a solution. Then he left the room. Grant wanted them to own the problem and fix it. When he came back, the leaders had come up with a creative solution, under the guidance of the Holy Spirit: Everyone would fast and pray every other meal and everyone would take turns praying half of the night. In this way, they all had food to eat and a bed to sleep in.

Grant used a simple MAWL approach as he coached and trained the leaders.

- **Model:** He led by example.

- **Assist:** He helped emerging leaders take the first steps and made sure they were modeling for others.

- **Watch:** He stepped back from assisting but provided feedback.

- **Launch:** He created space so that the new leaders could take full responsibility.

Whereas a ministry is usually about what one leader can do with the help of others, a movement is what God can do when leaders let go of control and multiply leaders. Using MAWL can be an effective diagnostic and planning tool for movement leaders, enabling us to ask: Who are the leaders we're equipping at each level? Are they doing the same for others?

# DEEPER: THE WORD

*But the word of God increased and multiplied.*

ACTS 12:24 ESV

A central cause of the spiraling decline of the church in the West is the loss of confidence in God's Word. Luke leaves us in no doubt why this movement of God grows and multiplies: It is because of the inherent power of God's Word. At Pentecost, the Holy Spirit propelled the worshippers out of the upper room onto the streets with the gospel. The work of the Spirit in Acts is about the progress of the Word.[8]

God's Word is God in action. God creates and upholds the universe by his Word. The story of the Bible is the story of a God who speaks and of a God who expects that we express our love by obeying his Word. In Jesus' Parable of the Sower, the Word is like a seed that grows and multiplies in the good soil of faith and obedience. In Acts, the sign that the Word has fallen on good soil and is bearing fruit is the creation and growth of the people of God.[9]

For Luke, the Word of God is found in the Hebrew Scriptures, in Jesus' life and teaching, and now in the apostles' message about Jesus.[10]

Acts tells the story of the progress of the Word from Jerusalem to the ends of the earth, overcoming every obstacle. The messengers are under continual pressure, yet God ensures the Word keeps moving on, never taking a backward step.[11]

Acts is built around several summaries that report the progress of the Word as a dynamic force.[12] Each breakthrough follows an account of persecution or conflict. Each advance causes an increase of disciples and churches, in both numbers and depth. The messengers play their part, but God directs and enables them.[13]

Disciple making movements have a high view of the Word of God as the power of God at work in the world, bringing salvation and the life of discipleship in community.

There's a restless urgency in the Gospels and Acts that escapes us today in our settled church life. Yet in Acts, the Word conquers the world. Powerful rulers and angry mobs cannot stop the spread of God's Word.

There are many ways we deny the power of God's Word and therefore stifle any hope that we will see disciple making movements in the West.

The first is to place ourselves above God's Word, deciding for ourselves what is right and wrong.[14] For many modern-postmodern scholars, the Bible only *contains* the Word of God, and we must decide for ourselves what that Word says. Movements of God that were once great have fallen into this trap and then faced decline. The cycle continues as new generations of church leaders embrace the spirit of the age.

An opposite error is to uphold the authority of the Word of God but confine its use to church meetings and academic institutions. Of all the preaching in Acts, Luke records only one message before a believing audience; the rest are before people far from God. The Word goes out into public places and homes, prison cells, markets, a lecture hall, a governor's palace, even a sinking ship.

Another mistake is to place spiritual experiences above the authority of the Scriptures, which the Holy Spirit inspired. Even a genuine work of the Spirit will atrophy if we keep it to ourselves. The Spirit came in power that we all might bear witness to Jesus.

A final way we deny the power of God's Word is by redefining our mission as economic, social, and political transformation. Acts is explicit: God's mission is all about the spread of his Word, bringing salvation and the creation and growth of the people of God. Transformed communities may result, but there is no guarantee. Jerusalem was not transformed. The cities Paul visited were transformed—into riots. Heaven on earth will come, but only on the other side of God's judgment.

In contrast to the above, disciple making movements view the Word of God as the power of God at work, bringing salvation and resulting in multiplying disciples and churches.

Luke provides one factor that explains the rise of this movement— the living Word proclaimed and taught in the power of the Spirit, to people far from God. Our methods, structures, and strategies must serve that reality. The Word believed, obeyed, lived, proclaimed, and taught is at the heart of every movement of God.[15]

The building block of every disciple making movement—whether they meet in a village hut, a prison cell, or a palace—is a group of people gathered around God's Word in the presence of the Holy Spirit, learning to take the next step in following Jesus and fishing for people.

You could start a group like that today.[16] Acts ends with Paul the missionary in custody, yet the Word goes out "unhindered."[17] Luke is challenging his generation—and ours—to take up the unfinished task, as the Word travels to the ends of the earth, reaching every place and every people.

# YOU ALWAYS RESIST THE HOLY SPIRIT! (6:8–8:3)

### AD 31/32

The crackdown by the religious authorities began with a ban on speaking about Jesus; then a flogging; now an execution.

Stephen was a man full of God's grace and power to heal the sick and speak with wisdom. Greek-speaking Jews from the Synagogue of the Freedmen opposed him.[18] Saul, who was from Tarsus in Cilicia, probably attended this synagogue.

Filled with the wisdom the Spirit gave him, Stephen is a formidable opponent. So his enemies trade debate for slander and violence. They drag Stephen before the high priest Caiaphas and the Sanhedrin, the same high priest and the same ruling body that had handed Jesus over to the Romans. They charge Stephen with some of the same offenses—that he rejected the temple and the law.

Stephen is on trial for his life; instead of defending himself, he puts his accusers on trial. The glory of God rests on him as he gives the leaders of Israel a lesson in history. Emboldened by the Spirit, Stephen builds his case on the Hebrew Scriptures. He speaks of Abraham, the father of the nation; Joseph and the captivity in Egypt; Moses, the great liberator and lawgiver; and finally, King David and Solomon.

He argues that at every turn in Israel's history, God was the initiator, often working outside of the promised land. God spoke to Abraham in Mesopotamia; he blessed Joseph in Egypt; he revealed his law to Moses on Mount Sinai.[19]

Stephen argues that the history of Israel was the history of rebellion. Freed from slavery, the people longed to return to Egypt. While Moses was receiving God's revelation on Mount Sinai, the nation was bowing down and worshipping a golden calf. From the beginning, Israel ran after other gods and tried to turn Yahweh into a national god they could control.

Stephen tells them God cannot be limited to one land, one people, one temple. His salvation embraces the entire world, and his people are a people on the move.[20] The current leaders of Israel are the children of those who rejected and murdered the prophets. They murdered the Messiah. They have broken the covenant, and God will judge them.

At these words, the Sanhedrin erupts with murderous rage—proving that what Stephen had spoken was true.[21]

Amid a rising tide of hatred, Stephen looks up to heaven and sees Jesus standing at the right hand of God in his glory; Jesus, the Son of Man, has been given all authority to rule and to judge the world.[22] All of God's plans and promises to Israel are fulfilled in him. He completes and replaces the temple and the law.[23] The one they murdered is now on the throne of the universe at God's right hand.[24] He is standing, ready to receive his servant, ready to judge those who condemn his servant.

Covering their ears and screaming, they rush at Stephen and drag him out of the city. Stephen falls to his knees, and like Jesus, prays for the forgiveness of his attackers as they stone him.

Stephen was the first witness to die for his faith in Jesus. What sustained him was not natural courage, but the Spirit's presence.[25] Although Stephen never left Jerusalem, his message and death paved the way for the gospel to move out from Jerusalem to the Samaritans and eventually to the Gentiles.

The day they killed Stephen, a severe persecution broke out against the church in Jerusalem. The Twelve remained in Jerusalem, but other disciples fled in all directions to Judea and Samaria and as far as Phoenicia, Cyprus, and Antioch—no doubt finding refuge among relatives and fellow believers.[26]

As Stephen died, a young man watched with satisfaction. For Saul of Tarsus, this was just the beginning. Saul was intent on destroying the movement. The word for "destroy" describes a wild beast tearing at raw flesh.[27] Saul regarded the idea of a crucified Messiah as blasphemy.[28] Previously, the authorities had targeted the movement's leaders; now Saul was going after the whole church, and ordinary disciples were on the run. Moving from house to house, he broke up the churches, jailed, and even killed both men and women.[29]

Saul was preparing a campaign to destroy this movement of Jesus' disciples wherever he found them. This great persecution will propel God's people out of Jerusalem into Judea, Samaria, the Phoenician coast, and Antioch.[30] The Word is on the move, and nothing will stand in its way.

## MOVEMENTS TODAY: HAIK HOVSEPIAN

When the Islamic revolution overturned the Shah in 1979, Iran was a nation of thirty-nine million people, most of whom were Muslim.[31] Although this appeared to be a dark time for Iran, Islamic rule prepared the way for an unprecedented move of God among the Persian people.

A decade before the revolution, God called Haik Hovsepian, a young Armenian Iranian pastor, to go as a missionary to the northern province of Mazandaran to reach Muslims. Few Armenian Christians shared a burden for the salvation of Muslims. If you were born as an Assyrian or Armenian, you were a Christian. If you were born a Persian, you were a Muslim. Ethnicity determined your religion.

By 1976, Hovsepian had started five churches meeting in homes with around twenty Muslim background believers. He believed one day there would be millions of Persian believers.

In 1981, the Persian church in Mazandaran had grown to sixty people, and Hovsepian turned the work over to the local leaders he had trained. He returned to Tehran, where he challenged the Armenian Christians to open their doors and their hearts to the Persian people and begin using Farsi in their services. New believers began pouring into the churches. The churches met secretly in small groups that soon multiplied. The government demanded that Hovsepian reveal the names of the Muslim background believers. He refused.

The Persian people grew weary of the harsh restrictions imposed on them by Islamic law. In 1993, Hovsepian drew international attention to the plight of Mehdi Dibaj, imprisoned by the Islamic courts for over ten years on charges of apostasy. The campaign succeeded, and Dibaj was released. Three days later, Hovsepian vanished. When they found his body, it was covered in stab wounds.

Despite the presence of government agents, hundreds of Persian believers honored Hovsepian at his funeral. These Muslim background believers, inspired by the boldness of Hovsepian, stepped into the leadership of a church-planting movement.

By 2008, there were a thousand churches that traced their origin back to Hovsepian's discipleship of just a few dozen Muslim background believers.

For centuries, Persians assumed that if you were a Christian, it was because you were an Armenian. Today, Persian believers refer to themselves as *farsimasihi* ("Persian followers of the Messiah"). The *farsimasihi* are sending and funding missionaries to the surrounding ethnic minorities—the Azeri, the Luri, and the Kurds.

Hovsepian saw beyond one church in Tehran to the possibility of a disciple making movement. Once the movement began to multiply disciples, churches, and leaders, it was no longer dependent on him. As tragic as Hovsepian's death was, it became a spark that lit an unstoppable fire that spread across Iran. Today, there are over one million Persian believers in Iran and around the world.[32]

When the risen Lord found the disciples, they were locked behind closed doors, hiding in fear. We are those disciples. Few of us have the natural courage to risk disgrace and rejection like Hovsepian. What we find in Acts are men and women who are no different from us. They had simply discovered the presence of Jesus in the face of hostility. He gave them the words to say and the courage to endure.

Like the first disciples, we all need to learn how to follow Jesus out, from behind closed doors into a world he loves, despite its rebellion. As we do that, he promises to never leave us.

## DEEPER: PERSECUTION

*The apostles left the Sanhedrin, rejoicing because they had been counted worthy of suffering disgrace for the Name.*

ACTS 5:41

Rejection casts its shadow over Jesus from the start.[33] At the temple, Simeon prophesied over the infant Jesus that he would divide Israel.[34] His hometown of Nazareth spurned him. The opposition that grew throughout his mission ended in his death.[35] He set his face to go to Jerusalem to what awaited him there. Though this was tragedy, it was a tragedy that fell within the plan of God. The darkest moment revealed the light of the glory of God: Jesus' greatest victory.

Jesus taught his disciples that persecution was a sign of the *present* age, not just of the very end.[36] He promised his disciples that they too would face rejection, but they were to rejoice because God would reward them.[37]

In the Garden of Gethsemane, the disciples slept while Jesus prayed. They fled when he was arrested. Not even Peter could stand. It was the hour when darkness reigned.[38] Satan stood behind the intimidation and threats of violence. Though the disciples failed, Jesus' victory opened the way for them to be restored.

The risen Lord taught them from the Scriptures, gave them their mission, and promised them power from on high. Transformed, it was his presence that gave them the courage and boldness they needed.[39]

After the resurrection, the focus of persecution shifted from Jesus to the disciples. Jesus had taught them not to fear men who can kill the body but to fear God who loves them and numbered the hairs on their head. Family and friends will betray and hate them. They will be brought before the authorities, but the Holy Spirit will teach them what to say.[40] Jesus' predictions were fulfilled in Acts and are still being fulfilled around the world today.[41] The Word progresses; the movement of God advances, but at a cost. Following Jesus leads to suffering, even death. Yet following Jesus also brings joy, boldness for proclamation, and God's protection.[42]

Persecution is not an extra to the missionary call; it is one of its essential elements.[43] We can't create the courage to endure such pressure. But we can find strength in Jesus' presence.

Despite warnings and threats from the authorities, "Day after day, in the temple courts and from house to house, they never stopped teaching and proclaiming the good news that Jesus is the Messiah."[44] The disciples attracted hostility because they acted and spoke in the name of Jesus. The persecution would cease if they stopped.[45] It was not their existence as a sect of Judaism but their uncompromising mission that provoked this violent opposition.

The disciples met rejection with patient endurance, a refusal to strike back, and prayer for their persecutors.[46]

Although they were arrested, threatened, and beaten, the number of disciples kept increasing. There is a repeated pattern in Acts—the combination of signs and wonders and the preaching of the gospel results in new believers and new churches planted—this happens despite and even *because* of opposition.[47]

Persecution was an essential part of Paul's calling as a missionary.[48] When he received his commission, Jesus told him he would suffer for his name. Paul and Barnabas fled persecution in city after city.[49]

Proclamation led to persecution and persecution led to proclamation, with every persecution leading to the planting of a new church.[50] With persecution in mind, Paul warned new disciples that they too would face many hardships before they entered the kingdom of God.[51]

Though the messengers are vulnerable, the Word of God is powerful.

When Jesus' disciples are persecuted, Jesus is persecuted. The risen Lord announced to Saul, "I am Jesus whom you are persecuting."[52] He is with his people who suffer for the sake of his name. Paul the apostle could endure prison, endless legal battles, and shipwreck because Jesus stood near him.[53]

When persecuted, the disciples prayed for boldness: the free, uninhibited, open communication of the gospel from person to person. It's a gift of God when we respond to persecution with faith and obedience. Boldness is at the heart of every disciple making movement.

History shows there is a greater threat to a movement than persecution—success. When movements succeed in gaining political and cultural power, they are most vulnerable.

Singaporean professor Nilay Saiya analyzed data from 166 countries and found that in countries where Christianity occupies a position of political and cultural power, it is weak and declining.[54] Christianity is more likely to thrive where it must compete freely with other faiths.

In Europe, Christianity has enjoyed state support for centuries, yet state-supported Christianity is in terminal decline. Churches with a favored position in society think they can exert influence. Instead, they tend to become civil religions, expressing their faith in rituals and symbols. Commitment levels fall as they drift from biblical orthodoxy to cultural accommodation.

It is possible to suppress the spread of Christianity through systematic, brutal persecution, but it's rare. Typically, persecution results in the vitality of Christianity. Right now, there are around one million followers of Christ in Iran, despite persecution from the Islamic regime. China will soon become the most populous Christian nation on earth, despite the opposition of its Communist rulers.

The sobering truth for Western Christianity is that political and cultural power is a greater threat to the vitality of the faith than persecution.

# THEY PREACH THE WORD EVERYWHERE THEY GO (8:4–25)

Persecution adds momentum to the movement's advance, as the disciples proclaim the Word everywhere they go.

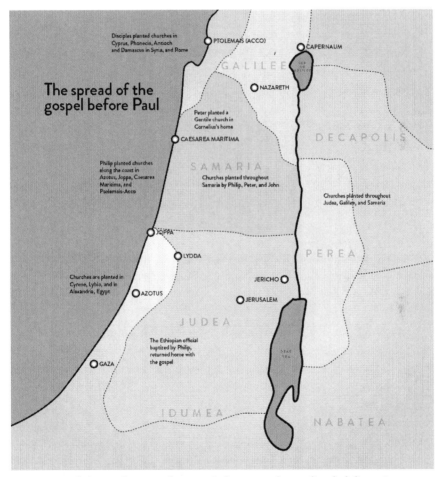

The spread of the gospel before Paul

Disciples planted churches in Cyprus, Phoenicia, Antioch and Damascus in Syria, and Rome

PTOLEMAÏS (ACCO)

CAPERNAUM

GALILEE

NAZARETH

Peter planted a Gentile church in Cornelius's home

CAESAREA MARITIMA

DECAPOLIS

Philip planted churches along the coast in Azotus, Joppa, Caesarea Maritima, and Ptolemais-Acco

SAMARIA

Churches planted throughout Samaria by Philip, Peter, and John

Churches planted throughout Judea, Galilee, and Samaria

JOPPA

LYDDA

PEREA

Churches are planted in Cyrene, Lybia, and in Alexandria, Egypt

JERICHO

AZOTUS

JERUSALEM

JUDEA

The Ethiopian official baptized by Philip, returned home with the gospel

GAZA

IDUMEA

NABATEA

*Even before Paul came on the scene, God was at work unsettling the believers in Jerusalem and sending them out to reach both Jews and Gentiles with the gospel.*

Philip the evangelist escapes north to Samaria; two to three days' journey from Jerusalem.[55]

Jews regarded Samaritans as half-breed heretics, yet Jesus included them in his mandate to reach Jerusalem, Judea, Samaria and the ends of the earth.[56]

Through Philip, a great number believed, and the first Samaritan churches were planted.[57] Philip didn't plan his mission, and the Twelve didn't authorize it. God turned persecution into an opportunity, and Philip took it. Philip was just one of the many believers on the run, who preached the Word everywhere they went.[58]

When the apostles hear that Samaria has received the Word of God, they send Peter and John to investigate. The Spirit has not yet fallen on the Samaritans, even though they believe and have been baptized. This is unusual; the pattern in Acts is that the Spirit is given immediately upon conversion.[59] The delay gives the apostles time to travel to Samaria and authenticate the Samaritan experience of Pentecost. Something similar will happen when the Spirit falls upon the Gentiles for the first time in the house of Cornelius.[60]

In Acts, the one salvation experience includes repentance and faith, forgiveness of sins, the gift of the Spirit, and baptism.[61] Acts doesn't provide a set order. Sometimes there is laying on of hands, sometimes not. Sometimes the Spirit comes before baptism, sometimes after.[62] We don't control how the Spirit works, but true conversion always includes repentance and faith, forgiveness of sin, the gift of the Spirit, and baptism. What is certain is God had grafted the Samaritans into the true Israel, and, filled with the Spirit, they are ready to engage in the missionary task.[63]

Among those who believe and have been baptized is Simon the sorcerer, a local celebrity known as "the Great Power of God." When he sees the Spirit is given through the laying on of the apostles' hands, he offers the apostles money. He wants to use the Holy Spirit to get rich and famous.

Peter responds, "May your money perish with you!" The gift of God cannot be bought and sold. Simon is disqualified from ministry and membership in the people of God because his heart is wicked, bitter, and full of sin. The fear of God comes upon Simon, and he urges Peter to pray for him. It's not clear if Simon's change of heart is genuine, but the warning is stark. God gives the Spirit; it is not given by celebrities or even apostles, and the Spirit cannot be tamed.[64]

People who seek money, power, and fame can corrupt a genuine move of God. As with Judas and then Ananias and Sapphira, threats to the integrity of the movement must be confronted. For God was active in both extending the movement *and* protecting its identity.

The apostles and Philip continue to proclaim the message about Jesus. Peter and John preach in many of Samaria's 140 towns and villages before returning home to Jerusalem, while the Spirit leads Philip into the desert.[65]

For the first time, the gospel goes beyond the Jewish people. The initiator of the breakthrough is God himself, and the catalyst is the death of the first Christian martyr and Saul's violent opposition. God propels Philip out of Jerusalem into enemy territory. With this opportunity, Philip obeys Jesus' command to go to the Samaritans. In Samaria, Peter and John show us again what it looks like for apostolic pioneers to devote themselves to prayer and the ministry of the Word.[66]

The work has only just started, yet Philip, Peter, and John don't stay in Samaria. They establish local churches and will return, or send others, to strengthen the disciples and identify leaders. Soon, we find Peter on one such tour.[67] Luke reports later that the church throughout Judea, Galilee, and Samaria enjoyed a time of peace and was strengthened. "Living in the fear of the Lord and encouraged by the Holy Spirit, it increased in numbers."[68] The movement was spreading, as the disciples in Judea, Galilee, and Samaria reached their own people.

They showed themselves to be a movement, as disciples, churches, and leaders multiplied. Philip preaching in Samaria was not a movement; it was one man's ministry. Thousands turning and believing was not yet a movement. The work in Samaria became a movement because Philip and the apostles raised up Samaritans as local leaders and pioneer missionaries. It's only by equipping and releasing insiders that a ministry becomes a movement.

When the disciples were scattered by persecution, they knew they had the authority to proclaim the Word, make disciples, and plant churches. It's a simple test of any movement: If God were to scatter us, would our people know what to do?

Stephen opened the door to this breakthrough with his vision of God—a God who could not be contained within Judaism. The Spirit pushed Philip through that door, Peter and John followed, and now there were disciples and churches throughout Samaria. The risen Lord had set the agenda—Jerusalem, Judea, Samaria, and the ends of the earth. And he was the one who brought the breakthrough, as the apostles obediently followed.

## MOVEMENTS TODAY: OUT OF AFGHANISTAN

Acts reveals that movements of disciples and churches are a work of God rather than human engineering. That hasn't changed.

Jalil fled his home in war-torn Afghanistan as a teenager and journeyed through Iran to Turkey where he worked and saved up enough money for a seat in a rubber dinghy to cross the Aegean and enter Greece. By God's grace, a Greek family took him in. For the first time he was free to seek answers to the questions he had about Jesus.

Some Iranians invited him to a Persian church, and after a year of conversations and a visionary encounter with Jesus, Jalil turned and believed and was baptized. Soon after, he met Will, an American missionary who was equipping Afghan believers to make disciples and plant churches—the very thing Jalil wanted to do.

Wave after wave of new refugees flooded into Greece, and God worked through Jalil, who led many to faith. He discipled these new believers in a simple, biblical pattern that was easily passed on, equipping them to share the gospel, make disciples, and plant churches wherever they went. Most refugees leave Greece within weeks or sometimes months, as they head to their preferred destination in Europe.

As the new disciples have spread throughout Europe, Jalil's impact has spread with them. Some have even returned home to the land from which they fled to reach their family and friends with the gospel.

God is at work in the upheavals of nations. The Arab Spring became the Arab Winter, and war came to Syria, Iraq, and Afghanistan. Into this tumultuous mix, God brought Will and Jalil together, and a door opened for the gospel. This is an unprecedented time—in 1,400 years of Islam, there has never been such openness to Jesus.

We may despair that the Western world has turned its back on Christ, but overnight the equation can change, and closed hearts can open. A movement of God is a work of God, not something we control. In Acts, Philip was a refugee from religious persecution when he fled to Samaria. God often works through seasons of upheaval to bring breakthroughs in the gospel's spread.

Our job is to sow faithfully, to teach disciples how to follow Christ, and make disciples themselves. When God shakes our world, we need to be ready.

# ON HIS WAY REJOICING (8:26–40)

Peter and John continue the mission among many Samaritan villages as they work their way back to Jerusalem. Meanwhile, an angel sends Philip south to the road that leads to Gaza, the last watering-place on the road to Egypt.[69]

Philip had proclaimed the gospel to thousands; now in the desert, he speaks to just one man. On the road, he meets a eunuch, the treasurer of the queen of Ethiopia returning home from worshipping in Jerusalem. The Ethiopian is a powerful aristocrat, a black African from a region on the Nile just south of Egypt in what is today Sudan; and he is wealthy enough to have a chariot take him to Jerusalem and to own a scroll of Isaiah. Under the law of Moses, castrated males were excluded from the people of Israel.[70] This devout Ethiopian could visit the temple in Jerusalem, but he could not step inside its inner courts.

As a eunuch, he could never be a full convert to Judaism. Yet Isaiah spoke of a day when eunuchs would be accepted among the people of God.[71] Finally, the promise was being fulfilled. The gospel was about to breach another barrier on its journey from Jerusalem to the ends of the earth. Once again, God was the initiator working through one of his servants.

Our mission can never focus solely on our neighborhood, our kind of people, our nation, or our culture. The mission of God is to every people and every place. It's also *from* every people and *from* every place—which means the West is no longer at the center. The movement of God encompasses the whole world.

The Spirit leads Philip to approach the eunuch, and as he does, he can hear him reading because in the ancient world people read aloud. He hears the words of Isaiah 53 about the Suffering Servant of the Lord:

He was oppressed and afflicted,
yet he did not open his mouth;
he was led like a lamb to the slaughter,
and as a sheep before its shearers is silent,
so he did not open his mouth.
…

Yet it was the LORD's will to crush him and cause him to suffer,
and though the LORD makes his life an offering for sin,
he will see his offspring and prolong his days,
and the will of the LORD will prosper in his hand.

—ISAIAH 53:7, 10

The Ethiopian wants to know who Isaiah was referring to. Philip is well-prepared to answer. Isaiah 53 was one of the key passages Jesus would have explained to his disciples who passed on Jesus' teaching to Philip.[72] Beginning with the text, Philip tells the eunuch the good news about Jesus. Through his death he justifies many and brings salvation, not just to Israel, but to the nations—even to this Ethiopian, who lives on the edge of the known world.[73]

Philip helps the official understand how the Scriptures are fulfilled in the life, death, and resurrection of Jesus.[74] This encounter shows how explanation of God's Word and the proclamation about Jesus is at the heart of the missionary task.

According to the pattern in Acts, Philip would have urged the Ethiopian to repent and believe in the Lord Jesus and to be baptized.[75] But when they come to water, it is the eunuch who announces his readiness for baptism. Led by the Spirit, Philip does not need any permission or direction from Jerusalem.[76]

The Holy Spirit then snatches Philip away to Azotus where he continues to preach in the Greek settlements along the coast to Caesarea. We can assume that in each place Philip began by connecting with the local Jewish population and through them to the Gentiles who, like the Ethiopian, had been attracted to the God of Israel. Later we learn of churches established in the Gentile cities of the coastal plain west of Judea and Samaria.[77]

The eunuch leaves rejoicing and becomes the first missionary to Ethiopia. We don't know for sure what happened when he arrived home. However, the church in that part of the world is ancient, with a heritage that goes back at least to the fourth century.[78]

God is fulfilling his purpose to spread his Word to the ends of the earth. The leadership in Jerusalem had to catch up to what God was doing through Philip and the unidentified believers who were scattered by persecution, preaching the Word as they went.[79]

The multiplication of disciples is possible because of the priesthood of all believers—every disciple has the authority from Christ to make disciples. Philip began the work, Peter and John helped strengthen and extend the work, but the Samaritans themselves and the Ethiopian eunuch were responsible for making disciples in their part of the world.

The Word was spreading from Jerusalem into Judea, Samaria, and beyond the borders of historic Israel. Long before Paul stepped onto European soil, the gospel had already gone to Africa.[80]

## MOVEMENTS TODAY: RETURN TO ETHIOPIA

Philip planted the seed of the gospel in Samaria and in the heart of the Ethiopian eunuch. Then the Spirit moved him on. Sometimes pioneers need to get out of the way for a disciple making movement to occur.

When Sudan Interior Mission (SIM) missionaries arrived in southern Ethiopia in 1927, most of the tribes were either Muslim or pagan. The missionaries labored for the next ten years and saw 150 new disciples formed into three fledgling churches.

Then, in 1935, Mussolini's fascist Italy invaded Ethiopia; and the Emperor of Ethiopia, Haile Selassie, fled to England. Two years later, the Italians expelled the missionaries.

During the years of occupation, SIM received no news from the church in Ethiopia. We now know that the Italians unleashed a ferocious attack on the new movement. Church leaders were imprisoned. Some were flogged until the flesh was torn from their backs; three died in custody. The leaders did not waver but used their punishment as an opportunity to proclaim the gospel.

Meanwhile, local evangelists penetrated deep into unreached regions. The evangelists were farmers who lived by faith, relying on whatever support other believers could provide. The movement grew rapidly.[81]

Five years later, when the Italian forces were driven out, they left behind an indigenous movement of churches with ten thousand disciples. By 1943, there were over two hundred churches and twenty-five thousand believers. The churches had worked out their own church life and leadership structures,[82] with no other guide than the instruction from the SIM missionaries to obey what they found in the Word of God.[83]

From the beginning, the SIM pioneers determined this would be an indigenous church. The focus of evangelism was not the mission compound but along the roads, under trees, and at communal events. Discipleship took place in small informal groups rather than classrooms.[84] The missionaries' goal was an Ethiopian church, led by local elders, not the missionaries. They did not establish a theological school; church leaders were instead trained informally through in-depth Bible studies. There was no salaried clergy, pastor-elders were volunteers living by faith.[85]

The SIM missionaries laid the foundation for an indigenous church, and at the right time God removed them, and the movement accelerated.[86] Back in England, God's people were united in prayer for Ethiopia, distressed that their prayers appeared to go unanswered and oblivious to a national movement of faithful disciples and churches that was forged in the furnace of persecution.

The SIM missionaries chose the patterns and principles of Acts over their culture. These were the days of Western colonial power, yet the missionaries had confidence that God's Word would do the work through ordinary Ethiopians, empowered by the Holy Spirit.

## DEEPER: BAPTISM

*"What can stand in the way of my being baptized?"*
ACTS 8:36

The answer to the Ethiopian's question, "What can stand in the way of my being baptized?" is, "Nothing!" For those who have turned to God and put their faith in Christ, nothing should stand in the way of their baptism.

Jesus was baptized by his cousin John, not for his own sins, but to identify with sinners and point forward to his death and resurrection on their behalf. In obedience to Jesus' command, the disciples called people to put their faith in Jesus Christ and confess him as Lord that they might be born of the Spirit. Then, they urged them to be immersed in water as the sign of their repentance and faith.[87] At the end of Matthew, Jesus' central command to make disciples of every people group is supported by three activities: going, baptizing, and teaching new disciples to obey everything he has commanded.[88]

In Acts, conversion has five aspects, all of which take place at the same time, usually on the same day. They are repentance, faith, confession of Jesus as Messiah and Lord, the gift of the Spirit, and immersion in water.[89] Luke gives multiple accounts of household baptism. On each occasion, household baptism follows household faith. Everyone in the household was saved and baptized because they all believed.[90] New Testament baptism is not adult or infant baptism but believers' baptism.

In the New Testament, a person was not baptized for one of two reasons. Either they did not want to repent and put their faith in Christ, or they did repent and believe but, like the thief on the cross, were physically unable to be baptized.[91]

Baptism did not guarantee salvation, but baptism always followed conversion.[92] To reject baptism was to reject the gospel message preached by Peter, Paul, and the early church. Withholding baptism from a new disciple who had repented and believed would have been unthinkable.

Who should baptize? Jesus commanded those who made disciples to do the baptizing. On a few occasions, Luke identifies the person doing the baptism. Peter didn't baptize Cornelius's household and associates; he commanded the unnamed Jewish believers who came with him to do it.[93] Paul was baptized by Ananias, a man described only as a disciple.[94] In pioneering contexts, Paul baptized new converts. He soon passed that task on to his coworkers and the newly formed church.[95] The Acts and the Epistles provide no restrictions on who could baptize a new disciple. Church leaders, such as Peter or Paul, followed Jesus' example and gave ordinary disciples the responsibility to baptize new believers.

In disciple making movements, the authority and responsibility to make disciples is released to every disciple. Every disciple is called to follow Jesus and make disciples by going, baptizing, and teaching new disciples to obey what Jesus has commanded. Movements ordain every disciple for ministry. To withhold the authority to baptize (or celebrate the Lord's Supper) undermines the authority of every disciple to obey the Great Commission.

If our practice diverges from the pattern of the New Testament, it will be one more indicator that we have drifted from what it means to make disciples according to the pattern Jesus laid down in the Gospels and Acts, and we need to find our way back.

## MOVEMENTS TODAY: ISRAEL THE UNTOUCHABLE

Disciple making movements teach the newest believers that they have the authority and responsibility to make disciples.

Kumar Pillai is a movement catalyst in northern India.[96] One of his disciples was an illiterate, low-caste Hindu who took the name Israel. Low-caste Hindus are known as "untouchables," their very presence brings ritual impurity. From generation to generation, they are restricted to occupations such as garbage collectors, sanitation workers, and street sweepers. From 4 to 9 each morning, Israel swept the streets.

Kumar trained Israel to share his new faith. Israel couldn't read, so his children helped him learn Bible stories by heart.

Israel shared the gospel with his relatives and friends, many of whom put their faith in Christ. That would normally be enough for a semiliterate, low-caste street sweeper. But Kumar trained Israel how to make disciples among his people.

On one occasion, Israel visited his community, and Kumar went with him. Israel led the son of a local Hindu priest to Christ, and as they walked to a local fishpond, Kumar asked Israel to baptize the young man. Israel was reluctant. With a smile on his face, Kumar told him, "You baptize him. I have a fear of water!" So, that day, Israel baptized his first disciple.

Later that day, Kumar and Israel visited Israel's elderly father. When the father heard that his son, a street sweeper, had been trusted to baptize a new Christian, he wept. His son, from such a low caste, had been honored with real responsibility.

Israel has since learned to read and write, and Kumar has trained him to plant churches. Typically, the churches are ten to fifteen people seated in a circle on the floor. They pray and sing; their only instrument is an Indian tambourine. They read the Bible together, using a 3-Thirds approach.[97] Out of their poverty, they give to needs within the community of faith and the wider community— and they are known for their generosity. Their giving pays for food, or a hospital visit, or school fees.

Israel has led seven other street sweepers to Christ. One of them, Abraham, is also planting churches. Israel has been the catalyst behind multiple streams of new disciples and new churches. He's lost count of how many, as it's hard to track while he is still working a full-time job as a street sweeper. He has won the award for the best street sweeper in his town three times.

At the heart of every movement of God, there are people like Israel. Jesus chose men and women like Israel. When Israel came to Christ, Kumar saw a disciple who could make disciples, baptize them, and teach them to follow Christ together. Kumar released authority and responsibility to Israel, backed up by training and coaching.

Can we see the Israels around us? We must shift our focus from what we can achieve, to helping the newest disciple reach their community. The skills aren't difficult, but the shift in understanding can be. That's why Luke wrote Acts.

# WHO ARE YOU, LORD? (9:1–30)

## AD **31/32–34**

When we left Saul, he was going from house to house, arresting and imprisoning those loyal to Jesus. His intention was to destroy the church.[98]

Damascus had a large Jewish community and was a natural refuge for disciples fleeing the persecution in Jerusalem.[99] Having obtained authority to hunt them down, Saul approaches the city, and the overwhelming light of God's glory strikes him down. To his surprise, the one who speaks is his sworn enemy, Jesus of Nazareth, the exalted Son of God! "Saul, Saul, why do you persecute me?" Jesus asks. To persecute his disciples, Jesus tells Saul, is to persecute him.[100] "It is hard for you to kick against the goads."[101] Like a stubborn animal, Saul is resisting God and wounding himself.

Saul, now blind and helpless, is led by his companions into Damascus as a captive of Jesus. Unable to eat or drink, he waits in darkness for God to make the next move.

Jesus could have told Saul everything he needed to know on the road to Damascus. Instead, he sends Ananias, a doubting disciple, who none the less has a part to play. Despite Saul's reign of terror, the Lord chooses him to be a light to the nations and to Israel. Saul—the one who has caused so much suffering to those who called on Jesus' name—will himself suffer for that name.[102]

At the house, Ananias welcomes his former enemy as a brother. Stephen's dying prayer, "Lord, do not hold this sin against them," is answered.[103] Ananias lays his hands on Saul while Jesus heals him. Then Ananias, a disciple, baptizes Saul, the soon-to-be apostle, and brings him into fellowship with the brothers and sisters in Damascus, some of whom were on the run from Saul.

Throughout this entire episode, Saul is passive—unraveled and remade by the living Lord. Saul will not stay passive for long, now the Holy Spirit has filled him.

The apostles in Jerusalem don't commission Saul. He doesn't need their authorization; he receives it from the Lord himself. His mission flows from God's mission. The scope is expansive. He will be a witness to Jews, Gentiles, and their kings—to *all people*. He will spread the gospel throughout the known world. He will suffer for Jesus' name. He will fulfill his calling by depending on the Lord who will rescue him from all his enemies. In his suffering and weakness, Saul will discover God's sufficiency. He will learn that the treasure of the gospel is in a fragile clay pot so that God's power is revealed.[104]

Immediately, Saul begins boldly preaching in the synagogues of Damascus. As he grows in power, so does the opposition.

From Galatians, we know that during his time in Damascus, Saul traveled to nearby Arabia to continue his missionary work (AD 32–34).[105] Arabia was home to the Nabatean kingdom, a thriving civilization with cities, seaports, and farming land. Cities such as Petra had synagogues where Saul could meet fellow Jews and Gentiles who were attracted to the God of Israel. Through these Gentiles, the gospel could spread to the wider community.[106]

Saul's mission in Arabia stirred up trouble.[107] When he returns to Damascus, the representative of King Aretas of the Nabateans tries to have Saul arrested.[108] Both Nabatean and Jewish opponents pursue Saul.[109] The disciples lower him over the wall at night, and he escapes. This won't be the last time he's chased out of town.

After three years, Saul completes his work in Arabia and Damascus and heads back to Jerusalem where he may have stayed with his relatives while building a relationship with the Jerusalem church.[110] The believers in Jerusalem know Saul by reputation: He had arrested and imprisoned many of them. It takes Barnabas, the "son of encouragement," to build a bridge and welcome their former enemy into the community of disciples.

Saul soon picked up where he left off in Damascus and Arabia; moving about Jerusalem, he preaches boldly in Jesus' name. Like Stephen, he engages the Greek-speaking Jews in their synagogues, perhaps including his former associates at the Synagogue of the Freedmen who had attacked Stephen. They now regard Saul as their enemy and make attempts on his life. The believers take him safely to Caesarea from where Saul sails to Tarsus, his childhood home and the capital of the Roman province of Cilicia, where he appears to have remained based for the next twelve years.[111] It's possible that the hardships Paul lists in his letters that aren't reported in Acts happened during these years (AD 34–42).[112]

We're so used to the story of Paul's conversion and call that we forget what a miracle of God's grace it was. Paul doesn't earn his place in God's purposes, nor does he advance this movement by the strength of his will and personality. Paul receives his call from God, and it is through God's power that he exercises his ministry. He is gifted, faithful, and courageous, but these traits were not enough. God taught Paul to rely on his power through his experiences of suffering and weakness. Every disciple and every movement pioneer should expect the same, because this is the way of Jesus.

Paul receives his mission from the risen Lord. The one blinded by God's glory will open eyes and lead people out of darkness into the light and from the power of Satan to God. God will forgive their sins and give them a place among his people.[113] The mission could not be clearer. Unlike our vague mission statements today, Paul knew what to do. He entered unreached fields with the gospel. He taught new disciples to love and obey Christ and brought them into the fellowship of God's people. He trained local leaders for the churches and mobile missionaries who joined him in taking the gospel into new fields. This is the core missionary task.

## MOVEMENTS TODAY: HASSAN'S STORY

Joanne and Mark are an American couple living in an Arab nation torn by rival Islamist militias. One day, while out with a teammate looking for a person of peace, Joanne met a man named Hassan, who was sitting outside his front door, drinking coffee, and watching people go by.

A secular Muslim in his early sixties, Hassan was on crutches because he had crushed his ankle in a motorcycle accident. The doctors could not restore the joint, and so Joanne offered to pray for his leg. There was no immediate change, but Joanne promised to visit Hassan again in a few days with her husband.

That night Hassan noticed his ankle was not as painful and went to bed without taking his pain medication. When he woke the next morning, his ankle no longer bothered him! That day he had an appointment with his doctor at the local hospital, which was controlled by Islamist militia. The elevator was out, so he walked the stairs up to the doctor's office. When he arrived the doctor asked, "How did you get up here?" Hassan told him he'd been healed through prayer in Jesus' name. Scared, the doctor ordered him to leave and never return.

When Joanne and Mark visited, they found Hassan was ready to follow Jesus and be baptized. They showed Hassan how to read the

Bible as a disciple, learning to obey and follow Christ. They taught him how to pray for his friends and family and how to share the gospel with them.

On finding out about Hassan's newfound faith, his brother (a Muslim cleric), and his son, (an Islamist militant), cast him out of his own house and threw away his belongings. Hassan remembers he felt like he'd "punched a beehive." With nowhere to go, Hassan and his wife went back to the village in the mountains where Hassan had grown up. Hassan's story spread widely throughout the district, and over thirty Muslims turned and believed in Jesus. What Joanne and Mark taught Hassan, he passed on to these new disciples. Hassan formed them into three churches, each in different villages, each with leaders Hassan had trained.

The disciples meet every day and discuss together who they have shared the gospel with and who they will share it with next. They take the Lord's Supper together and care for one another's financial needs. When two young men who decided to follow Jesus were thrown out of their family homes, one of the women in the church took off her wedding ring and sold it to cover their rent.

Hassan has been arrested and held for interrogation for over two weeks. When he was released, he met with one of the team to read the book of Acts together. As Hassan looked at Paul's journeys, he exclaimed, "Everything that has happened to me is written right here in this book!"

That day he discovered three lessons from the life of Paul: 1) Go in pairs. 2) Expect persecution. 3) When they get serious about killing you, it's time to run. To this day, Hassan is still on the run. Acts is a living book to him. Like Paul, Hassan has lost everything for the sake of the gospel.

Joanne, Mark, and Hassan—among many others—are playing their part in an unprecedented move of God among Muslims around the world. They read the book of Acts with fresh eyes, and so can we. We can learn from their example and discover where God is at work in our neighborhoods. Who knows, we might even find our own Hassan.

# FEARING THE LORD, ENCOURAGED BY THE HOLY SPIRIT (9:31–43)

So far, Luke has been using the term *church* for individual local congregations of disciples. For the first time, he uses *church* (singular) to describe multiple local churches across regions.[114] Luke has already mentioned the disciples in Samaria and Judea, and now we find there are churches in Galilee.[115]

The church is enjoying a period of peace. The persecution that began with Stephen's death has eased; the spearhead of the attack has met the Lord. God strengthens the church throughout Judea, Galilee, and Samaria. He brings encouragement through the Holy Spirit, and the fruit is new disciples and churches.

Luke describes a healthy, growing movement, yet the Lord has more for his people, and he is about to disrupt their peace. The growth in disciples and churches is taking place in Jerusalem, Judea, Galilee, and Samaria—what was once the nation of Israel. But what about the call to reach the nations? This dynamic movement is in danger of settling down and neglecting the core missionary task. Successful movements face the temptation to play it safe and protect their gains rather than risk them for a better future.[116] When that happens, God disrupts them.

Luke's attention moves away from Jerusalem. When we last heard of Peter, he was on mission in Samaria, preaching in many villages.[117] Now he's on the road again, consolidating and expanding the movement further and further away from Jerusalem.

Lydda is northwest of Jerusalem on the road to Joppa. The churches in the region are the result of Philip's mission from Azotus to Caesarea and the influx of refugees from the persecution in Jerusalem.[118] While Peter is with the disciples in Lydda, he heals Aeneas. When the people of Lydda and the towns in the Plain of Sharon see the change in Aeneas, they turn to the Lord. News of this spreads to Joppa, twelve miles west on the Mediterranean coast. At Joppa, a disciple named Tabitha has died, a woman who cared for the poor.[119] The disciples delay her burial and call for Peter.

Through Peter, the risen Lord raises Tabitha to life. The news spreads, and many people believe. This is what it means for a movement leader like Peter to make the ministry of the Word and prayer his priority.[120] This didn't involve constantly shutting himself away in a private place of prayer and sermon preparation. The Word is out, bringing the reality of God's transforming love to people who are far from him.

Peter consolidates and extends the work in Joppa while staying at the house of Simon the tanner. Luke often mentions the names of hosts as a reminder of the important role that hospitality plays in the mission. Peter is following the example of Jesus who taught his disciples to enter unreached towns, looking for the people God had prepared.[121] Simon the tanner lived by the seaside, as the tanning process required access to water. A strict Jew would not stay at the house of a tanner who handled animal carcasses. Peter is not bound by Jewish laws and customs, but he is bound to the risen Jesus who has fulfilled them, and so he stays where he and his message are welcomed.

Even though Peter is no longer in Jerusalem, Joppa and Lydda were still Jewish cities, and his ministry is still limited to Samaritans and Jews. However, that will change with a request from Caesarea, the headquarters of the Roman occupation.

## DEEPER: SIGNS, WONDERS, WORD

*When the crowds heard Philip and saw the signs he performed, they all paid close attention to what he said.*

ACTS 8:6

Acts is the story of the continuing ministry of the risen Lord through his disciples.[122] As they proclaimed the gospel, the disciples continued to perform miracles in Jesus' name. Signs and wonders revealed the power of the living God who brings salvation to the ends of the earth.

Through miracles, God is shown to be the central character in this story. Jesus is present, and the power of his Spirit is available as the Word goes out from Jerusalem. The disciples experience God's powerful presence when they pray, share meals, heal the sick, proclaim the gospel, and face persecution.

The transition from a Jewish movement to a global movement was marked at every stage by God's intervention. Visions, angels, signs, and wonders confirmed God had brought the Gentiles to salvation apart from the Jewish law.[123]

God determines when and how he will move in power, yet miracles do not guarantee a particular outcome. Some see a sign and then close their hearts, bringing greater judgment upon themselves.[124] For example, no town saw more miracles than Capernaum, yet Jesus condemned its people because they refused to turn and believe.[125] When Paul healed a lame man in Lystra, the crowd thought he was a god one moment and then stoned him the next.[126] Miracles alone do not bring people to repentance and faith.

Miracles authenticated the apostles' unique role as witnesses. But Stephen, Philip, the disciple Ananias, and Barnabas also ministered in power.[127] Faced with violent persecution, *all* the believers prayed that God would enable them *all* to speak his Word boldly and that God would stretch out his hand to perform signs and wonders as his Word went out.[128] In these last days, God pours out his Spirit on *all* of his people.

In Acts, miracles accompany the proclamation of the Word on about half of the occasions.[129] There are miracles of inspired speech, miracles of healing, miracles of protection and rescue, miracles of judgment.[130] There is a close relationship between demonstrations of God's power and the spread of his Word, yet references to the Word are found in many contexts apart from signs and wonders, while every mention of signs and wonders in Acts also comes with a proclamation of the Word.[131] Miracles cannot lead to saving faith without a person hearing and receiving the truth of the gospel.

Without the message of the gospel, the meaning of a sign can be distorted.[132] The greatest sign of all, the sign to which all miracles point, is that of Jesus' life, death, and resurrection.

Miracles can give rise to faith and discipleship, but also unbelief and persecution.[133] As Jesus was the miracle worker who must also suffer, so his disciples were miracle workers who must also suffer. Both martyrdom and miracle can serve the spread of the gospel.[134]

God's power did not prevent Peter from being thrown into prison, or Stephen and James from being killed, or Paul from being shipwrecked.[135] Miracles are intended for the glory of God and the authenticity of his message, not always for the comfort of his people.

Luke did not expect signs and miracles to end with the death of the last apostle. In the age of the Spirit, the progress of the Word is still accompanied by visions and God's guidance, bold witness in the face of persecution, and signs and wonders. Luke establishes the unique apostolic authority of Paul and the Twelve, but once they move off the stage, the church continues as a Spirit-empowered missionary movement.[136]

Schnabel makes an important point, "Since Luke does not treat the history of the early church as an entirely unique period of the history of salvation, it can be assumed that he was convinced that what God was doing through Jesus Christ and through the power of the Spirit, Christians in all churches should experience and be involved in."[137]

The disciples were aware of their supreme dependence on God for the growth of this movement. Paul had strategies, and he made wise decisions based on his understanding, but God could disrupt Paul's plans. On one occasion, Paul and his team were probing the unreached field of Asia Minor when twice the Holy Spirit stood in their way.[138] After weeks of frustration, finally a Macedonian man appeared to Paul in a vision, and a new door of opportunity opened. If the apostle Paul needed the presence and power of the Spirit, so do we.

From Acts, we learn the Spirit continues to be poured out on all of God's people that they might be witnesses to the Lord Jesus throughout the earth. There's continuity between the apostolic age and ours. But the power of the Spirit is not given just for our personal blessing; the Spirit leads God's people out of the upper room into a world that is far from him.

You don't have to fly to the Middle East to step out into your neighborhood to offer prayer and begin a conversation about Jesus. You may or may not see miracles, but God is always present, and he is faithful to work in the lives of those who are far from him. All around the world, the offer to pray in Jesus' name softens hearts and surfaces people who want to know more about following him. Go in the power of the Spirit, and have a simple, effective method for discipleship. Step out and discover what God can do.

# DON'T CALL IMPURE WHAT GOD HAS MADE CLEAN (10:1–48)

## AD 37

While Peter is traveling further into Gentile territory and staying in Joppa, to the north in Caesarea, the angel of God appears to a Roman centurion named Cornelius. The port city of Caesarea was the right place for a breakthrough in the mission to the nations. It was the capital of the Roman occupation, the heart of their military and commercial might. Built by Herod the Great to honor Caesar Augustus, it was the headquarters of Roman governors such as Pontius Pilate, Antonius Felix, and Porcius Festus. Although Caesarea was a pagan city loathed by many Jews, it contained a large Jewish community.[139]

Centurions, who commanded sixty to eighty soldiers, were the backbone of the Roman army. Cornelius was a man of status and rank who earned sixteen times the pay of a regular soldier.[140] He had a good relationship with the Jewish community, and his family were devout people who feared God, gave generously to the poor, and prayed continually. Like the Ethiopian official, he was one of the many Gentiles who rejected pagan gods and were drawn to the one true God of Israel.

God was already at work in Cornelius's life, preparing him for the encounter with Peter and the gospel. When movements spread quickly, it is because of people like Cornelius, whom God has prepared to welcome the messenger and the message. The gospel then travels rapidly across networks of preexisting relationships.[141] Finding the God-prepared insider is the key that opens an unreached community.

Meanwhile, in Joppa, Peter is on the rooftop praying when God commands him to kill and eat unclean animals. He refuses. Then he hears the Lord's command not to call anything impure that he has made clean. The Spirit tells Peter to get up and go with the men who have just arrived downstairs. Peter welcomes them, and the following day, the group of ten set out to walk the thirty miles north along the coast to Caesarea.

Peter arrives and finds Cornelius waiting with a house full of his relatives, servants, friends, and associates. In the ancient world, this was Cornelius's *oikos,* or household.[142] Luke shows how one household can become the open door to a community.[143]

Luke gives us a summary of Peter's message, which includes an outline of the life and ministry of Jesus, like we find in the Gospels.[144] Peter speaks of Jesus' birth, baptism, anointing by the Spirit, his acts of healing and deliverance from Satan's power, his death and resurrection, and his command to bear witness to the nations. Finally, as Jesus had taught him, Peter explains how all the prophets bore witness to Jesus.[145]

Up to this point, Peter and the apostles had largely confined themselves to the Jewish people, but now the message is to go beyond. Jesus is Lord of all, Judge of all, and the source of forgiveness for all who believe in him—including Cornelius and his Gentile household.[146]

An angel had spoken to this God-fearing man, yet Cornelius and his household still need to *hear* the gospel from Peter and *respond* to be saved.[147] Angels and visions prepared the way for the messenger, but were not enough by themselves. It was the same when Jesus confronted Saul on the road to Damascus. The Lord still sent Ananias to explain the gospel and baptize him. Today, reports of Jesus appearing in dreams and visions to Muslims only increases the urgency for messengers to explain their meaning.

The Spirit interrupts Peter's message and falls on everyone, and they begin speaking in tongues and praising God. The Lord pours the Spirit upon his people, just as he had done at Pentecost. The Jewish believers are amazed that the Gentiles have received the Holy Spirit just as the disciples had. At Pentecost, Peter announced *everyone* who called on the name of the Lord would be saved. Now Peter understands the implications of his own preaching! The movement of God is not limited to the Jewish people. God had included the Samaritans, and now God is including the Gentiles.

Peter's objection to entering Cornelius's house had been based on the purity rules of the Hebrew Scriptures. Now he understands God has cleansed these unclean Gentiles through faith in Christ and removed the barrier to the Gentile mission.[148]

The Jewish believers are content for Gentiles to become disciples provided they also become Jews. They are uncomfortable with a movement spreading among Gentiles that is outside of their control. But movements can never be controlled. This story still speaks today—in India, movements spreading among low-caste Hindus might be led by semiliterate street sweepers and sanitation workers. In the same way, a movement in the Texas prison system might be led by serious offenders with long prison sentences. In his day, John Wesley was accused of "prostituting the ministerial function to the lowest and most illiterate …

persons of almost any class."[149] The Methodist movement swept the world primarily through the efforts of such people.

Peter was a reluctant missionary to the Gentiles. This was not his initiative, or that of the Twelve, or of the church in Jerusalem. This was a work of God. Although there were many Gentiles in Israel who could have been the focus of missionary outreach, there was no plan to reach them. The Lord intervened. He prepared Cornelius; he overcame Peter's objections and led him to Cornelius's house; he sent the Holy Spirit upon them with visible signs to confirm their salvation apart from Jewish identity. God had included the Gentiles among his people through repentance and faith in Jesus, evidenced by the Holy Spirit and baptism. Though they were far off, they too now have the Spirit and can join Jews and Samaritans in the movement of God.[150] God was gathering his people from all the peoples of the world.

A few days later, Peter returns to Jerusalem, leaving behind a new community of disciples meeting in the home of Cornelius, probably under his emerging leadership. What did these new disciples have? Peter had passed on what Jesus had taught him from the Scriptures and from Jesus' own words and deeds. They knew about the significance of his death and resurrection and his command to bear witness to the nations. Cornelius and his family already led a life of generosity and prayer. Peter would have showed them how to celebrate the Lord's Supper as they ate together. They had the Holy Spirit who inspired their worship and life in community. After a few days, the church that met in Cornelius's house had many of the same characteristics as the first church in Jerusalem.

But this will come as a shock to those back in Jerusalem to whom Peter will have to defend his actions.

## MOVEMENT OF GOD TODAY: DEEPAK'S STORY

The Holy Spirit still opens eyes today.

Joey looked at Deepak and asked, "Why do you hate Muslims?"

Indignant, Deepak replied, "I don't hate Muslims!"

"Then you must fear them."

Again, Deepak dug in his heels, "No, I don't hate them, and I'm not afraid of them."

Challenging his brother in Christ, Joey pressed in further. "Then why in the last two years have I never heard or seen you share the gospel with a Muslim?"

Deepak had come to Christ from a Hindu background, and, as a pastor, he'd trained his people to share the gospel, make disciples, and plant churches. Now he was leading a growing network of churches and training other churches. Momentum was building in his city and among the unreached people groups of the region. They had planted hundreds of churches and trained hundreds of workers.

However, Deepak was ignoring his neighbors in his homeland of India, where over 200 million Muslims live.

Deepak went home and prayed, and God revealed the resentment against Muslims that had taken root in his heart. He confessed his sin and went to work, drawing together nine leaders to work with him. He invited an experienced missionary among Muslims to train them. Then Deepak and his team trained the workers who went out among their Muslim neighbors to share the gospel and read the Scriptures together. Soon there were stories of new disciples and new churches.

It took Joey's searching questions to unlock Deepak's heart.

Deepak and Peter are not alone. We all suffer from "people blindness"—the inability to see beyond our people to the places and people groups that are far from God. The fear of Islam is just as big an inhibitor for Chinese, Indian, and African believers as it is for Westerners. We all have our blind spots. Cornelius's story is a reminder of God's determination to gather one people from every ethnicity, culture, and language. He will disrupt our settled contentment and take us beyond our focus on people who are just like us to the glorious diversity of every people group and every place. We need to be ready.

## DEEPER: HOUSEHOLD CONVERSIONS

*The following day he arrived in Caesarea. Cornelius was expecting them and had called together his relatives and close friends.*

ACTS 10:24

The story in Acts begins in a house and ends in a house.[151] When the Spirit came at Pentecost, he filled the entire *house* where they were meeting. Acts closes with Paul confined to the *house* he was staying in and the Word going out unhindered. The movement travels from Jerusalem to Rome primarily by the means of receptive households.[152]

The house is a focus of mission in Luke's Gospel. Jesus turns the house into a place of healing, teaching, and relationship but also of conflict and division.[153] Jesus sends the Seventy out on a mission to the towns he is about to visit, instructing them on how to enter an unreached community and identify a receptive household. The focus has shifted from the temple and the priesthood to ordinary people and the world they inhabit.

Near the end of Jesus' journey to Jerusalem, he invites himself into the home of Zacchaeus the tax collector. To fulfill his mission to seek and to save the lost, he *must* stay at Zacchaeus's house.[154] When Jesus left, it was Zacchaeus who stayed as a witness to his community. Jesus modeled what he taught his disciples to do. What he does with Zacchaeus parallels the instructions he gave to the Seventy before sending them out.[155] The purpose of their mission is to find receptive households before moving on to the next village.

Conversion stories make up about one-quarter of Acts.[156] Among these stories are four accounts of the conversion of households: Cornelius, a centurion; Lydia, a female merchant; a Roman jailor; and Crispus, a synagogue president.[157]

Of all the examples of household conversions in Acts, one stands out: the account of the conversion of Cornelius, his friends, and family. Luke tells this story four times, making it the most repeated story in Acts.[158] Luke wants to get our attention. It is not the story of one person's conversion; it is the story of the founding of a church.

Jesus' example and teaching show that reaching households is an important aspect of how the movement spreads.[159] There are parallels between the instructions Jesus gave the Seventy and the mission of Peter to Cornelius's household.

**The parallels between Jesus' instructions to the Seventy and Peter's mission to Cornelius's house.**[160]

| Luke 10 | Acts 10 |
|---|---|
| The Lord appointed the Seventy and sent them out (v.1) | God intervened through a vision to send Peter to Cornelius's household (vv.9–20) |
| They were told to carry no moneybag, no bag, no sandals, and to greet no one on the road (v.4) | Peter went dependent on God and the people he would reach (v.48) |
| [Jesus] sent them on ahead of him, two by two, into every town and place where he himself was about to go (v.1) | Peter traveled with six companions and entered the city of Caesarea (vv.23–24) |
| They were instructed when first entering a house to say, "Peace be to this house!" If someone who promoted peace was there, the disciples' peace would rest upon them (vv.5–6) | Peter was welcomed into a household of peace by Cornelius (v.24–26) |
| They were to remain in the same house, eating and drinking what was offered, for the laborer deserves his wages (v.7) | He and his companions remained in a Gentile household for some days, eating and drinking what was set before him (v.48b) |
| They were to heal the sick who were there and say to them, "The kingdom of God has come near to you" (v.9) | There were powerful words and signs demonstrating God's saving presence (vv.34–47) |

Led by the Spirit and by the example of Jesus, the messengers in Acts focus their attention on receptive homes as a new center for the movement. In the ancient world, the household included parents and children, other dependents, relatives, friends, and slaves.[161] By reaching households, not just individuals, the communities of disciples embraced a diversity of people who would not normally relate to each other—Jews and Gentiles, slaves and free, rich and poor.

In the crowded cities of Antioch, Ephesus, and Rome, most people lived in multi-story tenements that could only fit a handful of people. A typical house had just one or two small rooms without running water, a kitchen, or a toilet.[162] Churches that met in typical houses must have been small and spread across the city. When Paul wrote to "the church" in Rome, he was writing to a network of churches meeting across the city.[163]

Only a small percentage of people could afford larger houses that could accommodate a group of thirty or more people.[164] Sometimes the mission in Acts required houses large enough to accommodate the missionaries and to provide space for the new disciples to meet.

The house was a place of evangelism, discipleship, and church life. As Acts unfolds, the household gradually replaces the temple as the place of God's saving presence.[165] Only by doing so can the movement break out of the confines of Judaism centered on Jerusalem and the temple and spread to the nations.

Movements today don't start with settled, paid clergy and grand buildings. They start with everyday obedient disciples telling their stories and gossiping the gospel in homes and everyday places.

In Acts, households of newly converted believers "mark the way-stations of the spread of the gospel from Galilee to Rome."[166] Household conversion stories provide several firsts in bringing salvation to the unreached peoples of the world: the first Gentile man (Cornelius), the first Gentile woman (Lydia), the first pagan (the Roman jailer), the first synagogue ruler (Crispus).[167] Their conversions led to even more Gentiles coming to faith. Each resulted in a new church.

Is it still legitimate to pursue a household strategy in the age of the fractured nuclear family? The breakdown of extended family relation-ships in an urbanized world inhibits the speed at which movements spread. In an urbanized world it's harder to reach entire extended families and social units. Relationship ties are weaker and more fluid. Households take on different forms. Yet relational networks still exist and are important. We are still social beings made in the image of the triune God. People are still more likely to adopt a new faith after a friend or family member converts to that faith. As the number of converted friends and family increases, so does the likelihood of conversion.[168]

For instance, in London there's a ministry reaching and discipling workers in the technology industry.[169] They do evangelism, disci-pleship, and even gather as church in and around the workplace. The spread of the gospel follows relational ties, but this can be challenging in a workplace setting, as their significant relationships live and work elsewhere. New disciples are therefore trained to take what they are learning into their homes and neighborhoods. The same is true for movements of disciples and churches spreading behind bars.[170] Social networks are different in prisons, and so methods need to be simple and adaptable. There also needs to be a strategy for the gospel and discipleship among the inmates' family and friends on the outside. The shift is to see the world through the new disciple's eyes and ask, "How can I help you reach these people?"

When someone comes to Christ, we tend to invite them into our group or our church. A movement approach is to take discipleship and church into the new disciple's world, to reach their relationships. Households look radically different today, but whatever form social relationships take, they are a key to the spread of movements.

If we question the legitimacy of a small gathering of people meeting in a home, a prison block, a café, or a university campus, we need to remember that in the ancient world, the typical house could only accommodate a handful of people. If you were wealthy, perhaps thirty to fifty. Yet these households, both large and small, were the building blocks of a dynamic movement.

The advance of this movement was not dependent on the provision of a building. The new disciples opened their homes to provide accommodation for the missionaries and a meeting place for disciples. Multiplying movements don't depend on facilities because that limits their ability to reproduce and remain sustainable.

A second lesson is that evangelism occurs in the networks of preexisting relationships.[171] In the ancient world, this happened through the extended household. But today, the nature of those networks of relationships varies from culture to culture. Whatever form they take, movements spread through networks of existing relationships. When movements encounter people, they don't just see individuals; they see the relational networks that surround each person. That's why movements mobilize the newest believers to share with their friends and family. When someone comes to Christ, one of the first questions should be, "Who needs to hear what God has done in your life?" And when someone is ready for discipleship, the questions to ask are, "When could we meet? Where could we meet? Who else do you know who would be interested in meeting with us?"

Movements don't extract people from their existing relationships; they bring the gospel, discipleship, and church to their world—just like Peter did.

The story of Cornelius is about the conversion of a people. As the account unfolds, the focus shifts from an individual (Cornelius) to *all* who hear the Word. At the end, Peter asks, how can we withhold baptism from *these people*? It's *they*, not just Cornelius, who ask Peter to stay longer. The gospel is not just about individuals; God is forming a new community of disciples who will learn to follow Christ together.[172]

Two things will halt the spread of a movement: methods that are unsustainable, and evangelism that focuses on reaching individuals rather than networks of relationships. The gospel could go to the Gentiles because the movement was not dependent on a temple and a priesthood in Jerusalem. The Word came into their world. Peter left after a few days, confidently knowing this community had the Word, the Spirit, and Jesus' command to continue the mission.

Today we still need to make the shift from the temple to the household, from the priesthood of the few to the ministry of the many. The gospel can go out, and disciples can meet in homes, cafés, prison cells, refugee camps, and workplaces. Everyday places can become sacred. The newest disciple can not only become a recipient of the gospel but, in the power of the Spirit, they can also become a minister of the gospel.

## MOVEMENTS TODAY: ABU YASSIM'S STORY

The story of Peter and Cornelius is still being played out today. Though the names and the setting changes, the pattern remains the same.

Gary and his team were trekking and praying through a mountainous region of the Horn of Africa. In one Muslim community, the head of the village, Abu Yassim, invited them into his home for a coffee ceremony. As they entered, Abu called to his four-year-old son, "Isa, shoo the calf out of the house so it doesn't disturb our guests."

"Why did you name your boy Isa?" one of the team asked. (*Isa* is the Arabic word for Jesus.)

Abu explained, "Four years ago, my wife was pregnant and, in a vision, a man came to me in white and said, 'I am Isa. One day, I will send someone from across the ocean to tell you my story; believe that man. As a sign to you that this is true, your wife will give birth tonight. It will be a son; name that son after me.'" Abu looked at Gary and asked, "Why did it take you four years to come?"

After the team shared the story of Isa, all nine members of the household turned and believed. They taught the new believers some basic stories from Scripture and encouraged them in their new faith. As they left for the next village, they wondered how best to help these new disciples learn to follow Christ, given neither Abu Yassim nor any of his household could read.

There were disciples in the next village, but it was a six-hour journey by foot. Bekele, the head of the village, had come to Christ through one of his sons who had been a student in the city. Now there were around 180 believers in the village.

Gary shared how Abu Yassim and his household had turned and believed and the need for their ongoing discipleship as they couldn't read the Scriptures. Bekele had a solution. "I have three sons who can read and know the stories about Jesus. I will give my son David to Abu Yassim as his son, and David can teach them."

Early the next morning, they hiked back over the mountains to Abu's village, and David became Abu Yassim's son. He guided his new family through a simple approach of reading the Scriptures for discipleship. Whatever Abu Yassim learned, he passed on to the entire village.

What can we learn from this story? Like the apostle Peter, Gary and the team were out praying, strengthening the disciples, and looking for God-prepared people. Like Cornelius, Abu Yassim became the doorway into an entire Muslim community. Gary will return when he can, but he could leave confident that God was at work through his Word and the Spirit.

Your world probably looks very different from the world of Abu Yassim, but wherever you are in the world, it's possible to walk around, praying and looking for the people God has prepared who welcome the messenger, the message, and the mission. All you need is faith and a simple pattern of discipleship that can pass from person to person and group to group.

# WHO AM I TO STAND IN GOD'S WAY? (11:1–18)

If Peter had previously objected to eating unclean food and was reluctant to enter the house of a Gentile, it is no surprise that the Jewish believers in Jerusalem feel the same and demand Peter explain himself.

The Jewish believers are not opposed to the salvation of Gentiles; they are concerned that Peter entered a Gentile home and ate with Gentiles, flouting the purity laws. If Jewish disciples did the same, there was a danger devout Jews would cut them off, and the mission to the Jews would grind to a halt.

Peter describes how the Gentiles had responded to the message concerning Jesus' life, death, and resurrection; how the Lord had poured out his Holy Spirit; and how Gentiles had been baptized and added to God's people. Peter explains it was God who set aside the purification laws and saved these uncircumcised Gentiles through faith in Christ alone, evidenced by the gift of the Spirit.[173]

Peter quotes Jesus, who said, "John immersed in water, but you will be immersed in the Holy Spirit."[174] Joel's prophecy—that the Spirit would be poured out on all people—has been fulfilled.[175] Jesus has poured out his Spirit upon them; they are part of God's restoration of Israel, the new people of God.[176] What else could Peter do but baptize these disciples?

When Peter finishes, their criticism turns to worship.[177] God had fulfilled his promise to Abraham, that through him and his descendants all the peoples of the earth would be blessed.[178] The church in Jerusalem embraced the Gentile mission, although unresolved issues will later resurface.

The hero of this story is not Peter, the reluctant missionary to the Gentiles, but God who brought Cornelius and Peter together, and through his Word and the Holy Spirit, achieved this vital breakthrough. Yet Peter played his part by leaving Jerusalem and going to unfamiliar ground, which strengthened and extended the limits of the movement. In this, he followed the example of Jesus, who went beyond the limits of institutional religion to take the gospel to people far from God.

Key to his understanding of what God was doing was his faithfulness to the teaching and example of Jesus and his openness to the work of the Holy Spirit. If God needs to disturb and reposition a leader of Peter's stature, how much more do *we* need his disruption to return us to his purposes?

Luke's attention now shifts from Jerusalem to the Gentile city of Antioch. Jerusalem was the birthplace of the movement but will not remain its center as the Word continues its journey to the ends of the earth.

There are several principles embedded in this story. As always, the breakthroughs in the movement of God occur on the fringe, not at the center. Peter is away from Jerusalem, strengthening and extending the movement. He's in a place where God can disrupt him. He goes on a journey to understand what God is doing. He looks for signs of the Spirit's activity that align with the teaching of Jesus and the Hebrew Scriptures. The Word and the Spirit enable him to interpret his experience and embrace what God is doing as the fulfillment of his promises. Now Peter is ready to return to Jerusalem and help God's people understand what God has done.

## MOVEMENTS TODAY: OUT OF ESSEX

David Bareham is a successful church planter and pastor in Essex, England, who, like Peter, discovered God had more.[179]

David launched the church in 1996, and since then it has grown steadily to five hundred people, helped by the influx of immigrants from Eastern Europe and Africa. Around forty nations are represented in their church family. Most years, they add about fifteen people to the church by conversion, many through the Alpha course. In addition, the church has planted four other churches in Essex.

Yet it troubled David that they were reaching so few of the local community. Most of their growth came from existing Christians.

Then he heard of Russell Godward, a local pastor, who had stepped down from his church to focus entirely on reaching people far from God. At first, he thought Russell was crazy. When Russell invited him to a training event, David agreed to go but arrived skeptical. I was with Russell that day, and I remember David's searching questions.

But David kept coming back for more. He attended three identical training events until he was sure there was something in this. The training covered the basic biblical foundation and skills in sharing the gospel and making disciples, followed by time in the community connecting with people and sharing the gospel.[180]

David kept pressing in because he wanted to see his church reach lost people in their community. He spent time with Russell out in the community, offering prayer and sharing the gospel. David believed if he were to see change in his church, he would have to embody that change himself.

It embarrassed him that, as a church leader, it was years since he had led someone to Christ. He felt he didn't have time to connect with people outside the church. If someone came to know Christ, he had no discipleship plan, apart from, "Come to church, listen to my sermons, join a life group, and sign up for Alpha in four months."

So David prayed he would lead someone to Christ every month. God answered his prayer, and David formed a discipleship group for new believers. Using a 3-Thirds approach, they worked through the Commands of Christ, learning how to follow Jesus and make disciples.[181]

While this was happening, David was working with his elders to gain support for the new direction. He'd been on a personal journey, and he didn't want to leave those in his church behind. On one occasion the elders needed more time to come to an agreement on the new direction, so he canceled a church training event and gave them the time they needed. All the while, David continued to share the gospel and make disciples.

Stories circulated throughout the church of the new decisions to follow Christ. They were baptizing people who had joined 3-Thirds groups with no church background and were going on to make disciples.[182]

As God was at work, the church culture was shifting, and the elders embraced the new direction. David recalls it took about one year for God to turn him around, then another two years to win wide support in the church, but it wasn't time wasted. All along the way, the gospel was getting out and people were turning and following Christ.

David has formed a team to take the training to every life group in the church. He and his team now train throughout Britain and Europe, helping other churches to reach out beyond their four walls.

When the church emerged from the pandemic, David took the opportunity for a reset. He restructured their Sunday gatherings. On the first Sunday of the month, the whole church comes together for a big celebration with a worship band. On the second and third Sundays, they meet on the same site, but in four regional gatherings, in a simpler format. Each requires a separate leadership and teaching team, creating the opportunity to develop more leaders. On the fourth Sunday, the church gathers in their 3-Thirds groups in homes. The restructure serves the goal of shifting the church from a consumer culture to a discipleship culture. It also creates room for new leaders to step up. In the mid-week 3-Thirds groups and Sunday gatherings, every disciple is wrestling with the meaning of Scripture and how they might obey it.

David led a healthy, diverse church of five hundred, but he wasn't content. His vision of the core missionary task was clear. His church was not making progress in reaching people far from God and forming them into disciples. So he immersed himself in learning and applying the essentials skills in disciple making. He built a relationship with Russell who trained and mentored him. He watched for the signs of God's activity and used those stories to draw others in. He took the eldership through the same journey he'd been on. He gave them time but continued to lead the way by example. Meanwhile, the evidence mounted as stories came in of new disciples and new groups forming. The whole process took three years and is still unfolding. David had a part to play, but it was God who was the initiator and guide throughout the process.

# A GREAT NUMBER TURN (11:19–30)

### AD 44–45

When Stephen was killed, the disciples in Jerusalem scattered. As a result the gospel went to Samaria, to an Ethiopian, and to the coastal cities between Azotus and Caesarea. Unidentified disciples fled to the Phoenician cities along the Mediterranean coast (today's Lebanon). They started churches in Tyre, Sidon, and Ptolemais.[183] Another group took the gospel to the island of Cyprus off the Syrian coast. Others went north to Antioch in Syria. As these refugees traveled, they spread the Word among the many Jews in each city; then something unprecedented occurred in Antioch.

Antioch was three hundred miles north of Jerusalem in what is now southern Turkey. It was the capital of the Roman province of Syria and one of the great cities of the Roman Empire, with a population of around 250,000 and a Jewish colony of over 25,000.[184] As a doorway for trade to the East, it was a melting pot of East and West, with Greeks, Syrians, Phoenicians, Jews, Arabs, Persians, Egyptians, and Indians making up the population.[185]

When the refugees reached Antioch, they shared the Word with Jews in the synagogues and with Gentile converts to Judaism and God-fearers.[186] These Gentiles became bridges for reaching pagan Gentiles. The hand of the Lord was with them, and a great number of people turned to the Lord.[187] Peter and John had strengthened the work in Aramaic-speaking Samaria.

Now, the church in Jerusalem send Barnabas to Antioch because he is a Greek speaker from Cyprus. Barnabas remains an important link between the churches in Antioch and Jerusalem, and between the Gentile mission and the Jewish believers in Jerusalem.[188] Jerusalem want to support the work, not control it. As Barnabas encourages the new disciples, more and more people turn to the Lord.

The opportunity in Antioch is so great that Barnabas leaves Antioch and travels 130 miles to Tarsus in search of Saul, who had been based there since he left Jerusalem eight years before.[189] Following his conversion, Saul had proclaimed the gospel in Damascus, Arabia, and Jerusalem

(AD 32/33). Then, from his base in Tarsus, he proclaimed the gospel and planted churches in Syria and Cilicia (AD 34–42).[190]

Back in Antioch, Barnabas and Saul meet with the church and teach large numbers of people, sharing the good news of Jesus with Jews and Greeks.[191] This is the first time Luke uses the word "church" to apply to Jews *and* Gentiles as the one people of God. What did it mean for these people to be "church"? Luke has already shown us in accounts of the church in Jerusalem.[192] Having established the pattern of church life, he doesn't repeat it every time he mentions a church, although he does give us glimpses in other locations that reinforce the pattern of Jerusalem.[193]

Because the Jews were embracing Gentiles, it's likely this mixed community had separated from the synagogue.[194] Antioch outsiders and government officials grasped for a label for this new group; they weren't Jews, and they didn't worship idols, so they gave them a new name— "Christians," or followers of Christ, a term only used by outsiders until the church adopted it in the second century.[195] Before this point, when the early Christians referred to themselves, they used a variety of terms, including disciples, believers, the church, saints, brothers and sisters, Nazarenes, and followers of the Way.[196]

During this year in Antioch, some prophets arrive from Jerusalem. Since Pentecost, all believers had been given the ability to speak prophetically, but certain men and women were emerging as recognized prophets.[197] One of them, Agabus, prophesies a famine throughout the Roman world. This prompts the disciples to raise money for famine relief in Judea, a reminder of the partnership between the Jewish and Gentile streams of the movement. The movement in Antioch is not under the control of Jerusalem, nor is it a rival. As the first church to include both Jews and Gentiles in full fellowship, Antioch becomes an equal partner with the Jewish church in Jerusalem.[198]

Movements don't cling to the safety of the center; they reproduce sending hubs like Jerusalem and Antioch. As Jerusalem had been a mission base for reaching Judea, Samaria, and Antioch, Antioch then became a hub for the Gentile mission. This would not have happened if Antioch had remained under the control of Jerusalem or if Antioch had sought to control the churches it planted.

Movements don't measure the health of a church by its size. A better gauge is the number of vibrant children, grandchildren, and great grandchildren it produces. Unhealthy churches, regardless of size, hold on to people and resources to meet their own needs. They grow fat. Movements reproduce new generations of disciples, churches, and leaders. They leave a legacy of descendants.

Healthy churches equip new disciples to share their faith with friends and family and to make disciples. Around the world, disciple making movements measure health by tracking the generations of churches that are planted: the number of first-generation churches that are planting second, third, and fourth generation churches. As they map the streams of new disciples and new churches, workers assess the health of these churches using criteria from Acts 2:36–47.[199]

# BUT THE CHURCH IS PRAYING (12:1–25)

## AD 41

Jesus had warned his disciples they would be seized and brought before kings and governors on account of his name.[200] He was right.

King Herod Agrippa I was the grandson of Herod the Great. When Agrippa was a boy, his grandfather executed his father, fearing he coveted the throne. Agrippa was sent to Rome with his mother to be brought up among the children of the Roman aristocracy. During that time, he had become a lifelong friend of Claudius, who was now emperor of Rome. In AD 41, Claudius restored the kingdom of Herod the Great to Agrippa. As "King of the Jews," Agrippa ruled over Judea, Samaria, Galilee, the Transjordan, and the Decapolis.[201]

Ten years has passed since Stephen's execution. The new movement has continued to grow and threaten the religious and political leaders of the nation. The mood has changed since the death of Stephen. Previously the opposition came from the religious and political elites; now the populace has turned against the movement.[202] Unlike the Sanhedrin, Agrippa has full authority to execute his subjects.[203] (His uncle, Herod Antipas, had used this same authority to execute John the Baptist.) Seeking the support of the Jewish traditionalists and nationalists, Agrippa has the apostle James arrested and beheaded. He then arrests Peter and schedules a public trial for after Passover—a trial in which Agrippa could determine the verdict and the sentence.

Peter had once told Jesus he was willing to die for him, and yet he denied him. Again Peter faces prison and death. This time, he is ready.

Peter is in jail, chained between two soldiers, while two others stand guard outside the cell door. Four squads of four guards rotate every three hours through the night and every six hours during the day. In this spiritual battle, there are two sides: a ruler with the power of the sword and God's people with the power of prayer.[204]

Peter doesn't know whether God will rescue him or if, like Jesus, Stephen, and James, he'll be executed. Despite this, in the middle of the night, he is at peace, asleep between two soldiers.

Suddenly an angel wakes him. At first, he thinks it's a dream. Once outside the jail, the angel leaves him, and Peter realizes it was real. He hurries to the house of Mary, John Mark's mother, where many disciples are spending the night in prayer for his release. It's a fine house, with servants and a gate that leads to a courtyard. Rhoda, the servant girl who answers Peter's knocking cannot believe it is him; nor can the praying believers when she runs back inside to tell them. Meanwhile, Peter, who had been released by an angel from his enemies, is locked outside by his friends.

Because it was not safe to meet at the temple, the gathering at Mary's home must have been one of many gatherings throughout the city praying for Peter's release. (The church in Jerusalem now numbered in the thousands.) Peter doesn't stay, because it is no longer safe for him to live in Jerusalem, but he leaves word for James, the Lord's brother, before traveling to "another place" beyond the jurisdiction of Herod. Leadership in Jerusalem is passing to James and the elders.[205] Peter leaves to continue his missionary work beyond Jerusalem, returning temporarily for the Jerusalem Council.[206]

The next morning, Herod demands a search, but Peter cannot be found. He may have been hiding among the thousands of Passover pilgrims heading out of Jerusalem in all directions.[207] As was the custom, the four guards on duty when Peter escaped received the same penalty he would have faced—death.

The story doesn't end there. A few years later, Herod is at his palace in Caesarea, dressed in his royal robes and seated on his throne, receiving the adulation of the cities of Tyre and Sidon. When he speaks, the crowd shouts, "This is the voice of a god, not of a human being!" In refusing to correct the people and give glory to God, Herod is immediately struck down. An angel's touch had released Peter from Herod's captivity, and an angel's touch brings about Herod's end.[208]

When Peter was released from a previous arrest, the believers prayed, "Now, Lord, consider their threats."[209] In Agrippa's case, God had waited long enough. He acted with justice. Herod lay dead, just four years into his reign. Let the rulers of this world beware: God rules over those who conspire against him and his people.[210]

Just as Pharaoh's oppression caused Israel to multiply, so Agrippa's oppression led to the church's increase.[211] God is in charge, not a human king. Despite fierce opposition, the movement continued to spread.[212] His servants may suffer, like his Son, but God's message of grace and truth is unstoppable.[213]

Throughout history, there have been many more tyrants like Agrippa, who have opposed God's people; it would be foolish to imagine that our mission cannot advance until they are deposed.

With this summary, Luke completes the story of the first church in Jerusalem. The focus now shifts from Peter and the Jerusalem church to Barnabas and Saul. In Antioch, we're about to see the first intentional mission to the Gentiles.

## MOVEMENTS TODAY: AYESHA AND NURA

Ayesha was born a Sikh somewhere in South Asia. Her father was from a high-status priestly family, but because her mother had been Catholic before she married, Ayesha grew up hearing stories about Jesus.

At sixteen, Ayesha was sent by her parents to serve in the Sikh temple, where she was beaten and mistreated. In her distress, she began reading the Bible and fell in love with Jesus.

Aged twenty-two, Ayesha met a missionary, and for the first time there was someone who could help her grow as a disciple. Ayesha would go on mission trips to the villages, and she learned how to proclaim the gospel, heal the sick, and cast out demons. On one trip, she met Nura, who had a Hindu background. Nura's brother had converted to Islam and was a religious leader. After Ayesha cast out demons from Nura, she too followed Jesus.

Nura grew in her faith, and every day she would pray for two and a half hours and read one chapter of the Bible. This was all she could manage because Ayesha was teaching her to read, and it took Nura an hour to get through each chapter.

Ayesha and Nura teamed up, and together they planted churches. Offerings from the church plants were used to support a local church planter, meet the financial needs in the community, and to rent a van every month to drive three hours to a secret location where they baptized new disciples.

Nura led a young woman called Nadia out of prostitution to faith in Christ. Soon Nadia was sharing her faith with others and teaching them to follow Jesus. Then one night, a local terrorist group kidnapped her. The terrorists sent a message that they would release Nadia in return for ransom money and Ayesha. Their only interest in Nadia was to get to Ayesha, the leader of this network of disciples and churches. In time, other attempts were made to kidnap network members. As a result, the network shut down. People stayed home behind locked doors, meeting only over the phone.

Ayesha and Nura were traumatized. Most of the churches in Nura's area disbanded. Ayesha fled with her family to another city. Eventually Nadia's family negotiated her release, but for the next six months it was unsafe for Nura to leave her home. Everything went quiet.

During this time, Nura led her older brother Baashir to Christ. With her brother's support, she was no longer a single woman alone in a patriarchal society.

Next door to Nura and Baashir lived a Hindu family with a temple in their home which drew worshippers. When the mother of the household became seriously ill, Nura and Baashir prayed for her, and she was healed. The whole household put their faith in Christ and destroyed their temple and its idols.

The Hindu background couple then led their Muslim neighbors to Christ and are now passing on to them what Nura and Baashir taught them. Immediately the Muslim couple began sharing their faith with their friends and family.

Encouraged by this, Nura and Baashir started going into villages, praying for the sick and casting out demons. The newly converted Hindu and Muslim couples came with them.

In one village they prayed for a girl who had been paralyzed for fourteen years. As they prayed for over an hour, the house filled with people waiting to see what would happen. The girl was healed and then walked down to the river to be baptized. Four others joined her. Within six months, eighty people had turned to Christ and were meeting in groups for discipleship.

From time to time, the terrorists issue threats, so the network goes to ground and limits communication to phone calls. They have learned when persecution comes to keep a low profile and wait to see what God does. While the messengers are harassed, God is with them and will make a way for his Word to continue to spread. In this case, he used a Sikh to reach Hindus and Hindus to reach Muslims.

An important indicator of a movement is that the message is being spread by insiders—people who have recently come to Christ within a people group and are given authority and the responsibility to make disciples.

Movements resist the temptation to professionalize the ministry and concentrate power in a few hands. We could call this a Western problem, but it's a human problem. In a movement, the role of gifted leaders is to equip God's people for service.[214] To do that we must have confidence that the Word and Spirit are available to ordinary people who commit to the core missionary task.

A friend of mine is a Western missionary multiplying disciples and churches among refugees—North Africans, Pakistanis, Afghans, Syrians and Persians. He has a saying, "The white man doesn't get wet." What he means is that although he baptizes the first wave of disciples, he immediately trains them to baptize the disciples they make while he stays dry.

It's so tempting to show supporters back home that you're the one getting the results. It's true on both the mission field and in local churches. However, movements release authority and responsibility but stay close to provide training, encouragement, and correction as new disciples make disciples.

To see a movement, we need to let go of *our* ministry and fan the flame of what God is doing through others.

## DEEPER: HOW THE FIRST CHURCH BECAME A MOVEMENT

*The law will go out from Zion, the word of the LORD from Jerusalem.*

ISAIAH 2:3

Luke tells us more about the life and mission of the first church in Jerusalem than any other church. From this one church came a disciple making movement that planted churches from Jerusalem to the ends of the earth. God brought this church into being and shaped its life and mission.[215] What God did in Jerusalem, he still does today.

## A God-Shaped Identity

This new community in Jerusalem was the creative act of the living God. The Father called it into existence through the message about Jesus, spoken in the power of the Holy Spirit. The mission is clear: bear witness to Jesus from Jerusalem to the ends of the earth.

Their God-shaped identity produced a way of life together. They were devoted to the apostles' teaching, devoted to sharing their lives, devoted to sharing meals and the Lord's Supper, and devoted to prayer. God's power was present to heal the sick and, through sacrificial giving, to provide for the poor. Every day, they met publicly and from house to house. Their hearts filled with joyful worship, and the people regarded them with respect. Every day, God added those being saved.

This is the life the gospel produces in a disciple making movement. When God is present among his people, this is what it looks like. What we read here is less about methods, which can change, and everything to do with the unchanging identity of God's people.

They filled Jerusalem with the message about Jesus, and the threats and intimidation grew violent. They chose not to sacrifice the message of Jesus for peace.

## A God-Ordained Mission

The disciples were not meant to settle down in Jerusalem and wait for the kingdom to come. God scattered them, and wherever they went, they took the Word with them. They won disciples and started churches. The church in Jerusalem became a multiplying movement as the gospel went to Samaria, Ethiopia, and the Phoenician cities along the Mediterranean coast. Others took the gospel to Cyprus; others went north to Damascus and Antioch in Syria. Most of them were unnamed, ordinary disciples.

Jerusalem was a center from which the gospel went out to the ends of the earth, but as the church in Jerusalem multiplied beyond its borders, it never sought to rule over the new churches.[216] Jerusalem sent Peter and John to strengthen and extend the movement begun by Philip in Samaria. They sent Barnabas, who recruited Paul, to strengthen and extend the work in Antioch. In both cases, there were no lines of authority stretching back to Jerusalem.

Out of the first church, God was forming a multiplying movement of disciples and churches.

## A God-Given Legacy

The apostles remained based in Jerusalem from where they traveled throughout Judea, Samaria, and Galilee, establishing and strengthening the churches. In Jerusalem, the apostles developed elders, led by Jesus' brother James, who oversaw the churches meeting across the city, preparing the way for the Twelve's departure. In a multiplying movement, everyone is doing themselves out of a job by developing the people around them.

In AD 41, Herod Agrippa made his move on the apostles, executing James the apostle and planning the same for Peter. It was time for the apostles to leave the city and pursue their calling to the nations.

The church in Jerusalem gave away many of its people. Stephen prepared the way for the Gentile mission. Philip took the gospel into Samaria and along the Mediterranean coast.[217] Jesus' brothers were engaged in missionary work.[218] They sent Agabus the prophet out from Jerusalem. John Mark, from Jerusalem, traveled with Paul and Barnabas. Barnabas was sent to strengthen and extend the work in Antioch and became a coworker with Paul. Silas–Silvanus, another coworker of Paul, was from the church in Jerusalem as well.[219] These are just the names we know. There are also the unidentified disciples who fled Jerusalem, taking the gospel with them.[220] They planted the church in Antioch, which became a new multiplying hub for the Gentile mission. This is how the church in Jerusalem became a sending center for a missionary movement.

Jerusalem was the first church and an example for every church to emulate. Luke tells us very little about the church's organization and method but a lot about its identity in Christ and obedience to the Spirit. They filled their city with the knowledge of Jesus, and thousands became disciples. The Word went out from Jerusalem in every direction, fulfilling the words of the prophets and Jesus. They gave away the gospel; they gave away their people, and they gave away their leaders to multiply disciples and churches from Jerusalem to the ends of the earth. All of this, in one generation.

The Jewish revolt against Rome erupted in AD 66. A Christian prophet brought a word to the disciples, saying the city would be destroyed, as Jesus had predicted.[221] The believers fled Jerusalem for the safety of Pella.[222] In AD 70, Roman armies destroyed the city and the temple. They led the survivors away into slavery. After forty years, the church in Jerusalem was no more. Yet her legacy continues because this one church in Jerusalem gave itself away to become a movement of churches.

Every generation needs to read the story of the church in Jerusalem and ask, "What does that look like for us today?" Here are some questions we might ask to help us respond:

*Is the gospel getting out through every disciple?* We like to limit our witness to lifestyle, which enables us to remain silent and safe. Jesus commanded his disciples to bear witness to the saving significance of his life, death, and resurrection. The gospel message proclaimed in the power of the Spirit created the life of the first church. The Word leads the way. Jesus trained his disciples in what to say, then sent them out to call people to repentance.

*Is conversion expressed in baptism and leading to discipleship in community?* When it could, the Jerusalem church met in public, but the life of discipleship was in face-to-face groups. They were gathered around the Word, learning to obey Christ, enjoying the Spirit's powerful presence, and learning to love and give.

*Are we growing leaders?* Thousands of disciples meeting in hundreds of gatherings across the city meant the Twelve shared leadership at every level. They developed leaders, such as Stephen, Philip and the Seven, James and the elders, John Mark, Barnabas, Silas, Agabus, and hundreds of other unnamed disciples. When persecution came, the disciples were ready. How are you growing leaders in the field? Workers who know how to share the gospel, make disciples, and start new churches with the characteristics of the church in Jerusalem.

*Am I giving away my life?* The church in Jerusalem gave away its leaders and its people to multiply. They didn't neglect their city, nor did they neglect the Spirit's urging to bear witness to Jesus throughout the entire world—to every people in every place.

The first church lasted just one generation. It gave its life away to spark a movement.

FOUR

# THE MOVEMENT INTO EUROPE

(13:1–15:34)

# SET APART BARNABAS AND SAUL
# FOR THE WORK (13:1–14:28)

## AD 45–47

Antioch in Syria was home to the first church with a serious mix of Jews and Gentiles. It was also the origin of a missionary band that would take the gospel to Jews and pagan Gentiles in the major cities of the Roman Empire. This is the first time we hear of a church other than Jerusalem at the center of a breakthrough in the mission.

It is spring, AD 45. Five men gather at Antioch in Syria to fast and to worship the Lord. In the room is Barnabas, a Levite from Cyprus; Simeon called Niger ("black"), possibly an African; Lucius from Cyrene in northern Africa; Manaen, a childhood friend of Herod Antipas, who had executed John the Baptist and played a part in Jesus' trial; and Saul, a Pharisee born in Tarsus and educated in Jerusalem.[1]

The diversity of this group reflects their location. Antioch was a wealthy city of 250,000 people of various religions and ethnic backgrounds. Around 10 percent of the population were Jews, who had settled in the second century BC and had attracted Gentile converts and God-fearers to their faith.[2] Only Rome and Alexandria were larger and more important to the empire. Antioch was an ideal base from which the movement could spread beyond Israel to the world.

Like the Jerusalem church, the Antioch church gather to worship, fast, and pray. The Spirit comes and launches Barnabas and Saul into the next phase of the mission. God's powerful presence leads and sustains the entire campaign. It is the Holy Spirit, not the church, who is the primary agent in calling and sending these missionaries.[3]

Acts 13–14 provides a picture of the movement of God advancing into new fields. What did that look like?

## *They Have an Expansive Vision*

Their mission is not confined to one location. Barnabas and Saul sail to Cyprus, where Barnabas was from. They walk the length of the island from Salamis to Paphos, no doubt evangelizing among the towns along the south coast. Four years later, Barnabas will return with John Mark to encourage the churches they plant along the way.[4]

Next, they sail from Cyprus to Perga, and then climb the steep roads up the rugged Taurus Mountains to reach Antioch near Pisidia. From there, the Word of the Lord spreads throughout the entire region, including fifty villages under Antioch's control.[5] They proclaim the gospel in Iconium, Lystra, Derbe, and the surrounding countryside. In Derbe, the entire city hear the gospel, and they win many disciples.

## They Connect With a Wide Range of People

In each location, Barnabas and Saul connect with all sorts of people: government officials, Jews and God-fearers, idol-worshipping pagans, a magician, the wealthy and powerful, men and women.

A pattern is set that continues throughout Paul's mission. They prioritize major cities where there are Jewish synagogues. If the city has a synagogue, Barnabas and Paul go there first to preach and teach. Because Barnabas and Paul were both Jews from the diaspora,[6] these are the people with whom they have religious, linguistic, cultural, and relational ties. At the synagogue, they meet God-fearing Gentiles who are closely connected with pagan Gentiles in the community. This way the gospel spreads through preexisting relationships to the entire city.

In Cyprus, they encounter Sergius Paulus, an aristocrat and Roman governor of the island. His is the first account of a pagan Gentile's conversion, one who has no background in Judaism.[7]

From Cyprus, Paul and Barnabas go on a long and difficult journey over the Taurus Mountains to the Roman colony of Pisidian Antioch. This could be another instance of the gospel following networks of relationships. We know that the governor's clan was a leading family of the region, with land and influence.[8] The governor may have written letters to his relatives, introducing Paul and Barnabas.

Around this time, Saul becomes known as Paul. In an increasingly Gentile world, he drops the use of his Hebrew name in favor of his Roman name.

## They Proclaim the Word With Power

The gospel is at the center of their mission.[9] Paul and Barnabas's message centers on the life, death, resurrection, and exaltation of Jesus as Savior and Lord. Signs play an important part in opening new regions to the gospel.[10] Healings accompany the Word in Pisidian Antioch and Lystra, and by a miracle of judgment in Cyprus.

Luke provides examples of their preaching to both Jews and pagan Gentiles, and they tailor their message to these audiences.[11] Among Jews, Paul expounds the Hebrew Scriptures, showing how Jesus is the crucified and risen Messiah. Among Gentiles, Paul speaks first about the God of Israel as the one true and living God before he speaks about Jesus the Lord and Savior.[12] They adapt the message to their audience without compromising the heart of the gospel.

## They Make Disciples and Form New Churches

Faith in Jesus leads to discipleship in community. When Paul and Barnabas are driven out of a city, they wait and then risk their lives to return and strengthen the disciples and churches and appoint local leaders.

Luke provides a condensed account of how they strengthen the churches on their return visits.[13] First, they teach the disciples to expect persecution, saying, "We must go through many hardships to enter the kingdom of God."[14] Second, they appoint elders. Third, they commit all the believers to the Lord with prayer and fasting. They leave, confident that the new churches and their leaders can trust God's Word and the Holy Spirit to bring them to maturity.[15]

They go out of their way to encourage the churches. At the end of their mission, the quickest and easiest route home is via Tarsus, but they don't take it because of their commitment to revisit the disciples.[16]

## They Multiply Workers

Paul and Barnabas take John Mark along as their assistant. Although he leaves prematurely, it shows the apostles' intention to train workers in the field. Paul finds workers in the churches he planted. Lystra and Derbe were smaller rural towns but yielded two of Paul's coworkers: Timothy from Lystra and Gaius from Derbe.[17]

Neither the churches in Jerusalem nor Antioch exercise authority over the conduct of the mission or the churches planted.[18] The two apostles do not settle down to lead the churches. Rather, they form new disciples into self-governing, self-sustaining, and reproducing churches.[19]

## They Meet Opposition

The mission brings Paul and Barnabas into conflict with evil powers and their representatives.[20] Their first confrontation occurs in Cyprus with a sorcerer and false prophet, Elymas. Satan is also at work in the violence of their opponents. When persecution comes, Paul and Barnabas are bold.

When a synagogue rejects them, they turn to the Gentiles. However, in the next town, they begin again in the synagogue. If the opposition grows to a dangerous level, they leave for the next city. When they are expelled from Pisidian Antioch, they shake the dust off their feet as a warning to their opponents and move on. After the persecution settles down, they return to strengthen the churches.

## They Travel Light

In contrast to established religions, this new movement is nimble and easily transplants to new locations. The faith that the missionaries proclaim does not strip Jews of their cultural and religious heritage.[21] Nor does it require Gentiles to take on those same markers of the Jewish faith, such as circumcision. Faith in Jesus does not require temples, animal sacrifices, or a priesthood—all of which are common to both Jewish and pagan religions. Instead, the disciples meet in homes. The missionaries serve at their own expense—either through support from other churches or by working to support themselves. The apostles appoint local leaders who do not, at least initially, require financial support.

## They Finish "the Work"

The journey began when the Spirit set Paul and Barnabas aside for "the work."[22] By the end of the journey, they had completed this work, which involved pioneer evangelism, forming new disciples into churches, strengthening them, and appointing local leaders. The churches became partners in the mission by reaching out to their city and region and providing workers for Paul as he pushed into new fields. The missionaries move on with confidence because they are assured of the presence and power of the Holy Spirit in the life of the new community.[23]

Between AD 45 and AD 57, Paul and his coworkers established churches in four Roman provinces of Galatia, Macedonia, Achaia, and Asia. Before they began there were no churches, but by AD 57 Paul could write, "there is no more place for me to work in these regions."[24]

Paul believed it was possible to complete his vision for a region. When Paul wrote, "I have fully proclaimed the gospel of Christ,"[25] he was referring to the scope of his mission:

- Pioneer evangelism;

- Training new disciples;

- Forming new churches;

- Establishing the faith and life of new churches; and,

- Equipping leaders to extend and strengthen the work in the region.

These were Paul's key apostolic tasks.[26] Once these tasks were fulfilled, Paul moved on to new regions.

Movements make room for movement pioneers like Paul and Barnabas, who take the gospel into places where it is not, make disciples, gather them into communities, strengthen those churches, and then appoint local leaders. This is the mission Jesus gave them, and the same mission is given to us.

If after all our theorizing around mission, we end up with something very different from what Paul and Barnabas do in these two chapters, we need to return to what Jesus did, what he trained his disciples to do, and what the risen Lord continued to do in Acts.

## MOVEMENTS TODAY: LONDON CALLING

Paul and Barnabas targeted major cities that were connected by road and sea to each other and to their regions. When Paul could stay long enough in a city, he worked to support himself. His hours each day in the workshop would have become an opportunity to connect with people and share the gospel.

Collin and Lyndsey Seale took a similar approach to Paul and Barnabas, pursuing movements of disciples and churches in a neighborhood of Austin, Texas that was home to immigrants and refugees.[27] They recruited and trained their own team and began visiting, looking for "people of peace." They went out into the community, visiting homes, offering to pray for people, sharing their story—all wrapped around the gospel. After one year, there were fifteen new churches meeting in different homes.

While this was going on, they both worked full-time jobs. Lyndsey was a project manager with Google. Collin ran his own business as a financial advisor. They wondered if what they were doing in the neighborhood could be transferred to the workplace.

Little did they know, God was prompting this idea and preparing them for a disciple making movement among their colleagues. Once they came to see the workplace as a mission field, they began to make some adjustments and apply the lessons from their neighborhood ministry.

God placed one of Collin's colleagues, Luke, on his heart, so he invited him out to lunch. As Collin listened to Luke's story, he heard a story of brokenness, and he offered to pray for Luke right then and there. Collin then confided, "I don't think I've ever shared my full story with you." He began to tell his story, wrapped around the gospel. Before he got far, Luke stopped him and asked, "How do you do that? How do you hand your life over to God?" Collin explained, and with tears flowing Luke surrendered to Jesus.

Over coffee or lunch, Collin began to disciple Luke by reading the Bible together. Soon after, Collin invited Luke and his wife, Beth, to the church that met in their home. Beth came to faith, too.

Luke began reaching out to the homeless in his neighborhood. At 3 a.m., he could be found with a flashlight, sharing the gospel on the streets. He started a house church for the homeless and began helping some find accommodation and work.

Within two months, Luke and Beth had told everyone they knew what God had done for them. The Seales found that as people came to Christ through their work relationships, the gospel began spreading beyond work relationships to families and neighborhoods.

Collin and Lyndsey discovered the most effective way to connect with people in the workplace was an offer of prayer. As they listened to their colleagues' challenges, they offered both practical help and prayer, finding little resistance to the offer of prayer.

Lyndsey met a young woman, María, at work who had just become a believer. María was keen to learn how to make disciples, so Lyndsey would bring her along to lunches with colleagues and show her by example how to pray and how to share. María was a magnet for broken people who began flocking to her. She formed a 3-Thirds discipleship group at Google and another training group for workers, as well as starting a church in her home made up of people connected through the tech industry.[28]

In 2018, through a series of experiences, the Holy Spirit led Collin and Lyndsey to move to London. They soon realized how strategic that decision was. London is a city where three hundred languages are spoken.[29] Less than 45 percent of Londoners are white British, and 37 percent of Londoners were born outside the UK. Through networks of relationships, the gospel can go from London to the world. Collin and Lyndsey were led to target a strategic city, just as Paul and Barnabas were in Acts.

Collin and Lyndsey's mission field continues to be the workplace. They train others to show care, offer prayer, and share their story wrapped around the gospel. London attracts people from around the world who still have close ties with friends and family back home.

In London's business district, a small group of employees who have been trained by the Seales meet in their company's lobby. They pray and then break into community care groups of two or three. For thirty minutes of their lunch break, they go out into London's financial district, offering prayer to people and engaging them in the gospel. They are well received. As a result, two hundred people have come to faith.

When someone comes to faith, the Seales have trained people to meet for discipleship over coffee or lunch. Workplace churches are forming, and some of the new disciples go out in pairs, looking for God-prepared people. One such person was Sandra, a hairdresser. After participating in the workplace training, she now has a small church of new disciples meeting in her home. Some of the new believers are Italians living and working in London. Sandra has gone with them on mission trips to Italy where they are sharing with friends and family.

What began in Austin, Texas through the faith and obedience of the Seales has grown into a workplace training ministry that has spread to London and cities beyond, including Chicago, Seattle, San Francisco, Dublin, Berlin, and Sydney.[30] This workplace ministry is one strategy for reaching global cities. People are trained in simple, effective methods of connecting, sharing, making disciples, and planting churches that can spread from the city to the suburbs and from global city to global city.

Paul and Barnabas never saw themselves as the answer to reaching a city and its region in depth. They planted the gospel in communities of disciples and entrusted the new disciples to the

Holy Spirit. They returned to strengthen the churches and appoint local leaders before moving on. The Seales have the same view: They see every city as a doorway to the world. The gospel is going out in the workplace and bearing the fruit of new disciples learning to follow Christ together and making disciples of others.

## DEEPER: THE MISSION

*You will receive power when the Holy Spirit comes on you; and you will be my witnesses in Jerusalem, and in all Judea and Samaria, and to the ends of the earth.*

### ACTS 1:8

It's not for us to determine our mission. The risen Lord gave his disciples their mission: "to preach the good news of Jesus in cities and towns in every region of the earth."[31] A conviction drives their mission—faith in Jesus is the only hope of salvation for every human being.[32]

From the beginning, Jesus called his disciples to follow him and promised he would train them to fish for people. Being with Jesus and learning to make disciples are two sides of one coin.[33] He showed them how to make disciples, and he sent them out. He commissioned them as witnesses to the nations.

The good news they proclaim is about the person and work of Jesus Christ.[34] Their message concerns the life, death, resurrection, and exaltation of Jesus, Lord and Messiah. The messages throughout Acts provide examples of what Jesus meant when he said, "Repentance for the forgiveness of sins will be proclaimed in his name to all nations."[35]

This is the Word of the gospel that is an unstoppable force in the book of Acts.

God's people are no longer restricted to Israel but includes everyone who repents and believes in Jesus. This good news must go out to the whole world, resulting in new communities of disciples that are growing in strength in every place and among every people. This is the heart of God's mission through his people as they live between the first and second comings of Christ.[36] It is by this standard that we must measure modern-postmodern attempts to redefine our mission.

The Word goes out through proclamation, discussion, and conversation, in the marketplace, synagogues, homes, and law courts.[37] Salvation comes to individuals and households: Cornelius the soldier, the Ethiopian official, Saul the persecutor, Sergius Paulus a Roman governor, Lydia and her household, a jailor and his family, and thousands more.[38]

The heart of the message is the story of the life, death, and resurrection of Jesus who now sends the Holy Spirit. The speeches in Acts to Jews and Gentiles reveal a belief in one God and Creator of the world who is Lord and who will one day judge the world. Jesus, who offers forgiveness of sins today, is the one who will be our judge on the last day. Everyone must repent and believe the gospel no matter their religious background.[39] Conversion includes repentance and faith in Jesus, the gift of the Holy Spirit expressed by immersion in water.[40]

When the Lord added new disciples to his people, discipleship was lived out in the community.[41] They were devoted to the apostles' teaching, to shared lives with one another, to shared meals (including the Lord's Supper), and to prayer. They shared their resources with their brothers and sisters. The Spirit was present in power, and the Word spread to unreached fields.

The churches that spring up are missionary communities whose witness is empowered by the Holy Spirit.[42] Whenever the movement settles down, the Holy Spirit nudges it forward into new unreached fields.

The newly converted Saul must proclaim Jesus' name to the Gentiles, to their kings, and to Israel. He must be a witness to all people, to open their eyes and turn them from darkness to light, and from the power of Satan to God, so that they may receive forgiveness of sins and a place among those who are sanctified by faith in him.[43]

This is not Paul's mission; it is the mission of God—Father, Son, and Holy Spirit. This is the mission God has given us.

Jesus did not discriminate when he poured out the Holy Spirit. *Everyone* is called to be his witnesses—young and old, men and women, rich and poor. When the Spirit falls in power upon a persecuted church, they *all* speak the Word of God with boldness. Apostles, prophets, evangelists, elders, and teachers play their part, but so do the unnamed disciples who take the gospel to Phoenicia, Cyprus, and Antioch.[44]

There are five elements in the continuing mission of the Lord Jesus in Acts:

*1. Entry: Going to places where the gospel is not known.* The good news is proclaimed in Jerusalem, Judea, Samaria, Galilee, and beyond historic Israel to reach Ethiopians, Roman soldiers, Syrians, Cypriots, Phrygians, Lycaonians, Macedonians, Achaians, the people of Asia Minor, Roman governors, a Jewish king, and the people of Rome.

*2. Gospel: Proclaiming the message about Jesus.* This is done through speeches; conversations with officials, inquirers, and philosophers; messages in public places, synagogues, and private homes; and testimonies in courts of law.

*3. Discipleship: Teaching people to obey Christ.* Salvation brings the obedience of faith, a life of learning to obey what Jesus commanded. That life begins with repentance and faith expressed in baptism; it soon becomes life in a community of joyful prayer and worship, loving generosity, and bold witness.

*4. Churches: Establishing communities of disciples.* Wherever the gospel is met with faith, new churches were formed. Discipleship took place in community. Peter traveled throughout Judea, Galilee, and Samaria, strengthening the churches.[45] Paul and Barnabas made it a priority to return to the churches they had planted to strengthen the disciples and churches.[46]

*5. Leaders: Multiplying disciples and churches.* The Word keeps on spreading from person to person and place to place. The outcome is a movement of multiplying disciples and churches. Jerusalem was filled with the knowledge of Jesus, and soon the movement spread throughout Judea, Samaria, and Galilee. Unnamed disciples took the gospel to Antioch; thousands responded, and Antioch became a base for planting churches in Greek and Roman cities. The word goes out from Thessalonica to the province of Macedonia; from Corinth to the region of Achaia; and from Ephesus, the Word goes out into the whole of Asia Minor.

God is at the heart of this movement. He is present in the proclamation of the gospel, in the making of disciples, and in the planting and strengthening of churches in unreached fields. He is the author of every breakthrough.[47]

This is what the movement of God looks like in Acts. Luke calls every generation to return to this pattern of faithfulness to the life and ministry of Jesus. This is not a formula for numerical success. This is not guaranteed to rescue your church from decline or save Western civilization. Jesus walked away from the crowds when they refused his invitation to discipleship. Nor can the movement of God be co-opted to any social and political agenda. At its heart is the return to the command to follow him while he teaches us to make disciples of the nations. We do not determine the outcome. That is in God's hands. What we *can* determine is whether we align ourselves with the mission of the risen Lord in Acts and allow his Word and the Holy Spirit to work through us as we pursue the core missionary task.

It begins by obeying Jesus' call to follow him and learn to fish for others. As you step out, keep asking the right questions. How can you share the gospel? What would it look like for you to teach disciples to love and follow Jesus in a way that they could teach others? How can you gather communities that reflect the life of the church in Jerusalem? How can you multiply leaders who make disciples and plant and strengthen churches from where you are to the ends of the earth? The resources you require are the living Word of God, the Holy Spirit, and your faithfulness to the mission.

# IT SEEMS GOOD TO THE HOLY
# SPIRIT AND TO US (15:1–34)

**AD 48**

Paul and Barnabas's Gentile mission was a significant breakthrough. Now Luke brings us back to earth by reminding us that every advancing movement faces threats and challenges from outside and within.

We have come to a major turning point in the gospel's journey from Israel to the nations. The movement began as a remnant within Israel with a calling to bear witness to every nation, but how are Gentiles to be included among God's people?

Some were arguing that Gentiles who believe must become Jews by submitting to circumcision and obeying the law. That view was challenged when the Spirit came upon the Gentiles who were meeting in Cornelius's house with no other precondition than faith in Christ alone.

In a meeting soon after the event, Peter won approval for his actions at Cornelius's house.[48] Years later, the trickle of conversions has now become a flood. Some Jewish believers fear being swamped by Gentiles. If they associate with them, the Jewish disciples risk being cut off by fellow Jews.

The Jerusalem Council is convened, not to hammer out a compromise but to confirm what God had done in saving the Gentiles apart from the law and to find a way for devout Jews and former pagans to live together as God's people.

How is the matter resolved?

- They identify the critical issue: Must the Gentiles be circumcised and obey the law to be saved?

- They debate the question among a delegation of missionaries to the Gentiles and representatives from the Gentile churches, apostles, and elders of the Jerusalem church.

- They emphasize how God had saved the Gentiles and given them his Spirit without them converting to Judaism.

- They return to the Scriptures, highlighting that it has always been God's intention to add the Gentiles to his chosen people.

- They find agreement—God had made it clear that Gentiles are not required to become Jews to be saved.

- They apply the decision. Gentile disciples are to abstain from sexual immorality and meat sacrificed to idols, as the law required. Gentiles who had table fellowship with Jewish believers should also abstain from consuming blood.[49]

- They communicate the decision in writing and send Judas and Silas in person to deliver the message to the Gentile churches.

The Jerusalem Council agrees that the entire law has been fulfilled in Christ, including circumcision, membership in Israel, and temple sacrifices. However, for the new Israel in Christ, which includes Gentiles, these commands still endure: to worship the one true God, to avoid sexual immorality, to care for the poor, to not worship idols.[50]

James, who appears for the first time as the leader of the church in Jerusalem, announces the decision that seems good to both the Holy Spirit and the assembly. James is the respected leader of the Jewish believers in Jerusalem. Accepting the Gentiles would make his job of relating to the Jewish people so much harder. The Enemy had sought to drive a wedge between the Jewish disciples and the growing number of Gentile disciples. Relying on the Word and the Holy Spirit, James makes sure that does not happen.

Since Pentecost, the Spirit had progressively pushed the movement beyond the boundaries of Judaism. He had spoken through Stephen's preaching; he had inspired Philip's mission to Samaria, and the Spirit had led Peter to the house of Cornelius.[51] The Spirit had set apart Barnabas and Saul for the first intentional mission to the Gentiles. God had made known his will through the work of the Spirit and his Word. Finally, the apostles, the elders, and the church in Jerusalem confirmed what God had done.

The story of Cornelius has been the story of three conversions: Peter, Cornelius, and the Jerusalem church. God was the author of each transformation.[52] The way was now clear for the Gentile mission.

## MOVEMENTS TODAY: A RELUCTANT MISSIONARY

Peter and the church in Jerusalem had not grasped the opportunity of reaching the Gentiles. There was no plan and no way of including them among God's people unless they first became Jews. The Holy Spirit had to convince Peter and the church in Jerusalem otherwise.

The question of the Gentile mission was resolved, yet any culture can be blind to reaching those who are different. The Holy Spirit is continually unsettling us, helping us see beyond the people just like us.

Joey Gordy was based in New Delhi, India, training local believers to make disciples among the unreached people groups represented in the city.[53] He partnered with Deepak, a local church leader, to set up a training hub. The strategy was to train local believers to reach unreached people groups in the city so the gospel would spread to their friends and family back home.

They selected a group for training and coaching, and within months there were four or five streams of reproducing disciples and churches in Delhi and nearby states.

After three months, one trainee was struggling to get started. Deepak and Joey sat down with David to help address the issue. David could continue if he was committed, they said; however, if not, David would need to leave, in order to free up a place on the team for someone else.

David left that meeting feeling convicted. As he traveled home, he prayed, "Lord if this is from you, lead me to someone from an unreached people group today." Across the road from his home was a settlement of Banjaara people, the Indian ancestors of the Romani, or gypsies.[54] David walked across the road and did something he'd never done before—he shared the gospel with someone.

That day, around thirty Banjaara people turned and believed. Excited, they took David to the next Banjaara settlement, and around two dozen people believed. Before the day ended, David had taken the gospel to three settlements, and in each, twenty to thirty people had turned to Christ. What David didn't know was the Banjaara were on Joey and Deepak's list of unengaged and unreached people groups.

Just as we've seen throughout Acts, when the gospel advances, the Enemy hits back. The other Banjaara were enraged when the new disciples stopped stealing cell phones and pickpocketing—two important income earners for the community. Some disciples were beaten, and a pregnant mother died from the attack. The police arrived, and everyone fled. David heard nothing for months. Yet, just as he did in Acts, God used these attacks as opportunities to further advance the movement.

David heard that the disciples had fled to a Banjaara camp hundreds of miles away and taken the gospel with them. They were baptizing new disciples and planting churches. These Banjaara were from the same tribe but were a different language group—another unengaged and unreached people group on Deepak and Joey's list. The gospel was going from camp to camp.

Now Deepak and David are working to develop leaders in this emerging movement; teaching them to read and helping them learn the skills they need to get jobs and provide for their community.

David looked out upon the Banjaara camp from the safety of his home, but he was blind to their existence until God intervened. Just as Peter stepped into Cornelius's house, David walked across the road and saw God's Spirit at work in this outcast community. Soon they became not just recipients of the gospel but ministers of the gospel to their people.

## DEEPER: DIVINE DISRUPTION

*Who was I to think that I could stand in God's way?*

ACTS 11:17

Paradigms are like maps—they are the way we see the world. A map is not reality; it helps us navigate reality. Sometimes our maps distort reality rather than explain it. That's when a paradigm shift is needed. Every paradigm shift begins with the disruption of the way we see the world.

In the battle over including the Gentiles, we have a case study of a paradigm shift in the disciples' understanding of their mission. Everyone agreed the gospel should go to the Gentiles, but there was no clarity about how non-Jews were to be added to the church. The question was, Do the Gentile believers have to become observant Jews to be included among God's people?

The key player in the shift was Peter, Jesus' leading apostle. Peter's credentials were impressive: chosen and trained by Jesus, filled with the Holy Spirit, an apostolic witness to the truth of the gospel. Jesus had commissioned Peter and the disciples to take the gospel to *every* people group, but it was not happening.

Before there could be a solution, Peter needed to discover there was a problem. God disrupted and confronted Peter with the gap between Jesus' command and the reality of the Gentile mission. Peter was not the initiator; he was reluctantly led to Cornelius's house before he finally understood what God was doing. From the beginning to the end, this significant change was a work of God.

God used Stephen, Philip, and the disciples who took the gospel to Antioch, to prepare the way for this shift. None of them were apostles. Breakthroughs in renewal and advance of movements almost always occur on the fringes rather than at the center of power.[55] Peter and the apostles in Jerusalem had to catch up to what God was doing on the fringes.

Peter was away from Jerusalem, strengthening and extending the churches, pushing further and further into Gentile territory. He was already outside of his comfort zone, attending to the core missionary task, ready to be disrupted. God was the author of this story. He shook Peter's world, then got him to the house of Cornelius and shook it again. God provided multiple convincing proofs through the Spirit and the Word of what he was doing.

Peter obeyed first and worried about what Jerusalem would think later. He decided, "who was I to think that I could stand in God's way?"[56] Like Jesus, Peter didn't wait for a consensus before he acted.

The matter was settled at the Jerusalem Council based on three overlapping authorities: 1) the leading of the Holy Spirit in the field with multiple confirmations; 2) the words of the prophets recorded in Scripture; 3) evidence of progress in the core missionary task—the gospel was bearing fruit among the nations.[57]

Peter didn't wait for agreement before he acted; nor did Paul and Barnabas. When the Spirit disrupted them at Antioch, sending them on the mission to Gentile cities, they obeyed. By the time of the Jerusalem Council, they had already planted churches among the Gentiles who now welcomed the news of their formal acceptance. The Council caught up to what God had done.

At the Council, Peter, Paul, and Barnabas told stories of how the Gentiles were turning to Christ and becoming disciples in churches that were reaching their cities and regions. James confirmed this work of the Word and the Spirit. The shift was complete.

There was no separate body made up of academic theologians or ecclesiastical representatives that Peter or Paul had to convince before they acted. They were hammering out their biblical theology in the field as they pursued the missionary task, guided by the Holy Spirit. This was what they brought to the Council.

If we want to see a movement of God, then like Peter, we should welcome divine disruption. This disruption was a work of God, not an abstract exercise. Peter's wrestling with the Word and the Spirit was away from the center and on the edges where he was receptive to God's intervention. He saw the signs of the Spirit's work, as salvation came to the nations and new communities of disciples were formed. He worked to win support for what God had done.

## MOVEMENTS TODAY: A TSUNAMI OPENS THE DOOR

Indonesia is the world's most populous Muslim nation. When Stan Parks arrived there in 1994, there was a total population of 121 million. Stan became part of an Indonesian research network that discovered there were 127 unreached people groups (UPGs), most of which had no believers, no workers, and no churches.[58]

Stan was part of a leadership team that knew the solution had to come from the Indonesian believers. At a meeting of over four hundred Indonesian church leaders, they shared the results of their research. There was a stunned silence before these leaders turned to God, confessing their neglect of the missionary task. They turned prayer into action, and within five years over one hundred of the UPGs had workers among them.

In 2004, the tsunami hit, which devastated Aceh. The province had been closed to the gospel due to Sharia law and civil war. The Aceh tsunami caused many Indonesian Muslims to question their beliefs because they believed that staunch Muslims like the Acehnese should be the last ones to suffer tragedy. The fact that Christians and

"Christian" nations provided 90 percent of the aid and aid workers was shocking to Muslims.

After the tsunami hit, Aceh opened its borders to the outside world. Many Indonesian and expat gospel workers responded, including Stan, his wife, Kay, and their three children who moved there for four months to help. Some of the workers sought training in reaching Muslims. God told Stan that in the same way seekers could discover God's truth from Scripture, believers could also discover the principles of disciple making and church multiplication in the pages of the Bible. Stan would sit on the floor with about thirty gospel workers who had come from around the country, and they would open the Bible together, learning the principles and practices of disciple making movements. Stan was not trying to convince the gospel workers of his approach. Instead, he told his Indonesian coworkers that he'd never done anything like this before, nor had he seen a multiplying movement, but suggested that together they could read the Scriptures and look for the patterns and apply them.

Even before they began to see fruit, their lives changed. They focused on obedience-based discipleship. They prayed as never before. They followed Jesus' pattern when he sent out his disciples looking for households of peace. There were miracles and healings, and entire communities opened up to read the stories about *Isa* (Jesus) from the *Injil* (Gospels). The workers sat down with locals in groups and searched the Scriptures together. They didn't teach but allowed people to discuss and think and ultimately come to faith in Christ.

Stan trained the first thirty Indonesian workers and then coached them as they immediately trained two hundred more believers. They would go through one lesson and then pass it on to their coworkers that same week.

The workers persevered despite the risks, and churches emerged that looked a lot more like Acts 2 than a traditional Western church. Most were first-generation, passionate believers, who knew what it is to be rescued from darkness.

The response to the tsunami seemed to be a spiritual turning point for Indonesian Christians. God was doing "a new thing" across Indonesia as a collaborative network was led by the Holy Spirit to put aside tradition and embrace a biblical approach to making disciples and being the church. This story comes via Stan, but the Holy Spirit was teaching the same principles to many people, and now movements have emerged in many parts of the Indonesian archipelago. At the time of writing, over forty UPGs are seeing multiplying movements of at least four generations of churches. Another forty UPGs are like the Acehnese people, who are seeing multiple streams of second- and third-generation churches. In the last two decades, hundreds of thousands of Muslims have become disciples of Jesus, and tens of thousands of churches have been birthed. Their goal is nothing less than ensuring every Indonesian has a chance to respond to the gospel of Jesus Christ.

FIVE

# THE GOSPEL GOES
# TO THE GREEKS

(15:35–18:17)

# LET'S GO BACK (15:35–16:10)

### AD 49

Following the Jerusalem Council, Luke shifts his attention back to the Gentile mission in the Roman provinces of Macedonia and Achaia (today's Greece), specifically the cities of Philippi, Thessalonica, Berea, Athens, and Corinth.

## Return to Antioch

Paul and Barnabas return to Antioch from Jerusalem to strengthen and extend the work there. When they first began work in Antioch, Paul and Barnabas were the only teachers and preachers mentioned; now there are "many others" who work with them, reminding us that movements multiply by creating space for new leaders to emerge.[1] Soon it will be time for Paul and Barnabas to leave Antioch and resume their pioneering work.

Paul and his team often began and ended a mission by strengthening the disciples and churches they planted. They decide to return and encourage the disciples in southern Galatia. Barnabas wants to bring his cousin John Mark, but Paul refuses. John Mark had left them prematurely on their last mission, and Paul is not ready to give him a second chance.

Today, we wonder why John Mark left prematurely; or why Paul and Barnabas couldn't sort out their differences. These are not Luke's concerns. His focus is on the spread of the Word despite opposition, danger, and a dispute between two leading missionaries. Paul and Barnabas find a solution in the creation of two teams. Barnabas takes John Mark and returns to strengthen the believers in Cyprus.[2] Paul recruits Silas and travels throughout Syria and Cilicia, building up the churches. These churches were the fruit of Paul's ministry while based in Tarsus in AD 34–44.[3]

## Building a Team on the Move

Paul and Silas travel west to visit the churches Paul and Barnabas had planted in Derbe, Lystra, and Iconium.

Silas, also known as Silvanus, was a prophet and a leader from the Jerusalem church. Silas's involvement shows that the Jerusalem church is now not only accepting the Gentile mission but actively supporting it.

Paul forms his missionary band as he goes. He adds Timothy in Lystra; and Luke, the author of Luke-Acts, in Troas. Others will join along the way. Paul regarded them as cofounders of the churches they planted and coauthors of some of his letters.[4]

Timothy's father was a Greek, who may have opposed his son's circumcision. His mother, Eunice, and grandmother, Lois, were Jews who had come to Christ two years earlier during Paul's mission to Lystra. They had raised Timothy to know the Scriptures.

When Paul recruits Timothy, he has only been a believer for less than two years, but the believers in Lystra and Iconium regard him well.[5] Timothy would have counted the cost of accepting Paul's invitation, for Lystra is where Paul was stoned and left for dead outside the city.[6]

There was a problem, though; Timothy was born of a Jewish mother, yet is uncircumcised. Jews would regard him as an apostate and worse than a pagan. So, Paul circumcises him to remove a barrier to reaching Jews. Paul does this because Timothy is Jewish; he does not expect Gentile believers to follow Timothy's example.[7] In Paul's own words, he became all things to all people to save some—even if it meant circumcision in Timothy's case.[8]

Movements are flexible in their methods as they pursue their mission. They are willing to change everything about themselves—except their core beliefs. Declining religious institutions do the opposite. They sacrifice biblical orthodoxy for "relevancy" and cling to their unchanging traditions.

Paul and his team travel from city to city, delivering the outcome of the Jerusalem Council and strengthening the churches. As in Jerusalem, the number of new disciples grows daily.[9]

## The Spirit Shuts and Opens Doors

Once they visit the churches, it is time to push into unreached fields—but where?

Twice the Holy Spirit stands in their way. The Spirit stops them from speaking the Word in Asia Minor and blocks their path into Bithynia. Luke doesn't tell us how or why the Spirit stood in their way.

They head for Troas, a port city linking Europe with Asia Minor. In Troas, the first of the "we" passages begins—Luke has joined the mission and writes himself into the story.[10]

In Troas, a Macedonian man appears to Paul in a vision and urges him to come and help! The next day, Paul, Silas, Timothy, and Luke agree together that God has spoken, and they book a passage for Neapolis, the port city of Philippi in Macedonia, northern Greece. The door into Asia Minor is closed for now; the door into Europe has opened.[11]

Through the obstacles, the Spirit guides them and ultimately leads them to where they need to be. God sometimes frustrates our plans before revealing his. He reminds us that it is his mission, not ours. Luke doesn't give us a formula for being led by the Spirit. Instead, he shows us how the missionaries step out in faith and obedience, and how, after some frustrating dead ends, the Spirit guides them to their destination.

Throughout this whole time, Paul moves with a team of coworkers. They are among the scores of people who passed in and out of Paul's missionary band as the need and opportunity arose.[12] Silas was a mature Jewish believer, Luke was an educated Gentile, and Timothy was a young disciple.

## MOVEMENTS TODAY: FROM NEW YORK TO THE ENDS OF THE EARTH

Today the Holy Spirit still closes and open doors.

Chris Clayman landed in Bamako, the capital of Mali a month after 9/11.[13] Posters celebrating Osama Bin Laden were everywhere. Eventually, God led Chris out of the city to live in a Wassoulou village. The Wassoulou are an ethnic group with a thousand-year history and at the time had no known Christians. Chris found Wassoulou who wanted to learn more about Jesus and began meeting with them. God opened a door. Then it shut.

Chris contracted one of the worst cases of malaria his doctors had ever seen. Overcome with diarrhea, vomiting, and fever, Chris could barely stand. His body began to eat itself. It was a medical emergency, and Chris was evacuated. Once home in Texas, doctors told him there was no going back to Africa.

Then Chris heard there was a growing population of West Africans in New York, and so he visited the city to investigate. There are over 1,600 ethnic groups in West Africa, so Chris could have met someone from one of the 1,599 other tribes. Yet on his first day in New York, the first person he met was Musa, a Wassoulou. He was the first Wassoulou believer Chris had ever met.

Musa had met Christ in a dream. When he became a disciple, his family tried to kill him, so he fled Mali. Years later, he was still praying that the first churches would be planted among his people, but he didn't know what to do. On a street in Harlem, God brought a frail Texas missionary together with a persecuted Wassoulou disciple. God had a plan.

Through Chris and Musa, the gospel went to the Wassoulou, first in New York and then to Mali where the first Wassoulou churches have now been planted. God used Chris's weakness to prepare him to open a new frontier in world missions.

Chris discovered that cities like New York can become gateways to reaching the world's least-reached peoples. In these cities there are concentrations of UPGs that create open doors for the gospel to go from group to group, city to city, and back to their homeland.

# THE GOSPEL GOES TO A BUSINESSWOMAN, A SLAVE GIRL, AND A JAILOR (16:11–40)

**AD 49**

The mission to Philippi shows us how the movement enters an unreached field and wins the first new disciples on European soil.[14] With God's help, the apostolic band overcame many challenges and formed a new community of disciples.[15]

Philippi was a Roman colony ruled directly by the emperor.[16] It had a population of between five to ten thousand, many of whom were army veterans. There was no synagogue, but there was a Jewish place of prayer outside the city.[17] There, the missionaries find a group of women who gathered to pray, read, and discuss the Scriptures. Such a group would have been open to hearing from a traveling Jewish teacher like Paul.[18] Among them is Lydia, not a Macedonian but from Thyatira, famous for its purple dyes. She dealt in purple cloth, a luxurious textile, the color of royalty.[19]

Lydia was a Gentile God-fearer and was either a widow or divorced.[20] The Lord opens her heart, and she believes and is baptized along with her household, which would have typically included relatives, slaves, and dependents. She is the first of many prominent Gentile women to be converted during Paul's mission to Europe.

Lydia was wealthy, and she owned a home large enough to accommodate her household and the four missionaries. Just as Jesus had entered Zacchaeus's house and ate, Paul and his companions enter Lydia's house and stay.[21] Soon Lydia's home becomes a gathering place for new disciples in Philippi. The house, not the temple or the synagogue, is where the new people of God gather and from where the Word goes out.

Disciple making movements utilize resources that are in the harvest. If we need to pay salaries, hire an auditorium, or build a facility, then we are planning for addition, not multiplication; and a culture of dependency is ingrained from the outset. Instead, new disciples must be trusted with the responsibility to support the life of the church and the spread of the gospel, using the resources they already have, whether that be homes, or working to support themselves, or giving sacrificially to support the work.

With a base established, Paul and his team continue their mission to Philippi. There they encounter a slave girl controlled by a spirit of the Python.[22] It enables her to tell fortunes and earn money for her owners. For days she follows Paul and his team, shouting, "These men are servants of the Most High God, who are telling you the way to be saved!"[23] Despite the accuracy of her claim, her influence is damaging. As Jesus had silenced demonic testimony with a word, so Paul finally sets her free in Jesus' name with a word.[24] At once, she loses the power to tell fortunes, and her indignant owners seize Paul and Silas and drag them before the magistrates.

They are angry over the loss of future profits, but they frame the charges politically as an attack by two Jews upon Roman customs.[25] Around this time Emperor Claudius had expelled Jews from Rome, and anti-Jewish sentiment would have infected a Roman colony like Philippi.[26]

A mob joins in, and the magistrates order Paul and Silas to be stripped and beaten with no chance to defend themselves. Paul and Silas were both Roman citizens, so their beating and imprisonment without trial is a crime. Why were the authorities unaware of their citizenship? Luke doesn't say.[27] The attack fulfilled Jesus' warning that his followers would be persecuted, imprisoned, and brought before rulers.[28]

They throw the two missionaries into the dank darkness of an inner prison cell and shackle their feet in wooden stocks—a punishment worse than being chained. There would be no food or access to a toilet.

At midnight, Paul and Silas are praying and worshipping while the other prisoners listen. A prison cell has become God's dwelling place. This is the third time that an arrest and prison provides the context for prayer.[29]

Suddenly an earthquake shakes the prison. Doors fling open, and the prisoners' chains fall off. The jailor is terrified. He would be liable to receive the punishment for any escaped prisoners. Paul saves him from suicide. The earthquake was not for an escape but to bring salvation to the jailor's household.

When the jailor cries, "What must I do to be saved?" Paul answers, "Believe in the Lord Jesus, and you will be saved—you and your household."[30] Paul has the jailor gather his household—his family and any slaves who served in the jail—and speaks the Word of the Lord to them. Everyone in the household hears and believes and is baptized.[31] Luke mentions the jailor's house or household four times. He wants us to realize how important it is to win households not just individuals. What constitutes a "household" varies from culture to culture; what is unchanging is that people, made in the image of God, live in the context of relationships. The most effective evangelism and discipleship strategies reach social networks, not just individuals.

The jailor washes the wounds of his two prisoners, and they wash his sins away through faith in Christ expressed in baptism. Then the jailor's house becomes a place of table fellowship for the new people of God.[32] They all eat and are filled with joy—yet another echo of the life in the church in Jerusalem.

Wealth and power stand against the mission, but through the suffering of the messengers, the gospel reaches the first pagan Macedonian household.[33] It is another breakthrough as the Word travels from Jerusalem to the ends of the earth, revealing the weakness of the messengers and the power of God.

The next morning the city magistrates decide that a beating and a night in jail is enough punishment for these two Jewish troublemakers; they agree to release them. Paul wants none of this; he doesn't want to leave with the believers in Philippi under a cloud of illegality and dishonor. He demands the magistrates apologize publicly and escort them out of jail.

A pattern emerges in Acts 16–18: The disciples are accused before officials and told to stop preaching, but they refuse, and the mission continues. This movement of God is shaking the pagan culture.[34]

Paul and Silas leave the jail and head straight for Lydia's house to encourage the new believers. The community of disciples, meeting in at least two households, now include a God-fearing businesswoman, her household, a pagan jailor, his family and other slaves from his household, perhaps a slave girl who used to tell fortunes, and some prisoners who listened as Paul and Silas worshipped in the darkness.[35] They also win other disciples in Philippi—later in his letter to the Philippians, Paul mentions Epaphroditus, Euodia, Syntyche, and Clement.[36]

Why did Paul and Silas leave Philippi when the work had just begun? There was no legal imperative to leave. They left because God had given them a vision to reach the region of Macedonia, not just one of its cities. So Paul and Silas leave with Timothy and head west to Thessalonica. Luke may have stayed to strengthen and extend the work, for the reference to "we" that began in Troas now ends here in Philippi.[37]

From the first day they believed, the Philippian disciples became partners with Paul in the gospel's spread. They supported his work as he moved on to Thessalonica, and then beyond Macedonia to Corinth.[38]

We see the same pattern of engagement in Philippi as in Paul's previous missionary journey in Acts 13–14. They connected with people far from God. They proclaimed the gospel, made disciples, and planted churches. Before leaving, they encouraged and strengthened the disciples. When they met obstacles, they trusted God to intervene. Later they returned to identify local leaders and strengthen the churches.

This is what the movement of God looks like—every people, every place from Jerusalem to the ends of the earth.

## MOVEMENTS TODAY: THE MUMBAI RED-LIGHT DISTRICT

In Philippi, the gospel touched every level of society, including a slave girl oppressed by Satan. Today, women in slavery are still being set free as they encounter the Father's heart.

Luxmi was the youngest of three children growing up in the foothills of the Himalayas in Nepal. At thirteen, she was sold as a bride to an older man who had no intention of marrying her. He took her to Mumbai and sold her for a profit to a madam in the notorious red-light district.

She eventually gave birth to a little girl named Sweeti. When Sweeti became a toddler, they tied her to a post while her mother worked. When Sweeti was ten years old, they sold her to another brothel.

In 2018, God called Rajiv and his wife, Uma, to move into the red-light district and lead the Hilltop of Hope ministry to prostitutes.[39]

According to Rajiv, the Mumbai red-light district resembles a fish market. Prostitutes are lined up, surrounded by pimps and madams fighting for customers. The love of money drives the whole enterprise. Some girls are sold into prostitution by their impoverished families; others are promised a good job and lured far from home; some are kidnapped.

One day, Luxmi met some followers of Jesus from Hilltop of Hope, some of them former prostitutes, who told her of Jesus' love. She was rescued from her brothel and embraced by a community of disciples, most of whom had similar stories. Incredibly, Sweetie was also found and rescued.

Sadly, Luxmi had not seen her family for thirteen years. She was desperate to see them but had no idea how she would be received. So she fasted and prayed, a common practice in disciple making movements, and then went on a three-day journey to find them and tell them what Jesus had done for her. Her sister embraced her with tears, but her brother rejected her for the shame she had brought on the family. After a mob from the village forced her to leave, she returned to the safe house in Mumbai.

Finally, her family relented, allowing her to return home, and they too came to follow Jesus, including her angry brother. However, her return was tinged with grief, as Luxmi had been diagnosed with AIDS. She died clutching her Bible to her heart. Sweeti is still alive and lives in a gospel-centered girls home outside Kathmandu.

Every year, fifteen thousand young Nepali girls are sold into sex slavery in India. Hilltop of Hope ministry rescues such women and their children. They connect with them in the red-light district, share the gospel, and make disciples. As the women are set free, they join a healing community with other women. They work through their trauma and learn a skill that provides an income. Hilltop of Hope has several houses where women escaping prostitution can learn to make a living by sewing bags in a tailoring center. Some return to the red-light district to rescue others and make disciples. Some return home to Nepal to be reunited with their family and share Jesus, and as a result, new churches have been planted.

In the last four years, three hundred women have been rescued from slavery by the Hilltop of Hope. One hundred of them have been baptized and are following Jesus in simple churches.

Hilltop of Hope use simple tools for sharing the gospel and making disciples. Church formation is no more complicated than Acts 2:36–47.[40]

Some of the churches meet in the middle of the red-light district. In a typical gathering, thirty or so women sit on the floor and sing worship songs in Hindi. They share their struggles and pray for and support each other. They listen to the Word of God and discuss how they can act on what they are learning. A trauma healing process is integrated into their 3-Thirds discipleship groups.

Some of the women are still trapped in prostitution, afraid of pimps and loan sharks. The fear is justified: One woman was caught fleeing to another city and was severely beaten; another had her throat slashed but survived.

The churches are islands of hope, offering a community that accepts them and opens the door to a new way of life.

When the women are ready, many escape, often with their children, to a safe house across the border in Nepal where their discipleship and trauma healing can continue until they are ready to return home to their village, restored. In recent years, movements of disciples and churches have swept across Nepal, so Rajiv has no problem linking the women with local believers.

Some women stay and go back into the red-light district to show God's love, to share the gospel, and make disciples. Pinki grew up as the daughter of a madam, but she is now a daughter of the King, making disciples. She recently baptized her mother, who is no longer a madam.

Rajiv says the heart of the movement must be love expressed in action. When one of the women is beaten by her pimp, it's important to show up; when a woman is dying of AIDS, she needs people with her. Love brings healing to a traumatized heart, as the women (and their children) hear the story of the waiting father who embraces his disgraced son, or the story of the woman who wept at Jesus' feet, or of the prostitute Rahab who put her faith in the God of Israel, from whom Jesus is descended. As they gather around God's Word, the women experience the Father's heart and know that they are loved.

Who are the people you need to show up for today? Who needs to know God's love through your actions? Do you know how to share the good news about Jesus with them? Do you know how to gather people around God's living Word and make disciples?[41]

# THESE MEN HAVE CAUSED TROUBLE ALL OVER THE WORLD (17:1–15)

## AD 49

Still recovering from their beating and captivity, Paul and Silas set out on foot, walking around one hundred miles. They pass through towns but don't stop; their priority is Thessalonica, the capital of Macedonia, and the key to reaching the whole province.[42] The city had significant political, economic, and religious influence over the province, with easy access via a good system of roads. The Macedonians, descendants of a great empire ruled by Alexander, were outward-looking.

## *Thessalonica*

Paul begins again by visiting the synagogue, where he engages Jews and Gentile God-fearers. The missionaries reason, explain, prove, and persuade.[43] They open the Scriptures just as Jesus had done and as he'd taught his disciples to do.[44] Their focus is on the death and resurrection of Jesus the Messiah fulfilling the law, the Psalms, and the Prophets.

Luke identifies three groups who respond: some Jews, many Gentile God-fearers, and many prominent women. They "join" Paul and Silas, meaning they probably form a separate group from the synagogue and meet in the house of Paul's host, Jason.[45] Paul will repeat this pattern when he separates from the synagogue in Corinth and bases himself in the house of Titus Justus.[46] Paul and his coworkers form the nucleus of a new community of disciples, which Paul later called "the church of the Thessalonians in God the Father and the Lord Jesus Christ".[47]

Their outreach in the synagogue lasts three Sabbaths, but the team must have stayed longer, perhaps three months, as there is time for Paul to work his trade, receive a gift from the Philippians, and appoint leaders.[48]

A few months after they leave, Paul writes a letter to the Thessalonian church—composed largely of former pagans—reminding them of how they have turned away from idols. This indicates a successful mission to pagans carried out by the apostles and the new disciples once they left the synagogue.[49]

The influence of the new movement troubles some Jews. The synagogue was losing Jewish members and God-fearers, some of whom were women of wealth and influence. They stir up a riot in the market-place and go looking for Paul and Silas, intending to bring them before the assembly of citizens. When they can't find them, they drag the disciple Jason and some other believers before the city officials.

They frame the charges carefully. The officials would not be interested in an accusation of Jewish heresy as they had no jurisdiction over Jewish disputes. Paul is accused of causing turmoil and acting contrary to Roman law. Further, they accuse the new community of treason because these people recognize a man called Jesus as king rather than the emperor.

News of the riot in Philippi may already have reached Thessalonica; in addition, the emperor had recently expelled Jews from Rome for disturbances over *Chrestus*.[50] Worst of all, a Roman governor had executed their leader for sedition.

The city officials realize their charges cannot be sustained, but they need a way out without aggravating the mob. They force Jason and the believers to post bond to ensure Paul and Silas leave without causing any more trouble.

That night Paul and Silas depart quietly for Berea, leaving behind a new community of disciples to continue the work.[51] Among the new believers were Aristarchus and Secundus, who later joined Paul's missionary band.[52]

The ruling of the magistrates means Paul and Silas cannot return for at least a year, when the officials' term of service ended. Instead, they send Timothy back to strengthen the disciples. When Timothy returns to Paul, he writes that he is encouraged as he hears of their faith, witness, and joy, despite severe persecution.[53] When the Thessalonians abandon their idols and turn to the true and living God, they become the ones who take the gospel to Macedonia, Achaia, and everywhere.[54]

## *Berea*

### AD 49/50

In Berea, they repeat the pattern of engagement from previous cities. They begin in the synagogue, explaining from the Scriptures that Jesus is the Messiah whose death and resurrection bring salvation.

Some Jews and God-fearers want to meet every day and search the Scriptures with Paul. Many come to faith, both Jews and Gentiles, men and women. As in Philippi and Thessalonica, some of the women were from the leading families of the city. It's likely they were connected with the synagogue and came to faith in Christ. Women of wealth and status played a role in opposing the gospel in Pisidian Antioch, but in other cities they played a role in advancing the movement.[55] The number of converts suggests the gospel spread from God-fearing Gentiles to their idol-worshipping friends and relatives. Paul did not limit the focus of his mission—he appealed to rich and poor, men and women, slave and free, Jews and Greeks, God-fearers and idol worshippers.

When Paul's opponents in Thessalonica hear what is happening, they come to Berea to stir up trouble. Soon Paul is on the run again, while Silas and Timothy remain behind to continue the work. Among the new disciples is Sopater, son of Pyrrhus, who later joined Paul's missionary band.[56]

As Paul sails south to Athens, he leaves behind a community of Jewish and Gentile believers. Some of them would have friends and relations in Athens to whom they could introduce Paul, just as the Jewish believers of Thessalonica would have introduced Paul to the Jews of Berea.[57]

Silas and Timothy were to join Paul as soon as possible. Their task was to ensure the new community of disciples could stand on their own feet. This allowed the missionary band to keep moving into unreached fields while they circled back to encourage and strengthen the churches. The details are sketchy, but Timothy and Silas joined Paul in Athens briefly, after which Paul sent Timothy to Thessalonica and Silas to Philippi before they all met up in Corinth.[58]

# TO AN UNKNOWN GOD (17:16–34)

### AD 50

When Paul arrives in Athens, it is still known as a center of culture and learning, but its glory days had ended five hundred years earlier. The city is no longer important politically or militarily, and the population has shrunk to around twenty-five thousand.

Paul is on his own, waiting for Silas and Timothy to arrive. Athens had a Jewish community that went back over four hundred years, so Paul begins in the synagogue, explaining from the Scriptures about the Messiah, Jesus.[59]

When he sees the city's devotion to idols, Paul is troubled. Every gateway and porch carries a protecting god. Every street, every square, has its shrine. There are temples, altars, and images dedicated to the worship of Zeus, Athena, Aphrodite, Apollo, Ares, Hephaistos the mother of the gods, Nike, the twelve gods, the mystery religions, and Emperor Augustus.[60] According to the Roman poet Xenophon, it was easier to find a god in Athens than a man![61]

Paul was zealous for God's glory revealed in Jesus Christ.[62] The Lord had called him to open eyes and turn Jews and pagans from darkness to light, from the power of Satan to God.[63] He was just one man, alone in a lost and dark place—but God was with him.

Paul seeks out Jews in the synagogue and pagans in the market-place—the hub of community life in a Greek city—and engages them with the good news about Jesus and the resurrection. Luke tells us that Paul "argued," meaning his teaching involved back and forth discussion in which the audience asked questions and commented.[64] This went on for an extended period. The philosophers of Athens hear about Paul and seek him out, but they aren't impressed, calling him a scavenger of ideas and a preacher of foreign gods.

Although Greeks and Romans accepted the worship of many gods, it was a serious matter to introduce a new god to a city, requiring official permission. According to the Jewish historian Josephus, the penalty for introducing foreign gods into Athens without authorization was death.[65]

They bring Paul to the Areopagus—the Council who approved new altars, temples, and additions to the religious calendar.[66] Before the

Areopagus, Paul focuses on the nature of God and how he can be known. His speech does not cover the totality of the gospel, just one aspect of it. Paul argues he is not trying to introduce a "new" god; rather, he is explaining the true nature of the "unknown god" whose altar he had discovered while walking about the city. This God, Paul proclaims, does not live in temples made by human hands.

Throughout his speech, Paul uses language and arguments shaped for his audience of philosophers.[67] Paul tells his audience that God created human beings to seek him and know him, yet their speculations and idolatry kept them from the knowledge of the one true God. In doing so, Paul seeks common ground with them, using their terms and ideas to challenge their beliefs.

Although Paul does not begin with the Jewish scriptures or the teaching about Christ, everything he says is grounded in the Scriptures and points forward to Christ. His starting point is God, the Creator and Lord of all. Paul declares that Gentiles who know nothing of God's revelation to Israel, cannot find God in idolatry or philosophical specu-lation. Humanity has failed to know God as he is.

With this foundation, Paul announces the coming judgment of the world by the One whom God has raised from the dead. Paul didn't want permission to add a new god to the Athenian pantheon. Instead, Paul calls his pagan audience to abandon their gods and turn to the living God who can only be known through faith in Jesus Christ. He turns the spotlight back upon his investigators and calls them and the citizens of Athens to repent.[68] Like Peter and John before the Sanhedrin, Paul cannot defend himself without preaching Christ—a pattern he will repeat in future investigations.[69]

Most respond with either cynicism or indecision. Yet even among the elite of Athens, the Spirit and the Word do their work. Some sneer, others want to hear more, but a few join Paul and believe. Luke names two among those who believe: Dionysus, a leading man of Athens and member of the Areopagus, and a woman named Damaris who Luke's readers may have known.[70]

In Philippi, the gospel touched every level of society. Likewise in Athens, Paul shows he can speak to Jews and God-fearers in the synagogue, to passers-by in the marketplace, and the philosophers of the Areopagus. The gospel is answered with faith, and before Paul leaves for Corinth, he will form these disciples into a new community. Paul must have left relieved; for once, he wasn't run out of town!

# DEEPER: THE GOSPEL FOR PAGANS

*The God who made the world and everything*
*in it is the Lord of heaven and earth...*

ACTS 17:24

When Paul preached before pagans, he didn't quote the Hebrew Scriptures; instead, he spoke about the God of Israel, the one true and living God, before he spoke about Jesus as Lord and Savior.[71]

Paul's message in Lystra shows us how he communicated with polytheists who knew nothing of the God of Israel. Before he could explain that forgiveness of sins could only be found in Jesus, Paul had to explain to his idol-worshipping audience who God is. He had to convince them there is only one true God to whom they must give account. Paul communicated the following truths to his Gentile audience.

- There is one true God who made heaven and earth and all things in them.[72]
- He is kind and loving and provides rain for harvest and food to eat.
- He fills our hearts with joy.
- God alone deserves to be worshipped.
- He no longer permits Gentile nations to go their own way. He calls everyone to abandon their worthless idols and turn to the living God.

Paul's approach in Athens was similar in Lystra. His starting point was God, the Creator and Lord of all, the God revealed to Israel. God cannot be found in idolatry or human philosophy. The one true God can only be known through faith in Jesus Christ. Paul's message contained these aspects:

- God is the Creator of all things, including humanity. He is not far from us.

- The time of ignorance is over; God calls everyone to repent.

- God has appointed the agent of his judgment and has confirmed it by raising him from the dead.[73]

There is one gospel that can be adapted for different audiences, but the essence remains the same. Yet many Jews and Gentiles rejected the gospel, some violently. This was not due to any lack of the Spirit's power or clarity of the message.

For Jews, it was unthinkable that the eternal God would make himself known through a crucified criminal. Greeks were impressed with human wisdom and lofty ideas. The story of a crucified and risen Savior made no sense to them. To follow Jesus, both Jews and Gentiles had to abandon important aspects of their culture and face conflict with their community.

Faithfulness to the gospel requires that movements maintain the tension with a fallen world. In contrast, many institutional church leaders today are confused about the biblical teaching on sexual ethics and marriage. The confusion follows major cultural and now legal shifts in Western society. What has always been the teaching of Scripture and the church for thousands of years is now out of sync with society and many believe it must be ignored or overturned. It won't end on this issue, for there are many teachings of the Bible that offend our contemporary culture—including the authority of the Bible, Jesus as God and Savior, God's judgment on sin, the cross as the only hope of salvation.

Some denominations have spent decades agonizing over issues that should not be contended, at the neglect of Christ's command to make disciples of the nations. Once they abandon the authority of the Word of God, there is no hope of renewal as their relentless institutional decline demonstrates.

The disciples in Acts had a different approach: They proclaimed the gospel; they were faithful to the gospel under community pressure; and they allowed the Word and the Spirit to create communities of disciples who were also faithful to the gospel in words and deeds.

This is a major point of divergence between the church in the West and the movement of God in Acts. Movements maintain the tension between their message and their society. Movements decline when they lower that tension because their core message becomes vague, muted, and compromised.[74]

# I HAVE MANY PEOPLE IN THIS CITY (18:1–17)

## AD 50–51

For a movement to spread, it must gain footholds in major centers that act as connecting hubs with their region and other centers. Corinth and Ephesus were the two most important cities that Paul visited as a missionary. He stayed in both places long enough to establish churches that reached out into the surrounding provinces of Achaia and Asia Minor.

## *Corinth*

The Romans had destroyed ancient Corinth one hundred years earlier in 146 BC. Julius Caesar rebuilt Corinth as a Roman colony and populated the city with army veterans and freed slaves. Many Greeks from the region also settled there. When Paul arrived, Corinth was the most prosperous city in Greece with a population of two hundred thousand. It was a commercial port city, well-connected by sea and land to cities along the Mediterranean coast and in the interior of Greece.

The Corinthians worshipped Greek and Roman gods and goddesses, as well as the emperor. Corinthian religion was infamous for its sexual immorality. The temple of Aphrodite, the goddess of love, overlooked the city from a nearby mountain. A thousand female slaves served there as temple prostitutes.

Paul writes how he came to Corinth "in weakness with great fear and trembling."[75] The cause of Paul's trepidation was that, in Macedonia, he had been driven out of one city after another. Corinth was different; for the first time since he left Antioch, five years before, Paul had a long stay in one place. The fruit of this ministry was a vibrant and volatile new church, meeting in households across the city and in the province of Achaia.[76]

In Corinth, Paul meets Aquila and Priscilla, recently arrived from Rome. They are among the Jews expelled from Rome by the emperor Claudius because of disturbances related to *Chrestus*—most likely referring to Christ.[77] They too are leatherworkers and provide Paul with work and a place to stay. They become partners with him in Corinth and Ephesus before eventually returning to Rome.[78]

Timothy and Silas arrive in Corinth after finishing their work strengthening the churches in Macedonia. They seem to have brought a gift from the churches to enable Paul to devote himself full-time to the proclamation of the Word.[79]

As usual, Paul goes to the synagogue, where some Jews and God-fearing Gentiles believe. Some mock and reject the message, so Paul shakes out his clothes in protest and declares that he is going to the Gentiles, bracing himself for the inevitable pushback.

Previously, rejection in the synagogue meant Paul was run out of town. Not this time. Jesus appears to Paul in a vision. He gives Paul three commands: Do not be afraid; keep on speaking; and do not be silent. Jesus also gave three promises: I am with you; no one will attack and harm you, and I have many people in this city.[80] The word for "people" is the same word used in the Old Testament for "Israel." The new people of God are emerging—composed of Jews and Gentiles—and Jesus' presence is the key to their identity, life, and mission.

Forced out of the synagogue, the home of Titus Justus becomes Paul's center of outreach and discipleship. Many believe and are baptized, including Crispus, the ruler of the synagogue, together with his household.

The inroads among pagan Gentiles show how important it was that the Jerusalem Council had allowed table fellowship between Jewish and Gentile disciples. No doubt Paul engages pagan Gentiles in the marketplace, as he had done in Athens. He is occupied with teaching the Word to unbelieving Jews and Gentiles and teaching the Word to new disciples. As the Word goes out through these new disciples, the surrounding region of Achaia is reached.[81]

Eventually, a storm breaks. The Jews who had rejected Jesus as Messiah bring charges against Paul before the governor of the province. Gallio was the representative of Rome; his ruling would set an important precedent for the legal status of this new movement.

The charge against Paul states that he is teaching the Corinthians to worship God in ways that are against the law. It's not clear if they meant against the law of Moses or Roman law; probably the latter, but the ambiguity may have been intentional. If Gallio had found Paul guilty, provincial governors everywhere would have a precedent, and the movement would have been severely restricted.[82]

Gallio is having none of this dispute. His job was to establish the peace and security of the province, not to settle Jewish religious quarrels. He rules that the issue is outside his jurisdiction; Paul had not violated any Roman law. The governor regarded the followers of Jesus as a group within Judaism, and Judaism was a legally recognized religion by the empire.[83] So, Gallio drives the complainants out of his court.

Watching these proceedings is an anti-Jewish mob that then grab Sosthenes, the new president of the synagogue (following Crispus's conversion) and beat him. Gallio ignores them.

The Word continues to grow and multiply in Corinth and spread throughout the surrounding province of Achaia.[84] Paul would later write to the Corinthians and all God's "holy people throughout Achaia," the province surrounding Corinth.[85] Jesus had fulfilled his three promises to Paul: I am with you; no one will attack and harm you; and I have many people in this city.

From Paul's letters, we have many details about the makeup of the Corinthian church.[86] Among the disciples were Jews, God-fearers, and pagans. Most of the believers were slaves or freed slaves with little or no education.[87] Some disciples came from the local elite and had money, power, and education. Crispus, the former ruler and patron of the synagogue, was wealthy. Titus Justus owned a house that was large enough to serve as a meeting place for the many Corinthians who believed. Gaius's home served as a base for Paul. Stephanus, whose entire household believed, also owned a house. Other people of social status included Erastus the city treasurer and Chloe.[88] Sosthenes, the new synagogue president who was beaten, may have later become a believer and a leader in the church at Corinth.[89]

### Finishing With Confidence

After Paul leaves Corinth, the churches meeting in various households continue the work. He left at a time of his choosing. Given the trouble the Corinthians later gave Paul, we might wonder, did he leave too early? No, Paul was confident of God's presence among his people through the Word and the Spirit to bring them to maturity. The continuing presence of the risen Lord mattered far more than Paul's presence.[90]

Paul and his team had achieved much in the three years since he left Antioch. The Spirit of Jesus blocked their path and then led them into Macedonia and Achaia where they planted five churches in important centers—Philippi, Thessalonica, Berea, Athens, and Corinth.

Paul had faced many obstacles, yet Jesus assured Paul of his presence and protection, fulfilling his promise to his disciples that as they make disciples of the nations, he will always be with them.

From Corinth, Paul begins his return to Antioch in Syria. He boards a ship with Priscilla and Aquila for Ephesus, the leading city of Asia Minor and the focus of Paul's next mission.

## MOVEMENTS TODAY: ZEAL CHURCH

The example of Paul and his team of planting churches in strategic centers is still being followed today.

Troy and Rachel Cooper moved to greater Los Angeles in 2017 with their seven children and a small team, with a plan to multiply disciples and churches.[91] Troy began by connecting broadly with church leaders and training in evangelism and discipleship, using simple tools.

The Coopers have modeled for their children how to share the gospel with their friends and how to read the Bible with their friends for discipleship. The gospel goes out from house to house and even to the skatepark. Together with their team, the Coopers planted Movement Church, the first of what they hoped would become a movement of disciples and churches.

During the pandemic in 2020, Troy Cooper and his team from Movement Church served at one of the outdoor events where hundreds of people gathered on Friday nights at locations scattered along the Orange County coast to worship God. For many, it became an opportunity to put their faith in Jesus and follow him in baptism.[92]

Troy and his team were baptizing new believers when they met Shane Nassirian. Shane had previously come to faith after someone had approached him on the Newport Pier offering to pray for him and God healed him from a severe case of sunburn. Shane had come to the event with his two friends who were ready for baptism.

Troy and the team baptized them and then explained that baptism was the doorway to discipleship and offered to help them get started. That night, Troy met with Shane and his friends and began to disciple them. Because it was the summer break, they were able to meet every day for the next two weeks. Troy and the team dropped what they were doing to teach Shane and his friends simple tools for evangelism (411) and discipleship (Commands of Christ) that could be immediately passed on.[93] Troy cast vision for discipleship in community using Acts 2:36–47 (Church Circle).[94] When Shane heard this, he knew it was the type of community he needed and his friends and family needed; and he asked Troy to help him make it happen.

The next day Troy met with Shane to cast vision for a movement of disciples and churches in Orange County.[95] Shane's heart broke for his city, and he saw the need for a movement of disciples and churches. He felt called to plant a church and to call it Zeal Church. The next day, Troy spent time with Shane meeting his friends and watching Shane share his story and cast vision for discipleship and a church community like the one in Acts 2. Troy soon discovered that Shane knew everyone and was proving to be a "person of peace."[96]

Shane and the group invited some more of their friends, most of whom were not Christians, to come to a night of worship at a friend's home. The word went out through social media, and thirty-six people turned up. Shane told the story of what God had done in their lives and asked if anyone was ready to follow Jesus. That night, they baptized four of their friends in the backyard pool. Watching was Troy and the team from Movement Church that had prepared Shane for this.

The next day Shane met with the four new disciples to take them through the same pattern of discipleship he had been shown by Troy.

As they learned to follow Christ as disciples, they were forming a new church. They were taught the Commands of Christ, which align with the characteristics of a healthy church in Acts 2:36–47, so discipleship and church formation were integrated from the beginning.

Gatherings for worship continued until the three friends launched Zeal Church. Meanwhile, behind the scenes were Troy and Rachel Cooper and others from Movement Church, discipling and coaching Shane and his friends.

After twelve months, Zeal Church had about thirty to forty people. Most were young adults from the overlapping social networks of Shane and his friends. Some had turned away from drugs; others renounced the New Age and witchcraft and, on a firepit, burned their idols and books on magic.

When other Christians questioned the legitimacy of Zeal Church, Shane went back to the example of the church in Jerusalem to make sure Zeal Church was committed to the same pattern.

After just twelve months, Zeal Church was ready to send out a couple to start Rise Church at Vanguard University in Orange County.

Troy Cooper can identify thirty-four church starts over the last two years that trace their origin back to Movement Church. They vary in size from six to fifty people. Three of the churches have reached four generations of new churches.

The network is having a national and global impact as it sends out and supports frontline workers, making disciples and multiplying churches in unreached fields.

The Coopers' story will be dismissed by some as unremarkable. In five years, they and their team have helped spark a network of relatively small churches. Some people have come to Christ. But here's what I notice from a movements' perspective: They have fresh stories of people far from God hearing the gospel and becoming disciples. Those disciples are being immediately trained and mobilized to share the gospel with their friends and family, teaching them to follow Christ in community. New churches are beginning to reproduce, and experienced workers have been sent out to unreached fields. Movements emerge from such environments.

All this follows the patterns of the movement of God in Acts, and it's happening in a Western context. Time will tell where this leads. Meanwhile, I plan to watch and learn.

Troy says a movement of God requires three things: *1) A big vision.* Many church leaders have a vision for a big church. God has a vision for cities and nations. Troy helped Shane see only a movement could reach Orange County. *2) A clear path.* Troy employs a simple 4-Fields strategy (Entry, Gospel, Disciples, Churches, Leaders).[97] The 4-Fields provides people like Shane with a place to begin and a direction to head in. *3) Simple tools.* When it comes to making disciples, most believers don't know what to do on Monday morning. No one has trained them. Troy modeled and trained Shane in simple and effective methods such as the 411, the Commands of Christ, the Church Circle, and the Brutal Facts.[98] As Shane's friends came to Christ, he trained them and formed them into a community of disciples with a vision to make disciples.

Jesus told his first disciples to follow him and that he would teach them to make disciples. His mission hasn't changed.

SIX

# THE WORD REACHES ASIA MINOR

(18:18–20:38)

# STRENGTHENING ALL THE DISCIPLES (18:18–28)

**AD 51**

Paul is on the move again, traveling to Ephesus, Caesarea, Jerusalem, and Antioch, then back through Galatia to Ephesus.

Before leaving Corinth, Paul cuts his hair and takes a vow, perhaps in gratitude for God's protection in Corinth. Luke doesn't give us the details, but it is a reminder that Paul still values his Jewish heritage. From Corinth's eastern port, Cenchreae, where there is already a church, Paul and his team set out to sea.[1]

The pioneering work in Greece was finished, and perhaps they wondered if the time was right to head for Ephesus, the capital of Asia Minor. On board the ship to Ephesus are his coworkers from Corinth: Aquila and Priscilla, who are the nucleus of the team Paul is forming for Ephesus. Their vision is for Ephesus to become the hub for a movement of disciples and churches across Asia Minor.[2]

Ephesus had a large Jewish population. Paul goes to the synagogue where they press him to stay longer, but he makes known his intended return to Jerusalem and Antioch. Aquila and Priscilla remain behind to continue the work, and before long a church is meeting in their home.[3]

Paul lands at Caesarea, the port city of Jerusalem. He travels the sixty-five miles up to Jerusalem before going north to Antioch, a journey of over three hundred miles, on foot.[4]

Each of Paul's missions began in Antioch and ended in Jerusalem. He was keen to maintain the relationship with leaders and churches that had such important contributions to the Jewish and Gentile missions. Paul was not establishing an independent movement; rather, he was an important figure in the one movement that began in Jerusalem and was now spreading out from Antioch.[5]

After spending time in Antioch, Paul sets off for Ephesus on an eight-hundred-mile journey, taking about nine weeks.[6] Going by ship would have been easier and faster, but instead Paul travels throughout the region of Galatia and Phrygia, visiting and strengthening churches he and Barnabas planted on their first journey—Pisidian Antioch, Iconium, Lystra, and Derbe.[7] Paul's missionary journeys out of Antioch began with church strengthening and ended with church strengthening. Each mission began with the proclamation of the gospel and was not completed until churches were established with local leaders and growing in strength.

While Paul is traveling, Apollos, a Jew from Alexandria in Egypt, arrives in Ephesus. Apollos knows of John's baptism, and his knowledge of Jesus as the Messiah is accurate but incomplete. However, his ministry of the Word in the synagogue at Ephesus shows evidence of the Holy Spirit. So, Priscilla and Aquila take him aside and explain the Way more accurately.[8] Apollos already believed in Jesus and had received the Spirit, so he does not need to be rebaptized.

Soon, Apollos is ready to visit the churches in southern Greece and contribute in teaching and evangelism.[9] Luke tells us the disciples in Ephesus wrote to the disciples in southern Greece recommending Apollos. So, there was already at least one church meeting in Ephesus before Paul returned. That church was the fruit of Paul's brief ministry in the synagogue and the continuing ministry of Priscilla, Aquila, and Apollos while Paul was away.[10]

# DEEPER: MOVEMENTS AND MONEY

*I have not coveted anyone's silver or gold or clothing. You yourselves know that these hands of mine have supplied my own needs and the needs of my companions.*

ACTS 20:33-34

### *Money in the Gospels*

When Jesus left Nazareth to be baptized by John in the Jordan, he walked away from his trade as a carpenter, leaving his mother in the care of his brothers and sisters.

Jesus called his first disciples away from their usual occupations to follow him while he trained them to fish for people. They left their fishing nets, boats, and hired workers and trusted God to provide. Peter trusted God to care for his wife, mother-in-law, and children. James and John left the family business in the hands of their father Zebedee. Matthew left his tax booth.

Sometimes God's provision was miraculous—the feeding of the crowds, the coin to pay the temple tax, the miraculous catch of fish— but not always. Jesus relied on the financial support of a group of wealthy women, including Mary Magdalene, Joanna, and Susanna, who sometimes traveled with him.[11] Jesus relied on the hospitality of people like Zacchaeus. When Jesus sent the Twelve and the Seventy on mission, he taught them to trust God for provision of food and lodging through people who, like Zacchaeus, would welcome them and their message.[12]

If generosity facilitates the spread of a movement, greed can stifle it. The Gospels give just one reason for Judas's betrayal—greed. Jesus warned that worry, riches, and pleasures choke the Word and prevent it from producing a crop.[13] Jesus taught that it is hard for the wealthy to enter the kingdom of God. The rich young man went away sad; his wealth was the one thing that prevented him from following Jesus.[14]

Jesus taught his disciples to give generously to the poor. He shared a common purse with the Twelve from which they met the costs of their mission and gave to the poor.[15] Jesus urged his disciples to give generously, trusting that their Father in heaven knew their needs and would provide.[16]

### *Money in Acts*

Just as money played a role in Satan's attacks on Judas, greed also threatened the emerging movement in the accounts of Ananias and Sapphira and Simon the sorcerer. The love of riches and the comfort and security that money brings undermine discipleship and the health of a movement. But we also find the community of faith displaying generosity. The believers did not regard their wealth as their own, but instead shared freely to meet the needs of the poor.

After being on the road with Jesus for three years, the Twelve, who were Galileans, probably moved their families to Jerusalem. They had to support themselves in what was an expensive city. Luke doesn't give us the details of how they did that, although he reports Peter's reply to the lame beggar at the temple: I don't have any silver or gold.[17]

Most likely, they relied on the generosity of the church community to support their families and to cover the costs of their mission in Jerusalem and beyond.

When the Greek-speaking widows were overlooked in the daily distribution of food, the apostles responded by appointing seven men of character and spiritual maturity to resolve the issue while the Twelve prioritized prayer and the ministry of the Word, ensuring the continued health and expansion of the movement.

Paul proclaimed the gospel without charge and did not want to be a burden on new disciples.[18] He stepped down the social ladder to support himself and his coworkers by working with his hands.[19] His coworkers Priscilla and Aquila supported themselves as leatherworkers as they served in Corinth, Ephesus, and Rome.

Paul accepted gifts from other churches only after he left them and only if the gift came without strings attached.[20] In his letters, Paul defended the right of missionaries to be supported by the churches.[21] While in Corinth, Paul worked as a leatherworker in the shop of Aquila and Priscilla,[22] but when Timothy and Silas arrived with a gift from the Macedonian churches, Paul put aside his trade and devoted himself full-time to the mission.[23]

Paul was in custody and unable to work for two years in Caesarea and then two years in Rome. Typically, prisoners were not fed by their captors and had to rely on friends and family. Fortunately, there were local believers in both places who could help. As a prisoner in Rome, Paul was responsible for paying for his accommodation. Rent was expensive in Rome, yet Paul's apartment was large enough for him, his guard, coworkers, and the many guests who visited. Luke doesn't tell us how Paul paid for it.

Jesus did not leave his disciples detailed instructions of how to fund the movement. He set an example and gave them his Word, the Spirit, and the missionary task. He promised that as they went to the ends of the earth, he would be with them. There was no map, strategic plan, or timetable; just a promise that the power of God's Spirit was enough to get the witnesses to every people and every place.

We are simply left wondering, *Who paid for Luke and Aristarchus's voyage to Rome with Paul? Who paid their living expenses when they arrived in Rome?* Luke doesn't say. He's not focused on organizational and funding issues; however, from Luke's account we can glean some money lessons for movements.

***Principle 1: Movements serve God not money.*** Peter's clash with Simon the sorcerer is a powerful illustration of Jesus' teaching that you cannot serve both God and money.[24] Leaders who use their position to gain money and power will corrupt a movement.

A disciple trusts God by placing obedience to his Word above the desire for money, comfort, and security. Just as a disciple who falls into the love of money will become unfruitful, so a disciple making movement that grows to love money will become unfruitful. Money does not fuel movements; commitment and faith does.

*Principle 2: Movements ordain everyone.* At Pentecost, the Spirit fell on *everyone*, and they all declared the wonders of God revealed in Jesus Christ.[25]

You cannot pay enough people to make a disciple making movement happen. Volunteers, not paid professionals, do most of the work in any movement. For every movement leader like Peter or Paul, there are hundreds, even thousands who devote their time and resources for the cause.

*Principle 3: Movements keep their options open.* In Luke's Gospel and Acts, there isn't one funding model. God provided a variety of funding sources for the advance of the movement. Some missionaries supported both themselves and others through their trade.[26] Some workers served at their own expense.[27] Even the grateful inhabitants of Malta honored Paul and his companions and supplied their needs for the journey to Rome.[28] Ordinary believers, wealthy individuals, and churches gave money and other resources.[29] Hosts opened their homes to traveling teams; homes which then became meeting places for new churches.[30]

*Principle 4: Movements travel light.* The challenge of funding a movement isn't only about raising money; it also involves keeping costs low. Jesus instructed his disciples to leave their wallets behind when they went out on mission. God provided through the people who welcomed them.[31] The pattern of God providing through receptive households continues in Acts.[32]

The movement Jesus started didn't require a temple, a priesthood, or any of the trappings of the ancient religions.[33] As the gospel spread, churches sprung up where they were needed, not where they could be afforded.

*Principle 5: Movements stay nimble.* There was no supply chain from Jerusalem to the churches started in Samaria or on the Phoenician coast; nor was there one from Antioch to the churches in Macedonia and Achaia. Authority and responsibility were continually released to the field. The new churches soon had their own local leaders and were responsible for their own funding. It wasn't long before these churches released resources and workers for new fields. In this way, the movement remained flexible and nimble, able to multiply. To organize and fund the movement centrally would have choked its life and growth.

*Finally* . . . The oxygen of a movement is the commitment of its people—to give, to go, to serve without pay, to open their homes, to work with their hands, and to trust that God goes with them as they take the gospel from Jerusalem to the ends of the earth.

# ALL OF ASIA MINOR (19:1–41)

## AD 52–55

The Spirit had previously prevented Paul from entering Asia; now it is time.[34] For most of his ministry, Paul had just enough time to preach the gospel and gather a group of disciples before he was run out of town. The three years in Ephesus will be Paul's longest recorded ministry in any location. This is his last major campaign as a free man. It is not just another stop along the way; it is the climax of his mission, and it touches the whole Roman province of Asia. For centuries to come, the churches formed there were among the most influential in the world.[35]

With over two hundred thousand people, Ephesus rivaled Antioch in Syria as the third most important city in the empire after Rome and Alexandria. The roads of Asia converged on Ephesus, making it the cultural, communications, and commercial hub of the region. In the first century AD, Ephesus experienced a building boom. They constructed new temples and impressive buildings, including The Temple of Artemis, which was one of the Seven Wonders of the Ancient World and attracted tourists from all over the Roman Empire.

Paul arrives in Ephesus early in the summer of AD 52. He meets a group of John the Baptist's disciples. They have not heard that John's prophecy of the coming Messiah has been fulfilled, nor have they received the Holy Spirit. Paul explains to them that Jesus is the One to whom John pointed. When they hear this, they are ready to be baptized in Jesus' name, and they are filled with the Holy Spirit when Paul places his hands on them.[36] As at Pentecost, they speak in tongues and prophesy, and a new church is formed.

For three months, Paul is given exceptional freedom to preach and teach about the kingdom of God in the synagogue.[37] Eventually, a group oppose Paul and ridicule his converts. Paul leaves the synagogue and forms a separate community with the new disciples.[38] This is the last record of Paul ministering in a synagogue.

Paul's outreach to Jews and Gentiles continues in the lecture hall of Tyrannus. There he teaches, debates, and persuades every day for two years. In the Greco-Roman world, business (including formal lectures for fee-paying clients) was done in the cooler part of the day, starting at dawn and ending at 11 a.m. A meal and an afternoon rest followed the morning's work, with more people asleep at midday than midnight. Paul's daily sessions were probably conducted outside of working hours, between 11 a.m. and 4 p.m., when both the hall and his audience would have been available. This would have left the mornings free for Paul to earn his living as a leatherworker.[39]

During this period, God does extraordinary miracles of healing, as well as deliverance from demonic oppression. Ephesus was home to magicians, sorcerers, and adherents to many forms of pagan religion; Paul's miracles show God's power over sickness and demons. New believers openly confess their sins and burn their sorcery books, valued at fifty thousand silver coins.[40] Hundreds of people turn publicly from their faith in magic to faith in Jesus.[41] As the movement advances, the Enemy is on the run. Jesus is fulfilling his promise that Paul would rescue people from the power of Satan, bringing forgiveness and inclusion among God's people.[42]

This is a period of unprecedented fruitfulness. Paul writes that God had opened "a great door" for effective ministry.[43] Luke records how "the word of the Lord spread widely and grew in power."[44] Incredibly, "all the Jews and Greeks who lived in the province of Asia heard the word of the Lord" through Paul, his team, and the believers they trained.[45]

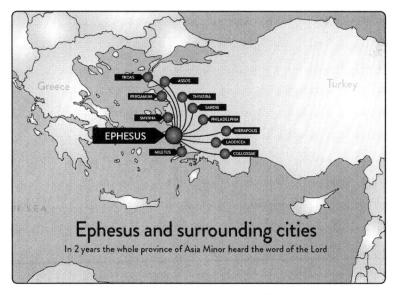

*All the Jews and Greeks who lived in the province of Asia heard the Word of the Lord (Acts 19:10). Map adapted from Arthur G. Patzia,* The Emergence of the Church.[46]

This was a movement, not one man's ministry, even if that man was Paul. While Paul was based in the school of Tyrannus, Epaphras established churches to the west in Laodicea, Hierapolis, and Colossae.[47] To the north, the churches of Smyrna, Pergamon, Thyatira, Sardis, and Philadelphia may have been started during this time.[48] Paul's team included Aquila and Priscilla, Timothy from Lystra, Philemon from Colossae, Aristarchus from Thessalonica, Gaius from Corinth, Tychicus and Trophimus from Ephesus, Stephanas, Fortunatus, and Achaicus from Corinth.[49] Apollos, who eventually returned from Corinth, was also a coworker.[50]

This is Luke's explanation of how Asia Minor was reached:

**The Word of God spread.** The Word was alive and active through Paul, his coworkers, and the new disciples so that more and more people accepted the gospel and were added to the new churches.

**The Word grew in power.** The Word was demonstrated in miracles, the shaming of the Jewish exorcists, and the public rejection of magic.

**The power of the risen Lord was at work.** The underlying cause of this advance was the power of God, not Paul's eloquence or gifted leadership or the manipulation of spiritual power.[51]

Paul completed his mission in under three years. When Paul wrote to the Corinthians, he sent greetings from all the churches in the province of Asia.[52] For centuries, Asia Minor remained one of the leading centers of the movement.

Paul decided to return to Jerusalem, passing through Macedonia and Achaia to strengthen the churches. Paul sent Timothy and Erastus ahead into Macedonia to prepare the way while he stayed in Ephesus a little longer.[53]

## Paul's Confrontation With Paganism

Before he leaves, Paul has one last battle to face. In Ephesus, he had many enemies, feeling as if he was "fighting wild animals".[54] The strength of the opposition was an indicator of Paul's impact. The gospel was shaking Ephesus and its pagan culture to the core.[55]

The goddess Artemis was supreme in Ephesus. They claimed she was the daughter of Zeus and Leto. Her cult was one of the most powerful in the ancient world. There were temples of Artemis from Spain in the west to Syria in the east. The temple at Ephesus contained a many-breasted image of the goddess that supposedly had fallen from heaven. Artemis was considered the founder and protector of Ephesus, and her image and name were everywhere. Her marble temple was the largest building in the Greek world, drawing many pilgrims, causing the city to prosper.

Paul's proclamation of the one true God revealed in Jesus Christ put him on a collision course with the goddess and her worshippers.

The silversmiths who made miniatures of the temple and its goddess would lose money if people turned from the goddess. Motivated by religious zeal and greed, a certain Demetrius calls a meeting of silversmiths in the great outdoor theater of Ephesus. The meeting becomes a mob.

They seize Paul's coworkers, Gaius and Aristarchus. Paul wants to face the crowd, but the disciples stop him. Paul had friends in high places among the Asiarchs—the leading men of the province—who kept him safe. Eventually, after the chief official of the city settles the crowd by reminding them of what their Roman overlords will do if they hear of this disturbance, the riot ends.

In Corinth, the proconsul had dismissed the charges against Paul, brought by unbelieving Jews. In Ephesus, the leading official dismisses the charges brought by unbelieving Gentiles. Two important legal precedents have been set for the protection of Paul and the wider movement.[56]

This marks the end of an era—Paul's last mission as a free man. He is ready to move on.

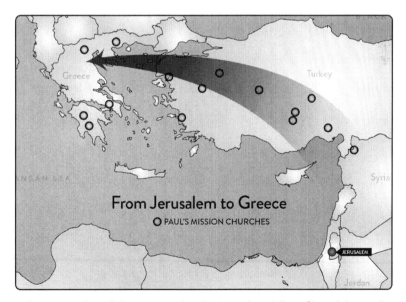

**From Jerusalem to Greece**
O PAUL'S MISSION CHURCHES

*"From Jerusalem all the way around to Illyricum, I have fully proclaimed the gospel of Christ"(Romans 15:19). See Paul Barnett,* Paul: Missionary of Jesus.[57]

## Paul's "No Place Left" Vision

Looking back, we see how Paul focused his mission on strategic centers to reach Roman provinces: Philippi for Macedonia, Thessalonica for Macedonia and Achaia, Corinth for Achaia, and Ephesus for Asia.

As he leaves Ephesus, Paul concludes he has fully preached the gospel in the whole of the eastern half of the empire. He had won disciples in unreached fields, formed churches, and multiplied workers. He had been a catalyst for a movement of God. Now he has no place left in which to work.[58] He has completed the work of an apostolic pioneer and is ready to return to Jerusalem and then to Rome.

Where are the Pauls today? Where are the people who proclaim the gospel where it has never been heard? Where are the people who will make disciples of those who are far from God? Who will plant churches where there were none? Who will raise up local leaders and head missionary teams of dedicated workers? Who are the people who will refuse to settle down but will continue to move on to unreached fields, appointing leaders and strengthening the churches they leave behind?

If we want to know why there are so few disciple making movements in the Western world, we need look no further than our settled patterns of church leadership. We need to return to the patterns of the movement of God in Acts.

Our mission is the spread of the Word in the power of the Spirit, bearing the fruit of the disciples and churches from wherever we are to the ends of the earth. Such a mission requires leaders like Paul, but also leaders like Priscilla and Aquila, Timothy, Silas and Titus, Junia and Andronicus, Apollos, Luke and Epaphras—as well as a host of ordinary disciples whose names are unknown. If we return to the mission God gave us, I suspect we might find our Pauls and Priscillas and Aquilas, and Timothys . . . and a host of ordinary disciples whose names are unknown.

### MOVEMENTS TODAY: ONE CHURCH'S JOURNEY TO MOVEMENT

Around the world, movement pioneers are applying the lessons of Paul's "no place left" strategy in their cities and regions.

Jeff Timblin has a heart for the nations, so when he planted Bridges church in Long Beach, California, the church caught his vision.[59] For thirteen years, Bridges has been sending teams into southern Ethiopia to plant churches in unreached villages.

In Ethiopia, Jeff learned the principles of disciple making movements by trial and error but never saw the connection to southern California. Back home he was leading people to Christ, but the church wasn't trained and mobilized to reach its community.

Jeff was in Ethiopia when God spoke to him. He says he didn't hear an audible voice, but what he heard was clearer than a voice. God told him to go to Dallas to a specific conference he'd heard about. He was to take a minivan with seven people whom God put on his heart.

At the conference he discovered a coalition of people who shared his heart for the nations and for multiplication movements. Importantly, they saw America as a mission field and were applying movement principles in their own back yard. Jeff had found his tribe, the NoPlaceLeft network.[60]

As the team drove the twenty hours back to Long Beach they debriefed, prayed, and planned what they would do next.

Back home, they began going out into their community, two by two, praying for needs, sharing the good news, looking for houses of peace where they could make disciples. Jeff started a church in his living room as a leadership hub, with the expectation it would multiply. Today that one church has started five churches.

Jeff wanted any changes to Bridges to flow from what God was doing as they stepped out into their community. He took time to bring his elders and the church with him. Meanwhile he was still active; he hooked into the NoPlaceLeft network for coaching and was learning from what was happening in other places.

Through training and coaching, Jeff and others have formed a network of movement practitioners across greater Los Angeles. They have begun a residency program to train church planters. Interns commit to six hours per week: two hours in the community looking for houses of peace, two hours meeting as church, and two hours training others. After two years, the residents graduate with a readiness to go wherever God leads.

In twenty years, Bridges had planted four churches across the United States. In the last four years, the network has planted around fifty churches across Los Angeles.

Jeff now has a vision to reach the 1.4 million people of Long Beach and north Orange County. He wants each one of them to hear the gospel from person to person. He's building a coalition to reach the twenty-four million people of greater Los Angeles.

He tells church leaders all they need for this journey are the essentials: a vision for no place left, a heart for lost people, and a willingness to trust in God for what happens to their church.

There's still a long way to go, but Jeff has made a start in aligning himself with the patterns and principles he's discovered in the life of Paul.

# DEEPER: THE DIFFERENCE TEAMS MAKE

*The Holy Spirit said, "Set apart for me Barnabas and Saul for the work to which I have called them."*

ACTS 13:2

### Paul and the Missionary Band

When the Holy Spirit called Barnabas and Paul out of Antioch to pioneer in unreached fields, the church in Antioch released them to form a missionary band.[61] The resulting apostolic band had its own identity and existence, distinct from any local church.

The goal of Paul's apostolic ministry was to establish and equip new, healthy churches in unreached fields. In a new field, the team existed as both a missionary band and a local church in formation. New disciples meant a new church start, but only a few joined Paul's mobile missionary band.

Paul's missionary enterprise was not under the authority and direction of the church at Antioch or Jerusalem or any other church. The missionary band received funds and personnel from the churches but operated independently of their leadership.[62] Paul expected local churches to take part in the mission locally and partner with his mission beyond. He called workers out of the local churches to join his team for varying lengths of time.

Once they established local churches, Paul and his coworkers began looking for new, unreached fields. Some stayed behind or returned to strengthen and extend the work. The churches continued the spread of the gospel in depth, planting new churches in their regions.

## Paul and Coworkers

Paul surrounded himself with coworkers, both mobile missionaries who traveled with him and local leaders in the churches. There are about one hundred names linked with Paul in the New Testament; thirty-eight of them are coworkers.[63] Many of these team members came from the churches he started.

Like Jesus, Paul trained his workers as they traveled and served together. Paul's coworkers traversed long distances by sea and on foot, sometimes with Paul, sometimes without him. It was a hard life— dangerous travel, violent opposition, lack of resources, persecution, and prison. They moved constantly while relying on support from the generosity of others and the work of their own hands.

The husband-and-wife team of Priscilla and Aquila was an example of the fluid network of leaders that Paul called "coworkers." Like him, they were leatherworkers. They moved from city to city, working their trade, and establishing households that provided a meeting place for a church.[64] In AD 49, they moved from Rome to Corinth where they worked with Paul in preaching and teaching. Two years later, they went with Paul to Ephesus, where a church met in their home.[65] After Paul left Ephesus, they stayed behind to continue the work there. By AD 56, they were back in Rome with a church meeting in their home.[66]

Paul involved coworkers when he wrote letters to the churches. Sosthenes, Timothy, "the brothers," and Silas are mentioned as co-senders in eight of Paul's thirteen letters. Paul's letters reveal how much he valued their service and how much he loved them. He used different terms for his team members: brother, companion, apostle, servant, fellow slave, fellow soldier, fellow prisoner, and fellow worker. These team members were not under the direct authority of their churches. Paul is their leader, yet these terms reveal relationships of equality. They are more than Paul's "assistants"; they are partners in spreading the gospel and strengthening the churches.

Paul's most frequently mentioned partners are Barnabas, Timothy, Luke, Priscilla and Aquila, Silas/Silvanus, Titus, and Tychicus. Some, like Timothy, were almost constant members of the team. Others worked with Paul for a time and then worked separately—Barnabas, Silas, and Apollos. Some returned to their churches.

Paul's partners acted independently and courageously. For example, while Paul was based in Ephesus, Epaphras started churches in the surrounding cities of Colossae, Laodicea, and Hierapolis.[67] Priscilla and Aquila oversaw and advanced the work in Ephesus while Paul was away. Timothy and Erastus checked the progress of the churches in Macedonia while Paul remained in Ephesus. Gaius and Aristarchus faced the anger of a mob while others restrained Paul from confronting the crowd.[68]

Paul's letters name seventeen women associated with his mission.[69] In Romans 16, Paul identified Phoebe, a "deacon" or servant of the church in Cenchreae (near Corinth) and a financial supporter of many, including Paul. He also greeted Mary, who had worked hard for the church. Junia and her husband, Andronicus, were pioneering missionaries who were in prison with Paul; he described this couple as "outstanding among the apostles."[70] Tryphena and Tryphosa were two women who "work hard in the Lord." Paul's dear friend Persis is another woman who worked "very hard in the Lord."[71] Elsewhere Paul referred to Euodia and Syntyche, two women who contended at his side in proclaiming the gospel.[72]

According to Acts, the living Word and the Holy Spirit are all the authority a disciple needs to share the gospel and make disciples. Every disciple has the authority and responsibility to make disciples wherever they are. In the New Testament, there are different gifts and ministries but no clergy and laity distinction.[73] Movements don't abolish the clergy; they ordain everyone for ministry.

Paul was a highly qualified theological thinker, who was of no use until he surrendered his religious pride to the supremacy of Christ. From that point, his great learning focused on becoming a servant, not the master, of God's purposes. He led from the front in a missionary movement that mobilized men and women, rich and poor, educated and illiterate.

Movements don't impose extra-biblical requirements on leadership. They don't use academic qualifications to filter out ordinary people. Their simple methods of training, equipping, and educating keep pace with the growth of the movement. Like Peter, Paul, and Luke, their best teachers have dirt under their fingernails. They learn their biblical theology in the field as they suffer for the gospel, make disciples, plant and strengthen churches, and multiply workers in unreached fields.

## MOVEMENTS TODAY: A CANADIAN ANTIOCH

Throughout Acts, Luke holds up the example of churches reaching out beyond themselves to multiply disciples and churches in unreached fields. What does that look like today?

I received an email from Jeff Bennett, the pastor of Habourside Fellowship in Ontario, Canada.[74] Jeff was frustrated with his attempts to equip his church to make disciples. Jeff was willing to go anywhere in the Western world and spend three weeks of his sabbatical out in a community making disciples with someone who could show him how. I knew just the person—Russell Godward in Essex, England. I connected them, and a few months later, Jeff was out every day with Russell, sharing the gospel and making disciples. They followed the example of Jesus as a pastor/shepherd who went looking for people far from God.

When Jeff returned to Canada, the first thing he did was to grab one of his team and walk across the church's parking lot to knock on a door. Jeff remembers sharing the gospel in sight of the church's front door.

Progress was slow at first, but Jeff recruited and trained teams to go out into the community every week. Three years later, they are now baptizing, on average, one new disciple every week.

One windy Saturday morning, one of the teams went out visiting when it was ten degrees below freezing, unaware that there was a man named Mark in the neighborhood who had cried out to God for help the night before. Addictions controlled his life, and he saw no way out. That Saturday morning, Mark stepped out of his building for a cigarette when the team met him, prayed for him, and shared the gospel. Mark turned, believed, and was baptized. When they asked him about meeting the next day for discipleship he said, "No. It's too important to wait. Can't we meet again tonight?" Mark is now sharing the good news with his friends and family who want to know more about the God who has set him free.

Harbourside Fellowship is growing by adding new disciples, and they are planting churches. There are three new churches in their community, and three church starts.[75] One church, begun by two college students, meets in the back room of a minimart. Another church meets in the basement of a bar; as a result, the bar owner has come to know Christ.

This growth became possible because Jeff embraced the gap between his experience and the ministry of Jesus in the Gospels and Acts. He wanted answers and was willing to give three weeks of his time to fly to England and learn from a man he'd never met before. Using a MAWL approach (model, assist, watch, launch). Russell *modeled* how to enter a community, share the gospel, and make disciples. He trained Jeff in some simple but effective methods in sharing the gospel and reading the Bible for discipleship. Russell *assisted* Jeff as he applied these tools in real life situations. He *watched* Jeff and gave feedback, and finally he *launched* him back in Canada ready to go.

Jeff wants Harbourside Fellowship to be an Antioch-like church, sending out people to make disciples in other places, just as the church in Antioch released Paul and Barnabas. He's praying for thirty Antioch churches across the cities and towns of Ontario, reaching its thirteen million inhabitants.

To see a multiplying movement, churches need to look beyond addition—adding people, adding groups, adding congregations, adding staff, adding sites. That is not the pattern of Acts. To add is to ask, *How big can we grow?* To multiply is to ask, *How can we have generations of healthy children, grandchildren, and great grand-children?* That's the pattern we see in the churches like Jerusalem, Antioch, and Ephesus. They gave their best away and became multi-plying hubs.

# WORDS OF ENCOURAGEMENT (20:1-12)

## AD 56

At the end of his mission in Asia, Paul returns to strengthen the churches in Macedonia and Achaia. The journey takes up to two years.[76] During a three-month stay in Corinth, he writes a letter to the Romans, preparing the way for his visit and the mission to the Latin-speaking world as far west as Spain.[77] He writes that he has fully proclaimed the gospel from Jerusalem to Illyricum, and now there is no place left for him to work.[78]

From there forward, Paul is focused on making his way to Jerusalem and then Rome—the two cities representing the two powers that Paul has disturbed—taking the gospel into the heart of the forces opposed to the movement of God.[79]

There is a plot to kill him, and it is too dangerous to return to Jerusalem by ship, so Paul backtracks on foot to Philippi in Macedonia, then travels to Jerusalem via Troas, Miletus, Tyre, Ptolemais, and Caesarea—visiting the disciples along the way.[80]

With Paul is Sopater from Berea, Aristarchus and Secundus from Thessalonica, Gaius from Derbe, Timothy from Lystra and Tychicus and Trophimus from Asia. These men represent the fruit of his pioneering work in what is now Greece and Turkey. They were coworkers with Paul in the mission of pioneering in unreached regions, proclaiming the gospel, making disciples, planting and strengthening churches. They carry with them a gift from the Gentile churches for the relief of the poor in Jerusalem. Paul wants the Gentile believers to acknowledge their debt to the church in Jerusalem and for Jerusalem believers to acknowledge that God has created the Gentile churches.[81] The Spirit was given to reach the nations; now the nations are returning to Jerusalem with gifts.[82]

References to "we" appear again in the text. It appears Luke joins Paul in Philippi before everyone meets up in Troas.

The week-long stay in Troas provides an opportunity for Luke to give another glimpse of church life in the pattern described in Jerusalem. They meet on the first day of the week at night, because most people would have been working during the day.[83] They meet in an upstairs room of a three-story house, which may have been a tenement building for the poor or the home of a wealthy person.[84] The latter is more likely, as accommodation for the poor could only cater for a handful of visitors.

They gather to "break bread"—to share a meal that includes the Lord's Supper.[85] They gather to hear Paul. Luke's word choice implies discussion rather than a monologue.[86] Paul has just written a long letter to the churches in Rome as a summary of the gospel. He may have covered this material for the disciples at Troas.

As the night wore on, the air would have become hot and stuffy. Eutychus, a boy, not yet a teenager, sinks into a deep sleep and falls from the third-story window. Fortunately, Paul restores him to life. They eat and celebrate the Lord's Supper. Then Paul continues ministering—until dawn!

Paul plans his last journey to Jerusalem so that he can visit five churches on the way, two of which were started by Paul (Troas, Ephesus) and three by others (Tyre, Ptolemais, and Caesarea).

The churches share the same characteristics as the church in Jerusalem.[87] They are devoted to obeying and spreading the Word,[88] the breaking of bread,[89] prayer and worship,[90] fellowship,[91] and sharing possessions;[92] and they all face persecution.[93]

In depicting these communities, Luke is showing us what the movement of God looks like. The outcome of God's mission is people learning to love and obey the Lord Jesus together as they reach out to their community. This pattern of discipleship takes precedence over human plans, programs, strategies, and structures.[94]

Today, there is no shortage of critiques of "the church" in the West. Critique without action breeds cynicism and despair. Movements, however, go beyond critique and ask, *How do we return to New Testament patterns and principles?* They ask, *What is to be done?* Luke calls every new generation to return to the essence of the church's life and mission. It is futile to complain about what others should be doing if we're not bridging the gap between the church in Acts and the church today.

Change begins on the fringes with disciples gathered around the Word, taking steps of obedience as they learn, trusting the Holy Spirit to guide them as they step out in obedience to what they already know.

## MOVEMENTS TODAY: NOPLACELEFT ARMY

The men and women of NoPlaceLeft Army are leading the way in turning a critique of the contemporary Western church into action, which reflects the life of the church in Acts.

Four years into their marriage, John and Lauren's relationship was spiraling downward when they moved to Fort Benning, Georgia in 2017.[95]

John, who served in the United States infantry in special operations, was wondering if there was any reality to the faith he professed. A friend connected him with Will, another soldier on base who shared the gospel with him. Will challenged John, asking him if Jesus was his Lord. When John replied, "Not really," Will explained to him that if he hadn't given Jesus full authority in his life, then he was living in the kingdom of darkness. That was the challenge John needed, and he surrendered to Jesus as King.

Meanwhile, Lauren was going through her own struggle of surrendering to God's will, particularly in relation to her marriage. She determined that John was the man God had given here and that no matter how hard it got, she was not giving up.

Will and his wife, Grace, invited John and Lauren into a discipling relationship and the two couples began meeting. Will and Grace helped John and Lauren with the issues they needed to work through in their marriage; and they also covered the Commands of Christ—such as "repent and believe," "be baptized," "love one another," "make disciples," and "pray."[96] The four of them began meeting; a new church forming there on their military base.

Lauren and John were surprised to hear that, despite their challenges, they too could make disciples and start a church. All they needed to do was to pass on what they were learning to others. They knew how to take a group through the Commands of Christ, and they could also share how their identity was changing as they followed Jesus together as a couple.

Their opportunity came when Will and Grace left for overseas missionary work. One day, while at the local pool, Lauren met a young mom named Sarah, married to Zach, who was a captain in the army. Lauren shared the gospel and invited Sarah to the gathering in their home. Sarah and Zach began attending every week. Zach had no faith but wanted to support his wife who was now following Jesus. Four months later he put his faith in Christ, and with Sarah he was baptized. As John and Lauren continued to pass on what they had learned, soon Sarah and Zach did the same—sharing the gospel and making disciples.

Not everyone responded like Sarah and Zach. Some new disciples didn't bear fruit. John and Lauren recall an entire year of hard work and hard lessons that challenged their identity in Christ but took them deeper with God and with one another.

They've also seen breakthroughs. A man named Avery arrived in Fort Benning for officer training. After some training from John, Avery shared the gospel with every soldier in his platoon. He baptized six of them, and now he and his wife, Amanda, have a church meeting in their home.

A typical church gathering on the base takes a 3-Thirds approach, beginning with mutual care, as people share their highs and lows for the week, followed by loving accountability as each reports on how they are following through on their commitments from last week. There's worship and prayer and a reminder from Matthew 28 that every believer has the authority to make disciples and form new churches. Then there's a Discovery Bible Study in which everyone takes part. Finally, they practice the skills they need to share the gospel and make disciples. The gathering closes with prayer and new commitments of action in the coming week.

One leader in the network is former soldier, Jim McKnight. Jim told me, they have a saying in the army: "If there's not one thing that everyone in your unit knows then nobody knows anything." In this network of disciples and churches, everyone is learning to share the gospel and make disciples among the people they know and the people they meet.

When someone comes to faith, they are immediately trained in the basics and told they are cleared to start a church with their friends. Jim says that sowing the idea at the beginning helps prepare people for what lies further down the road.

They tell new disciples that they're being launched to start a church, not because they're *trained* but because they're *in training*. Everyone is encouraged to come back next week so the group can follow up on how they got on.

Their pattern of discipleship and church is simple enough for any disciple to pick up and begin a new gathering, whether they go around their local community, around the nation, or around the world. Jim is convinced that the ministry of every believer is essential for the growth of any movement.

So far, the network of churches has baptized over five hundred disciples and planted forty-four churches around the United States and another ninety overseas. Workers sent out by the movement have planted churches in Central Asia, South Asia, and Kenya.

NoPlaceLeft Army have fresh stories of people learning to follow Jesus together and drawing in others. They have workers who are sent out around the world, multiplying disciples and churches. Although they aren't on most people's radar, they're experts in their field and worth learning from. Committed to the core missionary task, they step out with the Word in the power of the Holy Spirit. They don't write the books or get invited to speak on stage, but they are heroes.

# YOU KNOW HOW I LIVED (20:13–38)

Between AD 45–57, Paul and his coworkers found churches in the Roman provinces of Syria-Cilicia, Cyprus, Galatia, Macedonia, Achaia, and Asia Minor.[97] He completes his mission to the eastern Roman Empire. Paul is pressing on to make it to Jerusalem by Pentecost.

With his ship moored at the harbor in Miletus, Paul sends a message to the elders of the churches in and around Ephesus to meet him. Paul has come to say goodbye. After Jerusalem, he is headed to Rome and then further west to Spain. His message to the Ephesian elders allows Paul to reflect on the missionary task. Paul's charge to the elders summarizes and concludes Luke's description of his missionary work in Acts 13–20.[98]

In giving us the contents of Paul's farewell speech in Ephesus, Luke shows us the sort of thing Paul included in his parting words to all the churches. Paul's focus is on the identity of the church and its future, which will not depend on him but on the Word and the Spirit of God.[99]

In Paul's speech, we find parallels with his letters. Three overlapping themes are described below.[100]

## 1. Wide and Deep

Paul preached the gospel *widely* to Jews and Gentiles, God-fearers and pagans, men and women, rich and poor, the elite and the illiterate.[101] At the heart of his ministry was the proclamation of the Word from house to house and publicly in the synagogue, in the lecture hall of Tyrannus, and the marketplace.[102] Paul taught anyone who would listen to his gospel about Jesus the Messiah and Lord.

Paul preached the kingdom of God *deeply* in continuity with the teaching of Jesus, the Twelve, and the Jerusalem church.[103] He explained the significance of Jesus' death, resurrection, and exaltation. He called everyone to repentance and faith in Jesus, the only Savior from God's judgment; they must serve the living and true God on his terms.[104]

By staying in Ephesus for almost three years, Paul wanted to ensure the new believers understood the gospel deeply and lived out the implications in their lives, including the responsibility to carry the gospel to their family, friends, city, and region. Paul taught them the whole will of God revealed in Jesus Christ. Night and day with tears, he warned each disciple to remain faithful. He shared the Word, and he shared his life. Paul reminded the elders of his tears, his humility, his hard work to support himself, his courage in persecution, boldness in proclamation, obedience to the Spirit, faithfulness to the task, and freedom in generosity. He loved them to the end.

## 2. God's Mission; God's Church

The speech contains many references to God, Jesus, and the Holy Spirit. Paul is continually drawing attention to God's authority and leadership of his church.

The fruit of Paul's mission was God's church, which God purchased by the death of Christ. These leaders are shepherds of God's church. The church does not belong to them; the church belongs to God and is in his care.[105]

When Paul and his coworkers appointed elders, they were acting under the authority of the Holy Spirit.[106] The Holy Spirit was present and active within the church, choosing and preparing those who were called to lead. It is the Holy Spirit who provides leaders as they are needed.

The future of the church does not depend on Paul or even these elders, but on God who called the church into existence.[107]

## 3. Paul's Work is Done; Theirs Continues

Paul uses the image of the pastor/shepherd to describe the task of the elder/overseer. Shepherds care for their flock by providing pasture and water and by protecting the flock from danger. They must watch over the integrity and quality of their faith, teaching, and character. They must watch over the *entire flock*—Jews and Gentiles, slaves and free, rich and poor, men and women, old and young. They lead the flock, and yet they are also part of the flock.

After Paul goes, these local leaders will face fierce opposition from outside and from within, just as Paul had done. When the Enemy sends savage wolves among the sheep, they must deal with it without Paul.[108] Paul raised local leaders; now they must enter the fight, as Paul moves on to new fields. Paul is leaving, confident that the risen Lord is active in the church through his living Word and present through the Holy Spirit.[109]

Paul's speech to the Ephesian leaders provides a window into his achievements across an arc from Jerusalem to beyond Greece. The speech shows how Paul pursued his apostolic mission by reaching key cities and their surrounding provinces as the Word went out through the people of God. Their mission continues, while his focus shifts to new fields in the west of the empire.

As Paul speaks to the elders of the Ephesian church, seven men watch and listen.[110] Paul's traveling companions are the fruit of his ministry throughout the eastern empire. They have learned from this apostolic pioneer, catching his passion and heart.

Compelled by the Spirit, Paul is going to Jerusalem, where the Spirit warned he will face prison and hardship. Paul obediently leaves, knowing he is a captive of the Lord and because of that will finish the race and complete the task Jesus has given him—testifying to the good news of God's grace.[111]

The elders gather around him. They kneel and pray. They weep, unsure if they will ever see Paul again. Luke writes, "After we had torn ourselves away from them, we put out to sea."[112] Paul's mission to the East is over; now to Jerusalem and then to Rome.

# DEEPER: LOCAL LEADERS

*Paul and Barnabas appointed elders for them in each church and, with prayer and fasting, committed them to the Lord, in whom they had put their trust.*

ACTS 14:23

Paul's mission was not completed until he formed disciples into churches and appointed local leaders. As the church in Jerusalem grew to thousands, the apostles would soon need local leaders. With the appointment of the seven, Luke provides us with a detailed account of the appointment process. They were chosen by all the disciples and were men full of the Holy Spirit and wisdom who could ensure the widows will be cared for. Following their selection, the apostles prayed and laid hands on them.[113]

Luke gives future generations the patterns and principles of leadership selection rather than a blueprint for every situation.

When Philip was in Samaria, leading thousands to Christ, Phillip, Peter, and John had not settled in Samaria, yet later Luke reports how the church throughout Samaria was growing in maturity and numbers.[114] We can assume they had appointed local leaders either during their mission or on a return trip to strengthen the new churches.

We know the apostles were based in Jerusalem until AD 41, when Peter was forced to flee by Herod. Either at that point or earlier, responsibility to lead the church in Jerusalem was passed to a group of elders led by James, the Lord's brother.[115]

In Acts 13, the Spirit spoke to a group of prophets and teachers in the church at Antioch regarding Barnabas and Paul's mission. Luke doesn't say if this group were "elders" but the context in which the Spirit spoke appears to be corporate worship, prayer, and fasting. The whole church is involved in releasing Barnabas and Paul to the mission.

The work of making disciples and planting healthy churches was given to Paul and Barnabas by the Spirit and was only completed when Barnabas and Paul appointed elders over each of the churches. It had taken between one to two years to move from pioneer evangelism to churches with local leaders.

Paul's speech to the Ephesian elders is as close as we get to a role description for local leaders in Acts. These elders represented multiple churches throughout Ephesus and possibly the region of Asia Minor.[116]

In Paul's speech, the terms *elder*, *overseer*, and *shepherd/pastor* refer to the one role.

From Paul's speech we learn that the church belongs to God, not the elders. Elders are under the authority of the Holy Spirit and the Word of God. The Holy Spirit has given these local leaders oversight of God's flock. They have God's living Word, which can build his people and give them an inheritance among all those who are sanctified.

Paul reminds the elders of his example in leadership, which in turn was modeled on Jesus. Publicly and from house to house, Paul called everyone to repent and believe in Jesus. Likewise, elders must proclaim the whole will of God, following the Shepherd who sought the lost. These elders are responsible to finish the task in their city and region, which Paul began.

Paul is leaving, and Satan will send wolves to draw disciples to themselves, rather than Christ. The elders must deal with the menace and be sure of their own faithfulness. They must care for *all* of God's people, whether they be rich or poor, men or women, young or old.[117]

The appointment of local leaders marks a new relationship between the apostolic band and the local church, which is characterized by partnership in the gospel. Paul brings the churches to maturity so that they can govern themselves under the authority of the Scriptures while he moves on to unreached fields. The churches continue the mission in their region and release money and workers to the missionary bands.

Local leaders allow the churches to multiply as a movement without the need for central control and funding. As the Word spreads, grows, and multiplies, a network of reproducing churches can emerge.

Paul did not attempt to govern the churches centrally; he appointed local leaders over each community of disciples. Each church was self-governing. A centrally governed network of churches cannot multiply beyond the ability of the center to organize and fund its activities. The greater the control from the center, the less likely it is that innovation and breakthroughs will come from the fringes of the movement.

SEVEN

# TRIALS AND TRIUMPH

(21:1–28:31)

# WHY ARE YOU BREAKING
# MY HEART? (21:1-16)

Paul's voyage to Jerusalem followed the pattern for small ships in the ancient world, which was to hug the coastline and put into port each night when the winds died down.[1] In several ports they sought out the local disciples, who welcomed them, provided hospitality, and tearfully sent them on their way.

Paul "compelled by the Holy Spirit" is going to Jerusalem, where he will face prison and hardships.[2] Yet in Tyre, the disciples urge him "through the Spirit" not to go to Jerusalem.[3] Then in Caesarea, the prophet Agabus ties Paul's hands and feet and announces, "The Holy Spirit says, 'In this way the Jewish leaders in Jerusalem will bind the owner of this belt and will hand him over to the Gentiles.'"[4] Despite this growing sense of foreboding, Paul, like Jesus, sets his face toward Jerusalem.[5]

Paul is both *compelled* by the Spirit to go to Jerusalem and *warned* by the Spirit that trouble awaited him there. The prophecy of Agabus confirms the Spirit's leading and warning. The believers in Tyre understand the same message through the Spirit, but still urge Paul not to go. Because Paul is determined, the disciples agree, "The Lord's will be done."[6] It is the Lord who directs Paul's mission, who empowers his witness, and whose presence gives Paul the strength to suffer.[7]

Wherever Paul visits, the disciples grieve his departure. If he survives this journey to Jerusalem, he will then go to Rome, and onto Spain.[8] Although they will be sad if they never see him again, the future of the churches doesn't depend on Paul or any other leader. Their identity is in God.[9]

Paul didn't start the churches he visited, yet he helped get them started. In his attempt to destroy the movement before he met Christ, he drove the disciples out of Jerusalem to Tyre, Ptolemais, and Caesarea where they spread the Word and planted the churches he now visits.[10]

In Tyre, they welcome their former persecutor as a brother and a guest.[11] Believers line the way to Jerusalem in each place to encourage and honor this servant of the Lord.

In the port city of Caesarea they stay at the home of Philip the evangelist before some disciples escort Paul on the four-day walk up to Jerusalem. There he stays at the home of Mnason, one of Jesus' early disciples. This would have been an opportunity for Luke to gather an eyewitness account of the early days of the Jesus movement, which he could continue in Jerusalem.

Paul doesn't know exactly what will happen to him in Jerusalem. On the road to Damascus, the Lord told Paul he would suffer for his name.[12] His arrest, imprisonment, and trials were not an interruption to his mission but part of God's plan. Through Paul, God will confront the two powers that oppose his purposes—Jerusalem and Rome.[13]

## DEEPER: PROPHETS

*I will pour out my Spirit in those days, and they will prophesy.*

ACTS 2:18

The story that unfolds in Luke's Gospel and Acts "is driven by the fulfillment of prophecies."[14] Prophecies are fulfilled because God has a plan and is guiding history.

Many of Luke's characters are prophets—Elizabeth, Mary, Anna, John the Baptist, Jesus, Peter, Stephen, Paul, Agabus and his group, the prophets at Antioch, Judas and Silas, and Philip's four daughters.

The Spirit of Pentecost is the Spirit of prophecy. Peter, with prophetic insight, discerned the fulfillment of the Scriptures at Pentecost. Peter knew the hearts of Ananias and Sapphira and prophetically announced God's judgment on their sin.[15] Paul's conversion and call came through a visionary encounter with Jesus, which led to a prophetic encounter with a disciple called Ananias.[16] The conversion of Cornelius and his household through Peter was brought about through visions and prophetic words. The prophets and teachers at Antioch discerned what the Spirit was saying and set apart Barnabas and Paul for the next stage of missionary advance.[17] The prophets Silas and Judas encouraged and strengthened the Gentile believers and explained the outcome of the Jerusalem Council.[18] Paul and his coworkers were led to begin their campaign in Macedonia through a vision resulting in the planting of churches in Philippi, Thessalonica, Berea, and Corinth. It was a vision that ensured Paul would remain in Corinth despite the opposition.[19] When the Ephesian disciples received the Holy Spirit they spoke in tongues and prophesied.[20] Agabus the prophet predicted famine in Judea and warned Paul of suffering and danger.[21] At the end of his missionary journeys, Paul predicted what would happen to him and the church in Ephesus.[22] In the midst of a wild storm, Paul predicted God would rescue all on board and that he would stand before the emperor in Rome.[23]

### The Characteristics and Function of the Prophet

Early Christian prophecy has some characteristics of Old Testament prophecy and some differences. Paul's letters show that New Testament prophecy was not taken as a literal transcript of God's words but something that needed to be considered and tested.[24] This helps us understand Agabus's prophecy that Paul would be bound by the Jews and handed over to the Romans, as Jesus was. That did not literally take place; the Jews rioted, and Paul was rescued and arrested by the Romans. Agabus got the main drift of what would happen, but not the details of how it would happen.[25]

Just as Jesus was anointed by the Spirit to proclaim God's Word, so his disciples are anointed as end-time prophets.[26] This is an age in which young men will see visions, and old men will dream dreams. As the Word goes out, the mission is characterized by God's leading, bold witness, and signs and wonders. "It matters not whether we are young or old, male or female, rich or poor, black or white, the Spirit of Pentecost comes to enable every member of the church, each one of us, to fulfill our prophetic call to be a light to the nations."[27]

The gift of the Spirit of prophecy on every believer does not mean equivalent roles for everyone. All can prophesy and speak God's Word boldly, but only some are called "prophets" in Acts.[28]

Prophets are integrated within the overlapping gifts of the Spirit by which Jesus leads his church.[29] One of the functions of prophecy is to discern the fulfillment of Old Testament Scripture, such as Peter did at Pentecost, and James the elder did at the Jerusalem Council.[30] Peter and Stephen are examples of how the interpretation of Scripture can be a prophetic activity.[31] Peter and Stephen function as prophets, but Luke is not concerned to give them the title. He doesn't tightly define and label the ministries he identifies.[32] He prefers a certain level of ambiguity and fluidity in describing ministries.[33] His greater concern is to show how the Spirit empowers all of Jesus' disciples to contribute to advancing the movement.

Prophets also apply the meaning of the Scriptures, strengthen and encourage the disciples, and at times, reveal the future. Prophets who serve in the power of the Spirit reveal the character and truth of their Lord, who is the great Prophet of the end-time.[34]

### *Prophets Today*

Today, Simon the sorcerer lives on among those who corrupt the work of the Spirit for money and fame. Yet Peter's response to Simon was not to quench the work of the Spirit but a powerful prophetic word, warning of God's judgment.[35]

In Acts, prophetic words and visions are catalysts for break-throughs in the advance of the movement.[36] Luke did not expect the Spirit of prophecy to be withdrawn before the mission is completed and Christ returns. In these last days, the Spirit continues to intervene to direct, encourage, and warn his people as the Word goes out from Jerusalem to the ends of the earth.

●

# THE ARRIVAL AT JERUSALEM (21:17–26)

## AD 57

In Jerusalem Paul meets with James and the elders. The Twelve had already departed Jerusalem around AD 41.[37]

Paul travels with Luke and seven other coworkers who represent the churches in Macedonia, Achaia, and Asia Minor. They carry with them a gift from churches to the poor of the church in Jerusalem. Paul's letters reveal how important this gift was for Paul. It was a sign of the unity between the Gentile churches and the church in Jerusalem.[38]

Paul is able to give a full account of the pioneering work in the province of Asia, as well as reports on the churches he visited in Macedonia and Achaia. The men from the various churches who accompanied him would also have provided living confirmation of his reports.

For their part, the leaders of the churches in Jerusalem tell of the many thousands of Jews who have come to faith in Jesus as Messiah. These Jewish disciples are continuing to live as Jews and are zealous for the law. They are troubled by false reports, which said Paul taught the Jews of the diaspora to abandon the law of Moses and to not circumcise their sons.

These are turbulent times in Jerusalem. Jewish nationalism is on the rise, fueled by the brutality of the Roman governor Felix. Paul's mission to the Gentiles is not viewed favorably by non-believing Jews. The Jerusalem elders are caught between the Gentile mission and the Jewish population they want to reach.[39]

The disciples in Jerusalem are under the constant threat of persecution from Jews who rejected Jesus as the Messiah. The movement in Jerusalem needs to show they are faithful to the law of Moses, to remove a barrier for Jews to identify with the gospel message. Jewish Christians in Jerusalem are not asking Gentile believers to come under the law—that had been settled at the Council almost ten years before. Rather, they want to show that Jewish disciples of Jesus maintained their Jewish identity.[40]

This is still an issue today. Some Muslims in the West want to leave their Muslim identity behind. They would never attend a gathering for Muslim background believers in Jesus. Yet most Muslims cannot hear the gospel if it comes packaged with Western values and forms. If they follow Jesus, it must be within their culture.

James and the elders have a plan. They ask Paul to show his adherence to the law by paying the expenses of four men who were about to complete a Nazarite vow. Paul agrees. Ironically, Paul's decision to honor his Jewish heritage puts him on a collision course with his Jewish enemies.

The attempt to reconcile Judaism with the Gentile mission failed. Five years later in AD 62, James, the elder and brother of Jesus, was executed on the order of the high priest Ananus.[41] When Jewish nationalism erupted into revolt against Rome, support for the Gentile mission was unacceptable within Judaism which was fighting for its existence against a Gentile enemy. Following the destruction of Jerusalem in AD 70, Jewish Christianity was declared heretical, and disciples of Jesus were no longer welcome in the Jewish community.[42]

Yet the failure of reconciling Judaism with the Gentile mission does not mean that James's plan was ill-conceived or that Paul should not have gone along with it. They were not ultimately in control of events, nor were their opponents. God was working out his purposes. God would keep Paul safe and get him to Rome. Jerusalem rejected the Messiah and would be destroyed, as Jesus prophesied. Great nations will rise and fall, and powerful forces will oppose the gospel. God rules over human history and will achieve his purposes through his people who depend on him.

If we are faithful to take his Word to the ends of the earth, we should expect no less of a battle today.

# THEY SEIZE HIM (21:27–23:10)

### AD 57

Paul goes to the temple to demonstrate his faithfulness to Judaism. While there, he is recognized by Jewish opponents from Ephesus. They seize Paul and denounce him as an enemy of the Jewish people, the law, and the temple—some of the same charges that were brought against Jesus and Stephen. They falsely allege that Paul brought a Gentile, Trophimus, into the temple. Paul came to the temple for purification, yet he is accused of defiling it.

The large outer court of the Gentiles was open to all, but signs written in Greek and Latin warned them not to go deeper into the inner sanctuary: "No foreigner may enter within the barricade which surrounds the temple and enclosure. Anyone who is caught doing so will have himself to blame for his ensuing death."[43] Even a Roman could be put to death for defiling the temple.

The mob drag Paul out into the court of the Gentiles and slam the temple gates shut. There, they could beat him or stone him to death without fear of defiling the temple.

This is the last temple scene in Acts. Jerusalem had rejected Jesus, Peter, John, Stephen, and now Paul.[44] As Jesus had prophesied, Jerusalem was ripe for destruction. Judgment will come at the end of the Jewish War with Rome in AD 70.[45]

News of the riot reaches the Roman tribune Claudius Lysias, the commander of one thousand men. He was stationed in the Antonia Fortress next to the temple. Soldiers kept watch from its towers and ran down a stone staircase into the temple's outer court when there was trouble—and during festivals this was often the case.[46] Lysias arrives with two centurions and two hundred soldiers. They rescue Paul and retreat to the staircase as the mob shout, "Away with him!"[47]

The commander is surprised to discover Paul is a Jew from Tarsus; he thought Paul was an Egyptian revolutionary.[48] Surrounded by soldiers, Paul, standing on the staircase, addresses the crowd in Hebrew.[49] He defends himself and his message, arguing he is a faithful Jew and of no threat to Rome. Paul, a Jew born in Tarsus, but brought up in Jerusalem, was a student of the law under Gamaliel. His zeal for Judaism led him to persecute the followers of Jesus. But Jesus appeared to him on the way to Damascus. Paul tells the story of his conversion and his call to serve the risen Lord.

But when the crowd hear that the Lord had sent him to reach Gentiles, they erupt again and demand his death. To claim that Gentiles could be saved apart from the law was an abomination. Paul was destroying Judaism by placing Jews and Gentiles on an equal footing before God.[50]

This is a tragic development. Israel was to be a light to the nations (Gentiles). Instead, taking their status as God's people for granted, they neglected a lost world. The same thing happens today when we settle down to enjoy the benefits of being God's people and neglect our calling to reach the nations.

The commander removes Paul to the safety of the fortress for questioning. From this moment until the end of the book of Acts, Paul does not leave Roman custody.

The Romans prepare Paul to be flogged. It was usual for slaves and non-Romans to be tortured before they were questioned. Without Roman citizenship, Paul would have been interrogated under torture and handed back over to the Jewish authorities with no legal protection.[51] The whip, like the one used on Jesus, was made of leather thongs, weighted with pieces of metal or bone, and attached to a wooden handle. If a man did not die under the flogging, he could be crippled for life.[52]

To inflict maximum harm, the soldiers stretch Paul out. Just then, Paul asks if it is legal to treat a Roman citizen this way. Lysias is horrified. To flog a Roman citizen without the ruling of a court was a serious offense. Lysias had paid a large bribe for his citizenship, but Paul was a citizen by birth.

The next day, Lysias brings together the Sanhedrin and the chief priests to find out why they are accusing Paul. The prisoner declares that his conscience is clear before God. As a follower of Jesus the Messiah, he is a faithful Jew.

The high priest Ananias, known for his cruelty, has Paul struck on the mouth—a violation of the law.[53] Paul snaps back, "God will strike you, you whitewashed wall!"[54] Jesus had also protested when he was struck during interrogation.[55] Stephen too denounced his accusers, even though he, like Jesus, was willing to forgive them.[56] Paul, Jesus, and Stephen all operated with both grace and truth.

Paul warns the high priest of God's judgment, and it eventually came. At the beginning of the Jewish War in AD 66, Ananias was murdered by nationalists for collaborating with Rome.[57]

Paul could not expect justice from the Sanhedrin. He knew if the Romans could be convinced that this was a dispute over matters of the Jewish faith—which it was—then as a Roman citizen, he was in a strong legal position.[58]

Paul identifies the issue upon which he would base his defense: The crucified Jesus had risen from the dead and appeared to him. So he announces, "I am a Pharisee, descended from Pharisees. I stand on trial because of the hope of the resurrection of the dead!" The court is split between Pharisees who believed in the resurrection and Sadducees who didn't. Another riot erupts, and for a second time the Romans rescue Paul.[59]

That night, the Lord stands by Paul, as he had done before and would do again.[60] Jesus assures Paul that just as he has been a witness in Jerusalem, he would now bear witness in Rome. On the journey, Paul would face assassination plots, prison, legal trials, a deadly storm, and a shipwreck. But Paul does arrive in Rome. His life and his mission were in the Lord's hands.

One lesson we can learn from the life of Paul, is to expect trouble. The message of the gospel, the mission of God in the world, will place us on a collision course with a world that is far from God. But the power of God is on display through the very weakness of his messenger.

Paul did not lead a campaign to overthrow the Roman Empire or capture control of the Sanhedrin. There were far more important issues at stake than political realities. As Paul stood before kings and rulers, he knew he was sent to open eyes that are blind, and free people from the power of Satan that their sins may be forgiven and that they may be added to the people of God. That was his mission.[61]

# YOU MUST TESTIFY IN ROME (23:12–35)

Frustrated by their legal attempts to silence Paul, some Jewish extremists bind themselves with an oath not to eat and drink until they have killed Paul. Those who accused Paul of violating the law were now planning to murder him.[62] If the chief priest and elders would request another hearing, the oath-keepers were ready to mount an attack in Jerusalem once Paul is outside the Antonia Fortress.[63]

Paul's nephew, who was in his twenties or early thirties, hears of the plot and reports it. The commander orders two centurions to put together a detachment of 470 soldiers on foot and horseback to take Paul through the night to military headquarters at Caesarea. Ironically, the plot against Paul is the very thing that enables his escape.[64] Nothing can stop God's plans. That night, Paul leaves Jerusalem and begins his long journey to Rome.

A letter from Lysias to the Roman governor Felix accompanies the troops, explaining how he rescued a Roman citizen from a mob, how he found that the dispute was about Jewish law, and that there was no charge for the prisoner to answer under Roman law.

In Caesarea, Felix places Paul under guard in Herod's praetorium, the governor's official residence by the sea.

# THIS MAN IS A TROUBLEMAKER (24:1–27)

## AD 57–59

Soon after Paul arrives in Caesarea, the high priest Ananias arrives with members of the Sanhedrin and an advocate, Tertullus. Paul is to answer their charges before Marcus Antonius Felix, governor of Judea (AD 52–59).

Born a slave, Felix owed his position to the influence of his brother who had been close to the emperor Claudius. A rising tide of unrest against Roman rule marked Felix's time in office, which the governor ruthlessly put down, alienating the Jewish population. The Roman historian Tacitus described the governor as "a master of cruelty and lust who exercised the powers of a king with the spirit of a slave."[65]

As was usual, Tertullus opens by praising the governorship of Felix, ignoring its flaws. He then brings the charges against Paul. He accuses the apostle of being a public enemy who causes riots among the Jewish people wherever he goes. Tertullus turns a religious dispute into a political one. He claims Paul is the leader of a dangerous movement that follows a man who is crucified by the Romans for claiming to be the king of the Jews.[66] Paul threatens the peace of the empire, which Felix was responsible to protect. Finally, the advocate accuses Paul of defiling the temple, a crime that the Romans agreed deserved death.

Paul counters by saying he came to Jerusalem to worship, not to foment rebellion. He asserts he is a faithful Jew who acknowledges Jesus as Israel's Messiah, and that the movement known as the Way is not a breakaway sect but the fulfillment of Judaism.[67] Paul explains he was in the temple for legitimate reasons when Jews from the province of Asia attacked him.

Paul then plays his trump card by asking: Where are my accusers? Where are the eyewitnesses? Finally, Paul brings his defense back to what he regards as the core issue—his belief in the resurrection of the dead. In doing so he frames the conflict as a dispute within Judaism, not sedition against Rome. Having heard both sides, Felix adjourns the matter until the tribune Lysias arrives from Jerusalem.

Under Roman law, Paul has no case to answer. Yet Felix has other considerations than the law. Rome deposed his predecessor, Ventidius Cumanus, and sent him into exile because he had failed to work with the

Jewish leadership.[68] Felix faced a dilemma: There were no legal grounds for convicting and executing Paul, but he could not release Paul without antagonizing the Jewish leaders whose support he needed to maintain order in Judea and keep Rome happy.

As a sign of Paul's status as a Roman citizen and his innocence, Felix relaxes the terms of his custody, allowing Paul's friends to visit and provide for his needs. Paul already has a relationship with the believers in Caesarea and has visited them on his way to Jerusalem. Wherever Paul went, he was met by communities of believers who warmly embraced him. Paul's coworkers, Luke and Aristarchus, also join him while he is in custody.[69] They provide food, clothing, books, and writing implements throughout Paul's two-year stay.[70]

Days later, Felix comes with his Jewish wife, Drusilla, and summons Paul to discuss his faith in the Messiah Jesus. Paul speaks of righteousness, self-control, and the coming judgment—suitable topics for this couple given their background. (Felix's third wife, Drusilla, was the daughter of Herod Agrippa I, who had executed the apostle James. Felix had paid a magician from Cyprus to convince Drusilla to leave her husband.) Paul offers them a chance to come to faith in Jesus and have their sins forgiven, but Felix is terrified and dismisses him.

Felix continues to engage with Paul, but Felix's greed and the desire for a bribe wins the day. From Felix's perspective, Paul is a leader in an empire-wide movement. He assumes Paul has access to money and could offer an inducement for his freedom. The governor needed an incentive if he was to alienate the Jewish leadership by releasing Paul. Two years passed until the leaders of the Jewish community in Caesarea went to Rome to protest Felix's violent suppression of a dispute between Jews and Gentiles.[71] As a result, Felix was removed from office.

# I APPEAL TO CAESAR! (25:1–12)

The new governor Festus needed to build a good relationship with the Jewish leadership. One of his first actions was to meet with them in Jerusalem. Paul was high on their agenda. They wanted him transferred for trial to Jerusalem so along the way they could have him ambushed. They hated Paul so much that they were prepared to risk a violent confrontation with Roman troops. However, Festus held the trial at his headquarters in Caesarea. There, the Jewish leadership repeat their charges against Paul. They accuse him of speaking and acting against the temple and the law. Paul reiterates he is a faithful Jew who upholds the law, respects the temple, and is loyal to the emperor.

Like his predecessor, Festus cannot afford to alienate the Jewish leadership. Yet Paul is a Roman citizen and the evidence against him is thin.

Festus wants Paul to agree to a trial in Jerusalem, but Paul knows he wouldn't get justice there. Paul has been told by the Lord that he must bear witness in Rome. He has been in jail for two years in Caesarea and now the governor wants to send him back to Jerusalem. He has lost confidence that Festus would guarantee a trial before a Roman court. Paul decides the only way out is to go above the governor's head, so he appeals to Caesar, the infamous Nero.[72]

Now Paul is no longer Festus's problem, but what will Festus write to the emperor regarding this case?

# YOUR GREAT LEARNING IS DRIVING YOU MAD! (25:13–26:32)

Soon after Paul appeals to the emperor, Festus receives a royal visit from King Herod Agrippa II and his sister Bernice. Agrippa ruled over the northern regions of Palestine. He also had authority over the temple and the appointment of the high priest. He was a friend of Rome and a favorite of Nero.

Agrippa was the last ruler in the dynasty of Herod the Great.[73] Herod had set the pattern for his descendants when he attempted to murder the infant Jesus. His son Herod Antipas beheaded John the Baptist. Jesus called Antipas a fox and was silent when he appeared before him. Herod the Great's grandson Agrippa I executed James the apostle and imprisoned Peter before the Lord struck him down.

Festus hoped Agrippa's knowledge of Judaism would help him frame the case for the emperor. His opinion would add weight to Festus's report. For Festus, this appears to be a dispute within Judaism about a man called Jesus, who died, but Paul says is alive. There is no legal reason Festus should detain Paul any longer.[74] It is the political realities of keeping peace with a volatile constituency that are keeping Paul in prison.

This is not a trial but a hearing to enable Festus to brief the emperor on his reasons for sending someone to the emperor who appears to be innocent.[75] It is an impressive turnout. Paul's hearing provides some theater and entertainment to important guests—a Jewish king, a Roman governor, the military commanders, and the leading men of the city.[76] Standing before them, alone, is a prisoner in chains. Through Paul's weakness, God is revealing where real power resides. The risen Lord is fulfilling his promise that Paul would be his witness before kings and governors.[77]

This is the climax of Paul's defense speeches in Acts. He speaks, not just for himself, but for the movement he represents.[78] Paul is sandwiched between the Jewish elite who want him dead, and the Roman authorities who find him innocent but fear the trouble his release would cause. Yet Paul doesn't consider himself a victim. Instead, he uses these hearings to bear witness to his Lord.[79]

Paul reaffirms his faithfulness to Judaism and identifies the central issue—does God raise the dead? Specifically, did God raise Jesus of Nazareth from the dead? As a faithful Jew, Paul recounts how he persecuted followers of Jesus, and how, on the way to Damascus, he discovered that Jesus of Nazareth was the risen Lord who shares God's glory. This Jesus commissioned Paul to serve in his mission.[80]

Ironically, as Paul stands before Jews and Gentiles in chains, he tells how Jesus promised, "I will rescue you from them."

Paul lists three elements of the mission Jesus gave him:

1. To open the eyes of both Jews and Gentiles so they could see the reality of Jesus, the crucified and victorious Messiah, Savior, and Lord.
2. To turn them from darkness to light. People are captive to Satan, but they can be liberated by embracing the truth about Jesus and turning to God in repentance.
3. To tell them that they may receive forgiveness of sins and a place among God's people, made holy by faith in Jesus.[81]

His mission was not to overturn the Jewish law and temple, or to challenge Roman rule. Instead, he was called to turn the Gentiles to a new way of life. The authority for his mission came from the crucified and risen Lord Jesus who is the fulfillment of the Hebrew Scriptures. And that is why the Jewish leaders, who rejected Jesus, wanted Paul dead.

Paul shifts from legal defense to gospel proclamation, prompting Festus to cry out, "Are you mad!" Festus cannot see how, as a member of the Roman aristocracy, he can believe in a crucified Jewish savior who has risen from the dead. Paul appeals to Agrippa's knowledge of the Scriptures, but the Jewish king will have none of it. Then Paul reveals the real purpose of his speech: He wants everyone listening—the Roman governor, the Jewish king, the military commanders, and the leading men of Caesarea—to become like him (apart from his chains!) and put their faith in Jesus.

Once again, Paul turns legal defense into gospel proclamation. He obeys Jesus' commission, at the risk of prison and death. He wants Jews like Agrippa and Gentiles like Festus to be included among the people of God.

Paul was confident that his life and ministry were in God's hands, and so before these powerful rulers he could freely proclaim the good news and call them to faith in Christ. Paul might have lobbied for all kinds of political causes or he might have demanded protection for the Christian community, but instead he offers salvation in Christ to these representatives of an oppressive empire. Paul trusted in the promise of Jesus, who said that when his disciples stand before rulers he would give them the words and the wisdom they needed.[82]

Festus and Agrippa reject the call to repent, but by now two Roman governors and a Jewish king have all agreed that Paul has done nothing under Roman law to deserve death or prison. Still, Festus will not release him. Like Pontius Pilate, he wavers between justice and expediency.

Paul was Jesus' chosen instrument who would proclaim his name in Rome. The Word continued its journey to the heart of the empire, and nothing stands in its way. Paul will testify before the emperor.[83]

Movement leaders must have the courage to stand before the rich and powerful with nothing but the gospel and the power of the Holy Spirit. Paul did not rail against the Roman state for its crimes against humanity. He spoke of Jesus and offered the forgiveness of sins and a life of discipleship to people who were far from God.

Most of us will not stand before kings, presidents, or prime ministers, but we all encounter people of power and influence. Can we stand before them with nothing but the cross of Christ and the call to repent and believe? Do we have the courage to risk shame and ridicule? Do we trust the One enthroned in heaven who laughs at the powers of this world?[84]

## DEEPER: RULERS AND AUTHORITIES

*We must obey God rather than human beings!*
ACTS 5:29

Acts is in two minds about the relationship between political power and the spread of the gospel.

The Messiah was crucified as a royal pretender on a Roman cross. Jesus warned his disciples they would be dragged before kings and rulers on account of his name.

The Sanhedrin opposed the new movement at every turn; their threats turned into violence. Yet the messengers determined to obey God rather than the authorities. Later, King Herod executed one apostle and imprisoned another. In Philippi, Paul and Silas were beaten and imprisoned by the city authorities. The last chapters of Acts show Paul unjustly accused and detained for a total of four years in Roman custody.

Yet for Luke, the primary opposition to the movement is not the Sanhedrin, Herod, or the Roman authorities but Satan, who works through sinful human beings.[85] Jesus' messengers may suffer, but God is able to remove a powerful king like Herod and ensure that Paul arrives safely in Rome to bear witness before the emperor. God rules over evil rulers, and the gospel continues to advance.

God works through the authorities to achieve his purposes. When Paul was attacked by Jewish and Gentile mobs, he was rescued by Roman authorities backed by Roman law. Gallio, the proconsul in Corinth, set an important legal precedent when he ruled that the disturbance within the Jewish community over Paul's preaching was not within his jurisdiction.[86] The city clerk of Ephesus dismissed the rioting crowd of Artemis devotees and warned them of the danger of Roman intervention unless they pursued their complaints against Paul through the courts.[87] In Jerusalem, it was the Roman garrison that rescued Paul from the murderous mob in the temple. It was Roman cavalry that rode through the night to get Paul to safety in Caesarea. During his hearings in Caesarea, one Roman governor would not convict him and the other declared Paul innocent.[88] Paul relied on his status as a Roman citizen to appeal to Caesar in Rome. On the journey to Rome, Paul was under the custody of a Roman centurion who showed leniency and kindness, and protected Paul on the journey. Awaiting trial in Rome, Paul was allowed to stay at his own accommodation, and his ministry continued at the center of the empire.

From this survey of Acts, it is possible to conclude the following about the relationship between governing authorities and the movement:

- The movement of God will be opposed by authorities corrupted by Satan.[89]

- Messengers are likely to suffer at the hands of the authorities for faithfulness to the gospel.

- Disciples must respect and obey the authorities unless this brings them into conflict with God's will.[90]

- God can judge and overrule civil and religious authorities.[91]

- God can work through the authorities and the law to protect his people and advance the gospel.[92]

- God's people may seek justice and protection before the law.[93]

- Legal trials and hearings are an opportunity to proclaim the gospel before rulers and authorities.[94]

- Disciples are not called to overthrow the state. What a broken and sinful world needs is forgiveness and the power of the Holy Spirit.[95]

These principles from Acts have great relevance for many disciples outside of the Western world where persecution is common. They often lack the power to defend themselves against ruthless governments and must cast themselves upon God as their only hope. When they read the book of Acts, they find their story in its pages.

In the Western world, persecution is on the rise. Society would like us to play the part of chaplain, serving but silent when it comes to the message of the cross. Fighting for our rights and winning back cultural and political power are not our priorities. God's Word is on a journey from Jerusalem to the ends of the earth. Not even the rulers and authorities of this world can stop it.

## MOVEMENTS TODAY: WANG MING-DAO

Conflict with the rulers and authorities is a recurring theme in Acts. For years, Paul's precious time was spent fighting the charges against him while remaining in Roman custody. Throughout church history, Christians have faced similar conflicts.

Following the revolution of 1949, the Chinese Communists set up state-controlled, Three-Self churches led by K. H. Ting. Progressive Christian leaders saw the Communist revolution as the manifestation of the kingdom of God on earth. They were more interested in reforming society than saving individuals. Ting insisted that Christians submit to political indoctrination, and to only worship in government sanctioned churches. In his writings and messages, Wang Ming-Dao rejected the ideological pressure that stripped the church of its message and mission. He placed the Word of God above political ideology.

In 1955, Wang and his wife, Jingwen, were arrested as counter-revolutionaries.

A year later, afraid of a long imprisonment or death for his wife and himself, Wang gave in to his interrogators and confessed to crimes he didn't commit. The Communists released them on condition that they join the government controlled Three-Self Church.

A broken man, Wang compromised his faith and his beliefs and confessed before the leaders of the Three-Self Church, "I am a counter-revolutionary offender. As a result of the patient attitude shown by the Government and the re-education given me, I have come to realize my errors."[96]

He was free for as long as he stood by his confession and joined the Three-Self Church. He tried, but he could not join a church that was under Communist control. After seven months, Wang and Jingwen were arrested again.

In jail, he was relentlessly mistreated by other inmates placed in his cell, and his health declined. Weak, emaciated, and depressed, he wanted to die. In his despair, God spoke to him through the prophet Micah:

> Do not gloat over me, my enemy!
> Though I have fallen, I will rise.
> Though I sit in darkness,
> the LORD will be my light.[97]

His biographer writes, "Now, with a life sentence before him and his health nearly gone, the shackles of fear fell off and a surge of courage renewed him."[98]

Wang withdrew his confession and declared he was in prison, not for criminal acts, but for preaching the gospel. In 1979, the government wanted to release him. Wang refused to leave unless the government admitted that it had wrongfully imprisoned him. Unwilling to apologize, the authorities led him to the prison door and pushed him out.[99]

He lived long enough to witness the explosive growth of the underground church, which, like him, refused to submit to government control. Despite his old age and declining influence, Wang remained a symbol of uncompromising faith until his death in 1991. Jingwen died one year later.[100]

Wang spent twenty years of his life in harsh prison conditions, knowing that for much of that time his wife was suffering too. Meanwhile, outside the walls of his prison cell, an underground movement of millions of disciples and thousands of churches, forged in suffering, was spreading.

When the Communists came to power, the Christian movement that had been in China for fifteen hundred years was threatened with annihilation. Thirty-one years later, due to the example of men and women like Wang and Jingwen Ming-Dao, there are between eighty to 130 million believers in China.[101]

There are some enduring lessons for movements today. The first comes from Wang's uncompromising refusal to bow to a political ideology because of his faithfulness to God's Word. He refused to exchange the gospel of salvation for the false hope of heaven on earth through social and political revolution. Second, like the apostle Peter, Wang found grace and restoration after breaking under interrogation. He was plagued by depression and ill-health, yet he remained faithful to the end. Third, the victory over Satan was not won cheaply. Wang suffered seemingly alone, while the numbers of disciples and churches multiplied throughout the nation. As in the book of Acts, the suffering of the messenger and the victory of the Word were interwoven. This movement was not just expanding; God was shaping its heart in the image of Jesus.

●

# NOT ONE HAIR (27:1–44)

## AD 59

God had vindicated his messenger before two Roman governors and a Jewish king. He will now vindicate him in a life and death struggle against the elements as we enter a world of "cargoes and harbors, of wind directions and sails, dinghies and anchors, and finally ... into the nightmare of storm and shipwreck."[102]

In the whole of classical literature, this is the most detailed account we have of the working of an ancient ship.[103] Why does Luke provide so much detail? It is because the message of this journey *is the message of Acts*—nothing can stop the progress of God's Word on its journey to the ends of the earth.[104]

The story bears all the marks of an eyewitness account. References to "we" return to the narrative, revealing that Luke is again traveling with Paul. So too is Aristarchus from Thessalonica, Paul's coworker in Ephesus. Later, Paul described Aristarchus as his fellow prisoner in Rome.[105]

Festus allows Luke and Aristarchus to travel with Paul; even though in chains, Paul is still treated with respect. He is handed over to a centurion named Julius who also treats Paul well, allowing him on deck and permitting contact with the churches along the way.[106] That contact provides both personal and practical help. Paul had to cover the costs of his appeal, including transport to Rome, his accommodation, and food.[107]

Paul is one of a group of prisoners on board, all headed for Rome. Many have already been convicted and destined to die in the arena.[108] Sailors were often slaves and could be Greek, Syrian, Phoenician, or Egyptian.[109] These are the Gentiles Paul has been called to reach.

There were no imperial ships for the transport of prisoners, and no private passenger ships, so Julius requisitioned passage on one of the many ships transporting grain from Egypt to Rome. The centurion would use a succession of ships to get his prisoners and their military escort to an Italian port, from where they would walk to the capital.

They sail north from Caesarea to Sidon on the coast of today's Lebanon. Julius allows Paul to meet with the disciples in Sidon and receive supplies for his journey. This church may also have been started by the disciples who fled to Phoenicia following Saul's persecution in Jerusalem.[110]

From Sidon, the ship sails around the north coast of Cyprus to Myra on the south coast of today's Turkey. Myra was a major port for Egyptian grain ships headed to Italy. They board a ship that was trying to squeeze in a second delivery before winter closed the Mediterranean.[111] It was a mistake.

With some difficulty, and behind schedule, they make it to Fair Havens on the south side of Crete. Winter is closing in. Paul, a seasoned traveler, warns them not to set out again, or the ship will be lost. Instead, they make a dash for Phoenix; a better harbor in which to spend the winter. The storm returns, and the ship is driven before the wind. The crew lighten the load by throwing cargo and tackle overboard.[112] For days, they do not see the sun or the stars. All hope is gone.

Paul is a prisoner, and yet in this crisis, he takes command. He stands up and reminds them of his warnings. He tells how the angel of his God had appeared and assured him he would stand trial before Caesar and that no one on board would perish. He challenges all those on board to trust God's promises.[113] Paul the prisoner never ceased to be Paul the missionary.

On the fourteenth night, the sailors try to escape in a lifeboat. Paul intervenes, and the soldiers cut it loose before the sailors can get away. Before dawn, Paul gathers the 276 sailors, soldiers, passengers, and prisoners together and urges them to eat. He reminds them that God had promised everyone will live. He takes bread, breaks it, gives thanks and they eat.

The crew throw the last of the grain overboard, and they wait for dawn. As the sun rises, they spot a sandy beach and head for it. Before they reach land, they strike a sandbar. Under the impact of the pounding surf, the boat begins to break up.

The soldiers ready themselves to kill every prisoner, including Paul. They know if any prisoner escapes, they will receive that prisoner's sentence. Julius, wanting to spare Paul, steps in. He orders those who can swim, to make for land. Those who can't, were to grab anything that might float and try to make it to shore. Not one life is lost.

In pursuing his calling, Paul faced riots, arrest, imprisonment, trials, and shipwreck. Yet God was at work the whole time, caring for his messenger and getting the message out to the nations. At the peak of the storm, when experienced sailors despaired, God assured Paul that all would be saved and that he would stand before the emperor. Paul was in chains, battered by storms, but the gospel would triumph.

## MOVEMENTS TODAY: WAR IN UKRAINE

Just as Jesus stood by Paul on a sinking ship, today he stands by his disciples surrounded by war.

David began visiting Ukraine on short-term mission trips almost thirty years ago.[114] On a visit to a Ukrainian prison, he saw how Jesus transformed the lives of prisoners and heard his call to stay. He fell in love with the country and with a Ukrainian woman, whom he married.

The ministry he pioneered brought humanitarian aid and the gospel to the Ukrainian people. David wanted to empower Ukrainians, and he successfully started a business that provided jobs and funds to support Ukrainian ministries.

Then war came to Ukraine, and everything changed.

Tens of thousands have lost their lives, and millions have been displaced as their homes were destroyed and their lives threatened. David's city began filling with refugees fleeing the war.

David's immediate response was to reorganize the ministry to provide short-term accommodation and food parcels. Soon, over one thousand people were lining up for food outside their facility. The city officials asked them to close the food distribution because it was too dangerous to have so many people concentrated in one place.

This became an opportunity to reset the strategy. The team realized they were showing people Jesus' love in action, but they were not telling them how they too could know him. They knew how to run Discovery Bible Study groups, so why not offer the opportunity to smaller groups of refugees?[115]

They set up an online system of registration which limited the distribution of aid to about eighty people at a time. They invited people in for tea and coffee. A table leader would ask about their experiences and needs. Then the leader would ask, "Can we read the Bible together?" Most said yes. The first story was always about Jesus calming the storm.

For five days a week, they ran thirty Discovery groups for around two hundred people and used that opportunity to distribute food parcels. Over the summer, they stopped distributing food but kept inviting displaced people to lead their own Discovery Bible Studies.

Lena and her family arrived at the center with nothing. They had fled their home, and while in the car, a mortar hit the car behind them, killing the driver and all the passengers. Lena realized that could have been them. At the center, they received food and shelter and the opportunity to talk about God, read his Word, and discover his love. Lena says, "I accepted God into my heart, into my soul and this helps me. I know I am not on my own, that the Lord is always close to me." Lena now leads Discovery groups for other displaced people.

The war has changed everything. People are open to the gospel. David can see that about one in ten Ukrainians are ready to take part in a Discovery group. The challenge is to multiply the groups beyond the ministry center. David and the team are working on how to help people run the groups away from their center, so that they can take them wherever they go on the refugee highway into Europe. When the war ends, people will return to their homes, and David's team wants the new disciples to start Discovery groups wherever they go; they want to see a vibrant disciple making ministry become a disciple making movement.

Just as a violent storm opened hearts for Paul, so the violence of war has opened Ukrainian hearts to seek after God. As C. S. Lewis said, "Pain is God's megaphone to rouse a deaf world."[116] Privilege and prosperity have made the Western world hard of hearing, but our privilege and prosperity won't last forever, and when it goes, those in the West may hear once again. Like Paul and like David in Ukraine, we need to be ready with the gospel and with proven methods of multiplying disciples.

# DEEPER: PAUL AND THE SHAPING OF A MOVEMENT LEADER

*We must go through many hardships to enter the kingdom of God.*
ACTS 14:22

About a quarter of the book of Acts tells the story of Paul's imprisonment and trials in Jerusalem, Caesarea, and Rome. Persecution, hardships, troubles, martyrdom, and disputes are the framework for

Acts. Suffering follows the expanding Word, and suffering provides the opportunity for greater expansion.[117]

On the road to Damascus, Paul suffers the loss of everything for the sake of the gospel. Suffering marked the whole of Paul's ministry; his apostolic call was also a call to suffer. He was Jesus' chosen instrument to proclaim his name to Jews and Gentiles, kings, and governors; and the Lord promised to show him how much he must suffer.[118] At the end of his final mission as a free man, the Spirit revealed that prison and hardship awaited him in every city.[119]

Paul's experience of hardship is normal for anyone pursuing movements of disciples that multiply disciples and churches. Nothing can stop the gospel, but its spread still causes grief and loss.[120]

If you asked Paul, "What was in it for you?" he would probably respond with, "I was the worst of sinners. God owed me nothing!" Or he might explain how in his darkest moments Jesus stood by him. He suffered but was never alone; his life was also filled with a joy that anticipated an eternal reward that far outweighed his light and momentary troubles.

The cross is at the heart of every genuine movement of God. Before Jesus strode into Galilee in the power of the Spirit, following the affirmation of the Father and the anointing of the Spirit, Jesus faced Satan alone in the wilderness. He won his victory through obedience to his Father's living Word, knowing that obedience would lead him to the cross. In his moment of crisis, Jesus chose the Father's will, the Father's Word, and the Father's way over Satan's shortcuts to power and success. Because of the joy set before him, Jesus endured the cross—the joy of the Father's love and the joy of welcoming prodigals home.

There's a repeated pattern in Acts; there is trouble and hardship for the messengers, and then the clouds part, and the glory of God is revealed for those with eyes to see.

Paul not only proclaimed the death and resurrection of Christ, but he also *lived* that reality, and he wanted his disciples to experience that same reality.

In Paul's hardships, God's glory was revealed for those who could see—for the sailors, soldiers, and prisoners whose lives God spared because of Paul's presence and prayers; for the barbarians of Malta who were healed and set free from demons.

Paul was becoming like Jesus. When Paul stood before Nero in chains, he stood as Jesus stood bound before Pilate and before Herod.

Paul saw Stephen forgive his assailants, and watched as he died, caught up in a vision of the glorious Son of Man.

"I want to know him," Paul writes, in "the power of his resurrection, and the fellowship of his sufferings, becoming like him in his death."[121]

It is rare for the movement of God to spread without suffering. The gospel moves, but never without pain.[122] There is victory but always through suffering. Paul learned to embrace his weakness and let God's power work through him. Suffering brought joy because he found Christ in his weakness.

Every disciple, every movement leader, is on a lifelong journey to learn and live out this truth. Failure to do so can destroy a movement of God. Jesus' victory alone in the wilderness set the pattern for his life and the example for us to follow. Sooner or later, every tree will be known by its fruit.[123]

# WE ARRIVED AT ROME (28:1–15)

### AD 60–62

The ship's company washes up on the island of Malta. The inhabitants were of Phoenician descent and were regarded as uncivilized barbarians who didn't speak Latin or Greek.[124]

Like a modern-day thriller, just when it seems the hero can relax, a snake strikes Paul's hand as he collects firewood. The locals assume he is a murderer under the judgment of the goddess Justice. But Paul had already survived so many dangers, a snakebite won't stop him getting to Rome.

Paul often established relationships with the leading figures in a community.[125] In Malta, Publius, the highest-ranking official on the island, welcomes and provides for them. Publius's father is sick with fever, and Paul heals him. News spreads, and soon people come from around the island to be cured. Paul was doing what Jesus did when he healed Peter's mother-in-law and ministered to the people of Capernaum who gathered at Peter's door.[126] On Malta, the risen Lord continued to heal through his servant.

Luke doesn't record Paul preaching the gospel or making disciples on the island. But throughout Acts, miracles serve the progress of the Word. Would the Paul we know have remained silent? No. Paul would have used the limited time to proclaim the gospel and gather new disciples into a community. After he left, Paul would have sent others to strengthen the churches in Malta. This is the repeated pattern of God's mission in Acts. Luke assumes by now we can fill in the gaps.

The islanders welcome this apostle to the Gentiles and show incredible hospitality. This is another sign of God's care for his servants as they take the gospel to every people group—even to these "barbarians" on the fringe of the civilized world.

As the story of Acts nears its conclusion, we can see how God's salvation is being proclaimed to all peoples. The Word has gone from Jerusalem to Samaria, to an Ethiopian, a Roman centurion, the Gentiles of Antioch, Jews, God-fearers, and pagans. Finally, the Word has come to the barbarians of Malta. From this array of peoples, God is forming one new people to display his glory to the world. Salvation is on its way to every corner of the earth.[127]

Spring comes three months later, and it is therefore safe to sail on to Rome. In appreciation to Paul, the islanders provide the group with all the supplies they need. Julius secures passage on a grain ship from Alexandria, which had wintered in one of Malta's safe harbors. They sail for Syracuse in Sicily and then to the Italian port city of Puteoli.

There, Julius allows Paul to stay with the community of disciples for a week while he replaces equipment and prepares to take his soldiers and the prisoners on the five- to ten-day journey to Rome.[128] For the duration of the visit, Paul's right wrist is chained to a soldier.

That there are disciples already in Puteoli is no surprise. Pilgrims returning from Jerusalem to Rome after Pentecost would have passed through that port city, bringing the gospel with them.

This will be Paul's first visit to Rome, but three years earlier he wrote to the church there and identified twenty-eight people he already knew and at least five churches meeting in homes throughout the city.[129] Luke can't tell us who planted every church. The movement of God out of Jerusalem is taking root at the same time in multiple locations.

News of Paul's arrival in Italy reaches the disciples in Rome. Some set out immediately and travel overnight to the Three Taverns to meet Paul, while others make it even further to the Forum of Appius. They are not ashamed to be associated with this brother in chains.

It is in these small details that we get another glimpse of the deep love that existed between Paul and his brothers and sisters in Christ. Wherever Paul goes on the journey to Jerusalem and then to Rome, there are tears, embraces, prayers, provisions of food and lodging. This movement is one big extended family.

When Paul wrote his letter to the churches in Rome, he spoke of his longing to visit them, and he sought their support for his mission to Spain.[130] Back then he didn't know he would enter Rome in chains, yet Paul can give thanks that after a journey of four months, the Lord has brought him safely to the heart of the empire.

Paul's original plan was to go from Jerusalem to Rome and then to Spain.[131] Instead, he faces many hardships, intensified by Satan and demonic forces. Yet God overcomes them all. Along the way, God reveals his glory to governors and kings, to pagan soldiers and sailors, to superstitious islanders, and the disciples watching on. Paul's entry to Rome, like Jesus' entry to Jerusalem, was God's triumph.

## MOVEMENTS TODAY: THE EARLY OFFER OF PRAYER

Whether it was on board a sinking ship or on an island, Paul connected with people far from God through the offer of God's help in times of need. Answered prayer became an opportunity to proclaim the gospel.

John McGinley was the senior minister of Anglican church Holy Trinity Leicester, in England. He'd just returned from a meeting with over twenty of his staff to discuss a proposal to train people to go into the community, offering prayer. It was bad news: "Steve, my team agrees this won't work in England. It may work in Australia, but it's different here. We will not be welcome if we visit people in their homes." Then he added, "But nothing is working here, so why don't we try it!"

Two months later, we trained seventy-five people from churches in Leicester and around the country to visit homes and pray for people. In five days, over 1,200 homes received a visit, and of those, over 400 welcomed prayer. Most of those who declined were still happy that we dropped by.

What happens when you offer to pray for people? Here are some responses I've heard: "Wow, I just got out of jail yesterday, and I'm trying to get back together with my partner and two sons. Pray for that." "Pray for me, my dearest friend died last week." "Can you pray I'll win the lottery?" "I can't believe it. Yesterday I asked God, 'If you're there, send somebody' … and you turn up!"

All around the world, one of the simplest ways to engage someone in a conversation about Jesus is by asking, "Is there anything I can pray for you?" It touches people you already know, as well as people you've met for the first time.

# WITH BOLDNESS AND WITHOUT HINDRANCE (28:16–31)

As Paul strode into Rome with his escort of soldiers, prisoners, and disciples, he was entering the world's largest city with around one million inhabitants, most of whom lived in cramped apartments in one of the many thousands of tenement buildings.

As a citizen who had appealed to Caesar, Paul could stay in his own accommodation, chained at the wrist to a soldier. The ground floor of an apartment building was reserved for shops. Rent in Rome was four times more expensive than in the rest of Italy.[132] Only the very wealthy could afford the second story. Paul needed to rent a third-floor apartment big enough to house himself, his guard, and his many visitors.

As a prisoner, Paul could not ply his trade.[133] He either had independent means or relied on the generosity of others to pay for his accommodation and living costs. Fortunately, he was free to receive visitors, and so the gospel still went out.

Now that Paul is in Rome, we might expect Luke to focus on his trial or his relationship with the churches in Rome. Instead, he concentrates on Paul's witness to the Jewish community, which numbered around twenty to thirty thousand people.[134] Paul meets with the Jewish leaders and tells them of the last two years of conflict and trials. He affirms his faithfulness to Judaism, his innocence before the law, and his belief that Jesus' resurrection fulfilled the hope of Israel.

The leaders had heard nothing of the matter from those in Jerusalem, suggesting Jerusalem had dropped the case due to lack of evidence.

The Jewish leaders come to his accommodation and sit with Paul from morning to evening as he explains about the kingdom of God. He takes them through the Hebrew Scriptures and teaches them about Jesus the King. This is the same message the risen Lord taught his disciples following the resurrection. It's the same message Peter preached at Pentecost. God's reign has come in the life, death, and resurrection of Jesus, the Messiah. He calls everyone to repent and believe for the forgiveness of sins.

As usual, Paul's audience is divided; some are convinced, and others will not believe. As had happened so often, a dispute breaks out among the leaders, which divides the Jewish community. Some would not embrace their King.

Paul gives a last prophetic warning from the words of Isaiah, confirming that no matter how much they heard and saw, they would not understand or perceive.[135] This was God's judgment because their hearts were hard. If only they would turn, God would heal them. There was hope: In Isaiah's day a remnant believed and survived God's judgment. The Jews of Rome were facing the same choice.[136]

Despite rejection and persecution, Paul never lost his love or his hope for ethnic Israel.[137] The mission to the Jewish people would continue, but now Paul must focus his mission in Rome on the Gentiles who are ready. For the mission of true Israel is to be a light to the nations.

There is both tragedy and triumph here. At the beginning of Luke's Gospel, Simeon predicted Jesus would divide Israel.[138] Tragically, as a people, Israel has rejected their Messiah, but the mission of faithful Israel, made up of Jews and Gentiles who put their faith in Jesus, will continue.

Paul is not alone in Rome. In addition to those named in his epistle, he has his coworkers with him. His prison letters mention Epaphras, Mark, Aristarchus, Demas, Luke, Tychicus, and Timothy.[139]

Paul can't pursue his trade, but he can dictate letters. During this time Paul writes to the Philippians and explains how his sufferings have advanced the gospel.[140] He is in chains and on trial for his life, but the gospel is still going out. He records how the knowledge of Christ is spreading throughout the elite Praetorian Guard, who were charged with the emperor's protection. In addition, there are now believers in Caesar's household, the body responsible for running the empire.[141] Also, because of Paul's example, most of the believers in Rome have become confident in the Lord and are proclaiming the gospel without fear.[142]

Paul isn't ashamed or frustrated by his imprisonment—he rejoices in it! The Spirit of Christ is working as the believers had prayed. He is ready to be freed, but he is also prepared to be condemned and executed. What matters to Paul is that Christ is proclaimed.[143] God's power is revealed in the weakness of his messengers who through their faith put the wisdom of the world to shame.

While Paul was in custody, Jesus' purpose, that the gospel would go from Jerusalem to the ends of the earth, was being fulfilled. This is the victory of God's Word.[144]

The Lord had brought Paul safely to Rome where he will testify before Caesar. For another two years, Paul welcomed all those who came to visit him. "He proclaimed the kingdom of God and taught about the Lord Jesus Christ—*with all boldness and without hindrance!*" (italics mine).[145] These are Luke's last words.

# ACTS ENDS, BUT THE MOVEMENT CONTINUES

This movement is of God, and nothing can stop it.[146] This is the gospel of the kingdom and the good news of Jesus Christ as one message.[147] The King rules over sin, death, and the devil; nothing can overcome his saving love.[148]

From the center of the empire, the Word will continue to spread and grow and multiply no matter what happens to Paul. Wherever the Word goes, it leaves in its wake disciples and churches to the glory of God.

Acts is not a biography of Paul or any of its human characters. Acts tells the story of a movement birthed out of the life, death, and victory of Jesus in fulfillment of the Scriptures. That movement grows through the spread of his living Word in the power of the Holy Spirit.[149]

Luke leaves Acts open-ended and unresolved. We don't know what happened to Paul.[150] What matters is the movement of God.

God—the Father, Son, and Holy Spirit—is the true hero of Acts. He completes the work as the gospel goes out through bold and embattled witnesses, leaving in its wake disciples and churches. Every place, every people.

We've reached the end of Acts, yet the story goes on. Why not write yourself into it? The Word and Spirit cannot be confined to our meetings. Step out into a lost world, confident that God has called you into this great movement that begins where you are and does not stop until there are disciples and churches among every people and in every place … from Jerusalem to the ends of the earth!

# APPENDIX: THE 4-FIELDS

# The 4-Fields
## Mark 4:26-29

The 4-Fields[1] answers five questions:

1. Entry: How do I enter a new field?
2. Gospel: What do I say?
3. Discipleship: How do I make disciples?
4. Church: How will I form healthy churches?
5. Leaders: How do I multiply leaders?

movements.net/4fields

# 4-Fields Discovery

Passage:

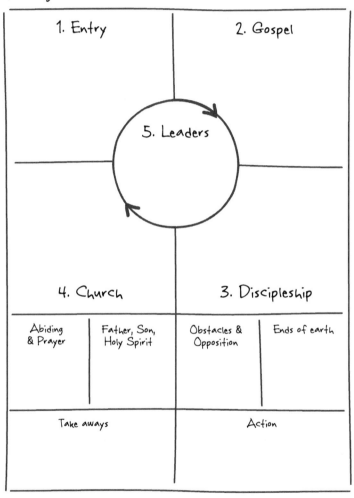

| 1. Entry | 2. Gospel |
| --- | --- |

5. Leaders

| 4. Church | 3. Discipleship |
| --- | --- |

| Abiding & Prayer | Father, Son, Holy Spirit | Obstacles & Opposition | Ends of earth |

| Take aways | Action |

# 4-FIELDS DISCOVERY WORKSHEET

Read a chapter of Acts and use the worksheet to answer these questions.

**1. Entry**
- What is the location?
- How do they engage people?

**2. Gospel**
- What is their message?

**3. Discipleship**
- How do they make disciples?

**4. Church**
- How do they start and strengthen communities of disciples?

**5. Leaders**
- How do they reproduce leaders?


**Abiding & Prayer**
- How do they go deeper with God through prayer and surrender?

**Father, Son and Holy Spirit**
- What is the evidence of God's activity?

**Obstacles & Opposition**
- What hardships and opposition do they face?

**Ends of the earth**
- How does the Word spread to every place and every people?

**Takeaways**
- What has God shown you?

**Action**
- What will you do?

movements.net/4fields-acts

# APPENDIX: 3-THIRDS DISCIPLESHIP

| First Third | Second Third | Final Third |
|---|---|---|
| 1. Mutual care<br><br>2. Worship<br><br>3. Loving accountability<br><br>4. Vision | 5. New Lesson<br>Discovery Bible Study<br>• Read the text and retell it in your own words.<br>• What does the passage teach us about God?<br>• What does it teach us about people?<br>• Is there a command to obey or an example to follow?<br>And/or a new skill<br><br>6. Practice the new learning | 7. Set goals<br>• How will you obey what you have learned?<br>• Who could you share with?<br><br>8. Commissioning and prayer |

Go to: movements.net/3-disciples

# APPENDIX: DISCOVERY BIBLE STUDY

David Watson is a pioneer of this approach, and these are the questions he recommends for a group of people who don't yet know Christ. He adapts the questions once they become disciples. This process can be used with any passage of Scripture, although there are sets of passages he recommends.

1. Ask everyone to share something they are thankful for.
2. Ask everyone to share something that is bothering them.
3. Read the Scripture passage. If you have access to an audio Bible, you may choose to listen to the passage.
4. Ask someone to repeat the story. Ask the group if the person left anything important out of the story.
5. Ask: "What does this story tell us about God? What does this story tell us about man? What does this story tell us about God's plan." Give them time to answer. Resist the urge to tell them what the story means. If they aren't getting it, read additional passages of Scripture or ask more questions.
6. Ask: "If this story is true, how does that change how we act?"
7. Ask: "What questions do you have about this story?"
8. Ask "Do you know anyone who needs to hear this story?" Encourage them to share the story with anyone they name.
9. Ask: "Is there anyone you know who needs help? What can we do to help them?" Have the group decide what needs to be done and commit to doing it before the next meeting.

movements.net/s/Discovering-God-Manual-Watson.pdf

# APPENDIX: THE CHURCH CIRCLE

The Church Circle
Acts 2:36–47

Those who repent and believe are added to the church.

Disciples are baptized and have the authority to baptize.

Prayer: Corporate and individual prayer.

Disciples are trained to share the gospel.

Love for one another expressed in deeds.

Worship: Corporate and individual worship.

Regular celebration of the Lord's Supper.

Giving to those in need and for the spread of the gospel.

Learning obedience to God's Word.

Recognized local leaders.

A dotted line circle indicates a group. A solid circle indicates the group identifies as a church.

movements.net/4-church

# APPENDIX: THE 5-LEVELS OF LEADERSHIP

Multiplying movements require five levels of leadership:[2]

1.  Seed-Sower: A disciple who shares the gospel.

2.  Church Planter: A Seed-Sower who learns how to make disciples and plant churches.

3.  Church Multiplier: A Church Planter who learns how to start churches that reproduce generations of new disciples and churches.

4.  Multiplication Trainer: A Church Multiplier who learns how to equip other church multipliers to achieve third- and fourth-generation churches.

5.  Movement Catalyst: A Multiplication Trainer who takes on a broad responsibility to reach an unreached population segment or region.

movements.net/5-leaders.

# The 5-Levels of Leadership

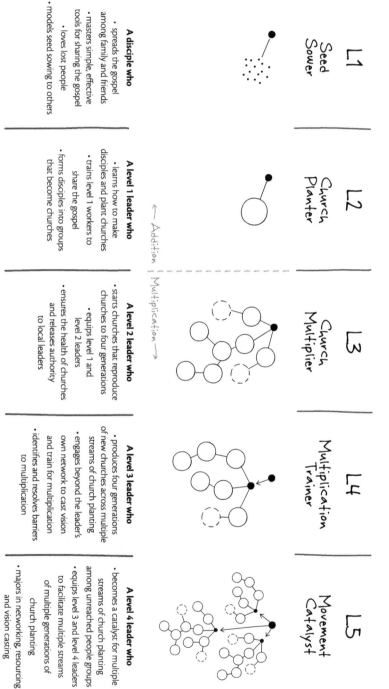

**L1**
**Seed Sower**

**A disciple who**
- spreads the gospel among family and friends
- masters simple, effective tools for sharing the gospel
- loves lost people
- models seed sowing to others

**L2**
**Church Planter**

**A level 1 leader who**
- learns how to make disciples and plant churches
- trains level 1 workers to share the gospel
- forms disciples into groups that become churches

← Addition

Multiplication →

**L3**
**Church Multiplier**

**A level 2 leader who**
- starts churches that reproduce churches to four generations
- equips level 1 and level 2 leaders
- ensures the health of churches and releases authority to local leaders

**L4**
**Multiplication Trainer**

**A level 3 leader who**
- produces four generations of new churches across multiple streams of church planting
- engages beyond the leader's own network to cast vision and train for multiplication
- identifies and resolves barriers to multiplication

**L5**
**Movement Catalyst**

**A level 4 leader who**
- becomes a catalyst for multiple streams of church planting among unreached people groups
- equips level 3 and level 4 leaders to facilitate multiple streams of multiple generations of church planting
- majors in networking, resourcing and vision casting

# BIBLIOGRAPHY

Addison, Steve. *Movements That Change the World: Five Keys to Spreading the Gospel.* Revised. Downers Grove, IL: InterVarsity Press, 2011.

———. *Pioneering Movements: Leadership That Multiplies Disciples and Churches.* Downers Grove, IL: InterVarsity Press, 2015.

———. "The Continuing Ministry of the Apostle in the Church's Mission." D.Min. diss., Fuller Theological Seminary, 1995.

———. *The Rise and Fall of Movements: A Roadmap for Leaders.* Cody, WY: 100 Movements Publishing, 2019.

———. *What Jesus Started: Joining the Movement, Changing the World.* Downers Grove, IL: InterVarsity Press, 2012.

———. *Your Part in God's Story: 40 Days from Genesis to Revelation.* Cody, WY: 100 Movements Publishing, 2021.

Addison, Steve, and David Bareham. "178-Becoming a Great Commission Church." *Movements*, November 29, 2018. https://www.movements.net/blog/blog/2018/11/15/178-a-local-church-takes-on-the-great-commission.

Addison, Steve, and Jeff Bennett. "275-Church to Movement in Canada." *Movements*, June 2, 2022. https://www.movements.net/blog/blog/2022/5/31/275-church-to-movement-in-canada.

Addison, Steve, and Chris Clayman. "172-Mali to New York and Back." *Movements*, September 5, 2018. https://www.movements.net/blog/blog/2018/7/18/172-mali-to-new-york-and-back.

Addison, Steve, and Troy Cooper. "285-LA Update." *Movements*, October 24, 2022. https://www.movements.net/blog/blog/2022/10/19/285-la-update.

Addison, Steve, and David. "282-Making Disciples in Ukraine." *Movements*, September 9, 2022. https://www.movements.net/blog/blog/2022/9/9/282-making-disciples-in-ukraine.

Addison, Steve, and Joey Gordy. "281-Joey's Story." *Movements*, August 25, 2022. https://www.movements.net/blog/blog/2022/8/23/281-joeys-story.

Addison, Steve, and Rajiv. "291-Mumbai Hilltop of Hope." *Movements*, January 13, 2023. https://www.movements.net/blog/blog/2022/12/2/291-mumbai-hilltop-of-hope .

Addison, Steve, and Jim McKnight. "284-NoPlaceLeft Army." *Movements*, October 6, 2022. https://www.movements.net/blog/blog/2022/9/23/284-noplaceleft-army.

Addison, Steve, and Stan Parks. "247-Multiplying Movements Among Unreached People Groups." *Movements*, May 6, 2021, https://www.movements.net/blog/blog/2021/4/27/247-multiplying-movements-among-unreached-people-groups.

Addison, Steve, and Terry and Amy Ruff. "194-Multiplying Movements in West Africa." *Movements*, June 27, 2019. https://www.movements.net/blog/blog/2019/6/18/194-multiplying-movements-in-west-africa.

Addison, Steve, and Lyndsey and Collin Seale. "198-Workplace Movements." *Movements*, August 7, 2019. https://www.movements.net/blog/blog/2019/8/8/198-workplace-movements.

Addison, Steve, and John and Lauren Sweatte. "286-John and Lauren's Story." *Movements*,

November4,2022.https://www.movements.net/blog/blog/2022/11/4/286-john-and-laurens-story.

Addison, Steve, and Jeff Timblin. "205-One Pastor Is Bringing Movements Home." *Movements*, November 28, 2019. https://www.movements.net/blog/blog/2019/11/21/bringing-movements-home.

Addison, Steve, and Don and Theresa Waybright. "288-Don and Theresa's Story." *Movements*, December 6, 2022. https://www.movements.net/blog/blog/2022/11/24/288-don-and-theresas-story.

Addison, Steve, and Justin White. "156-Growing Workers for NoPlaceLeft." *Movements*, February 27, 2018. https://www.movements.net/blog/blog/2018/2/25/156-growing-workers-for-noplaceleft.

Albert, Eleanor. "Christianity in China." *Council on Foreign Relations*. October 11, 2018. https://www.cfr.org/backgrounder/christianity-china.

Allen, Roland. *Missionary Methods: St Paul's or Ours?* 4th ed. London, UK: World Dominion Press, 1956.

———. *The Spontaneous Expansion of the Church*. 3rd ed. London, UK: World Dominion Press, 1956.

Anderson, Allan. *An Introduction to Pentecostalism: Global Charismatic Christianity*. Cambridge, UK: Cambridge University Press, 2004.

Barnett, Paul. *Paul: Missionary of Jesus*. Vol. 2. After Jesus. Grand Rapids, MI: Eerdmans, 2008.

Barnett, Paul. *Paul and His Friends in Leadership: How They Changed the World*. Abingdon, UK: Bible Reading Fellowship, 2017.

Bauckham, Richard. "James and the Jerusalem Church." In *The Book of Acts in Its Palestinian Setting*, edited by Richard Bauckham, 4:415–80. The Book of Acts in Its First Century Setting, Grand Rapids, MI: Eerdmans, 1995.

Beasley-Murray, G. R. *Baptism in the New Testament*. Carlisle, UK: Paternoster, 1962.

Bharath, Deepa. "Hundreds Gather in Huntington Beach to Be Baptized with Cold Dunk in the Ocean." *Orange County Register*, July 25, 2020.

Blue, Bradley. "Acts and the House Church." In *Vol. 2, The Book of Acts in Its Graeco-Roman Setting*, edited by David W. Gill and Conrad H. Gempf, 119–222. Book of Acts in Its First Century Setting. Grand Rapids, MI: Eerdmans, 1994.

Bock, Darrell L. *Acts*. Kindle. Baker Exegetical Commentary on the New Testament. Grand Rapids, MI: Baker, 2007.

Boda, Mark J. *Return to Me: A Biblical Theology of Repentance*, edited by D. A. Carson. New Studies in Biblical Theology 35. Downers Grove, IL: InterVarsity Press, 2015.

Boer, Harry R. *Pentecost and Missions*. Grand Rapids, MI: Eerdmans, 1961.

Bowers, Paul. "Fulfilling the Gospel: The Scope of the Pauline Mission." *Journal of the Evangelical Theological Society* 30 (June 1987): 185–98.

Bruce, F. F. *Paul: Apostle of the Free Spirit*. Revised. Exeter, UK: Paternoster Press, 1980.

———. "The Acts of the Apostles Today." *Bulletin of the John Rylands Library* 65, no. 1 (1982): 36–56.

———. *The Book of Acts*, edited by Gordon D. Fee, Revised. New International Commentary on the New Testament. Grand Rapids, MI: Eerdmans, 1988.

Busco, Elizabeth E. *The Reformation of Machismo: Evangelical Conversion and Gender in Colombia*. Austin, TX: University of Texas Press, 1995.

Casper, Jason. "Researchers Find Christians in Iran Approaching 1 Million." *Christianity Today*, September 3, 2020. https://www.christianitytoday.com/news/2020/september/iran-christian-conversions-gamaan-religion-survey.html.

Clayman, Chris. *Superplan: A Journey into God's Story*. Monument, CO: WIGTake Resources, 2018.

Clinton, J. Robert. *The Making of a Leader: Recognizing the Lessons and Stages of Leadership Development*. Revised. Colorado Springs, CO: NavPress, 2014.

Cole, Carolyn. "Beach Baptisms Draw Large Gatherings to the Shore." *Los Angeles Times*, August 13, 2020.

Cook, Harold R. "Who Really Sent the First Missionaries?" *The Evangelical Missions Quarterly* 13 (October 1975): 233–39.

Cooper, Troy. "4Fields Discovery: Gospels and Acts." Blog. *Movements*. https://www.movements.net/training-timothys.

———. "Church Circles Discovery: Epistles." Blog. *Movements*. https://www.movements.net/training-timothys.

Corley, Felix. "Obituary: Haik Hovsepian Mehr." *The Independent*, February 1, 1994. https://www.independent.co.uk/news/people/obituary-haik-hovsepian-mehr-1391238.html.

Cotterell, Peter F. *Born at Midnight*. Chicago, IL: Moody, 1973.

Cunningham, Scott. "'Through Many Tribulations' The Theology of Persecution in Luke-Acts." *Journal for the Study of the New Testament Supplement Series* 142. Sheffield, UK: Sheffield Academic Press, 1997.

Davids, Peter H. "Miracles in Acts." In *Dictionary of the Later New Testament & Its Developments*, edited by Ralph P. Martin and Peter H. Davids, 1085–92. Compendium of Contemporary Biblical Scholarship Series. Downers Grove, IL: IVP Academic, 1997.

Davis, Raymond J. *Fire on the Mountains: The Story of a Miracle—the Church in Ethiopia*. Grand Rapids, MI: Zondervan, 1966.

DeYoung, Kevin, and Greg Gilbert. *What Is the Mission of the Church?: Making Sense of Social Justice, Shalom, and the Great Commission*. Wheaton, IL: Crossway Books, 2011.

Elliot, J. H. "Temple Versus Household in Luke-Acts: A Contrast in Social Institutions." *HTS Theological Studies* 47, no. 1 (1991).

Ellis, E. Earle. "Paul and His Co-Workers." *NTS* 17 (71, 1970): 437–52.

———. "Paul and His Coworkers." In *Dictionary of Paul and His Letters*, edited by Gerald F. Hawthorne, Ralph P. Martin, and Daniel G. Reid, 184–88. A Compendium of Contemporary Biblical Scholarship. Grand Rapids, MI: InterVarsity Press, 2009.

———. "The Role of the Christian Prophet in Acts." In *Apostolic History and the Gospel: Biblical and Historical Essays Presented to F. F. Bruce*, edited by W. Ward Gasque and Ralph P. Martin, 55–67. Milton Keynes, UK: Paternoster, 1970.

Ferdinando, Keith. "Mission: A Problem of Definition." *Themelios* 33:1 (2008): 46–59.

Flew, R. Newton. *Jesus and His Church: A Study of the Idea of the Ecclesia in the New Testament*. London, UK: Epworth Press, 1938.

Foster, Richard J. *Streams of Living Water: Essential Practices From the Six Great Traditions of Christian Faith*. Grand Rapids, MI: Zondervan, 2001.

Frame, John M. *The Doctrine of the Word of God*. Vol. 4. A Theology of Lordship. Phillipsburg, NJ: P & R Publishing, 2010.

Gaechter, Paul. "The Hatred of the House of Annas." *Theological Studies* 8, no. 1 (1947): 3–34.

Galanos, Chris. *From Megachurch to Multiplication: A Church's Journey Toward Movement.* Lubbock, TX: Experience Life Church, 2018.

Garrison, David. *A Wind in the House of Islam: How God Is Drawing Muslims Around the World to Faith in Jesus Christ.* Monument, CO: WIGTake Resources, 2014.

———. *Church Planting Movements: How God Is Redeeming a Lost World.* Midlothian, VA: WIGtake Resources, 2003.

Gaventa, Beverly Roberts. *The Acts of the Apostles.* Abingdon New Testament Commentaries. Nashville, TN: Abingdon Press, 2003.

———. "Theology and Ecclesiology in the Miletus Speech: Reflections on Content and Context." *New Testament Studies* 50 (2004): 36–52.

Gerlach, Luther P., and Virginia H. Hine. *People, Power, Change: Movements of Social Transformation.* Indianapolis and New York: The Bobbs-Merrill Company, 1970.

Getachew, Ato. "The Genesis and Growth of the Kale Heywet Church," http://www.ekhc.org.et/ history.htm. Accessed February 24, 2006.

Gill, John. "Wang Ming-Dao (1900–1991): Faithful Amid Political Coercion." *The Gospel Coalition*, August 3, 2018. https://www.thegospelcoalition.org/article/ wang-ming-dao-faithful-political-coercion.

Green, Chris. "The King His Kingdom and the Gospel: Matthew, Mark and Luke-Acts." In *God's Power to Save: One Gospel for a Complex World?*, edited by Chris Green, 104–37. Leicester, UK: InterVarsity Press, 2006.

Green, Gene L. *The Letters to the Thessalonians.* Pillar New Testament Commentary. Grand Rapids, MI: Apollos, 2002.

Green, Joel B. "Good News to Whom? Jesus and the 'Poor' in the Gospel of Luke." In *The Gospel of Luke in Jesus of Nazareth: Lord and Christ: Essays on the Historical Jesus and New Testament Christology*, edited by Joel B. Green and Max Turner, 59–74. Grand Rapids, MI: Eerdmans, 1994.

———. "Persevering Together in Prayer: The Significance of Prayer in the Acts of the Apostles." In *Into God's Presence: Prayer in the New Testament*, edited by Richard N. Longenecker, loc. 2440–2711, Kindle. Grand Rapids, MI: Eerdmans, 2001.

———. "Salvation to the End of the Earth: God as the Saviour in the Acts of the Apostles." In *Witness to the Gospel: The Theology of Acts*, edited by I. Howard Marshall and David G. Peterson, 83–106. Grand Rapids, MI: Eerdmans, 1998.

———. *The Gospel of Luke*, edited by Gordon D. Fee. New International Commentary on the New Testament. Grand Rapids, MI: Eerdmans, 1997.

Hartley, Karen. "Biography of Haik Hovsepian-Mehr," *Truett Journal of Church and Mission* 2, no. 1 (2004): 43–57.

Harvey, Thomas Alan. *Acquainted With Grief: Wang Mingdao's Stand for the Persecuted Church in China.* Grand Rapids, MI: Brazos Press, 2002.

Hawthorne, Gerald F. *Philippians*, vol. 43, Word Biblical Commentary. Waco, TX: Word Books, 1983.

Hengel, Anna Maria Schwemer, and Martin Hengel. *Paul Between Damascus and Antioch.* Louisville, KY: Westminster John Knox Press, 1997.

Hengel, Martin. *Acts and the History of Earliest Christianity.* Philadelphia, PA: Fortress Press, 1979.

———. "Paul in Arabia." *Bulletin of Biblical Research* 12 (2002): 47–66.

———. *Poverty and Riches in the Early Church: Aspects of a Social History of Early Christianity*. Kindle. Minneapolis, MN: Fortress Press, 1974.

———. "The Origins of the Christian Mission." In *Between Jesus and Paul*. London, UK: SCM, 1983.

Hoekendijk, Johannes C. *The Church Inside Out*, edited by L. A. Hoedemaker and Pieter Tijmes. Translated by Isaac C. Rottenberg. London, UK: SCM, 1966.

Holmas, Geir Otto. *Prayer and Vindication in Luke-Acts: The Theme of Prayer within the Context of the Legitimating and Edifying Objective of the Lukan Narrative*, edited by Mark Goodacre. Library of New Testament Studies 433. London, UK: T&T Clark, 2011.

House, Paul R. "Suffering and the Purpose of Acts." *Journal of the Evangelical Theological Society* 33, no. 3 (September 1990): 317–30.

Howell, Don N. Jr. "Confidence in the Spirit as the Governing Ethos of the Pauline Mission." In *The Holy Spirit and Mission Dynamics*, edited by C. Douglas McConnell, 36–65. Evangelical Missiological Series 5. Pasadena, CA: William Carey Library, 1997.

Jenkins, Philip. *The Next Christendom: The Coming of Global Christianity*. New York, NY: Oxford University Press, 2002.

Johnson, Andrew. *If I Give My Soul: Faith Behind Bars in Rio de Janeiro*. Kindle. New York, NY: Oxford University Press, 2017.

Kee, Howard Clark. *Good News to the Ends of the Earth: The Theology of Acts*. London, UK: SCM, 1990.

Keener, Craig. *Acts*. Cambridge, UK: Cambridge University Press, 2020.

———. "Why Does Luke Use Tongues as a Sign of the Spirit's Empowerment?" *Journal of Pentecostal Theology* 15, no. 2 (2007): 177–84.

Kienzler, Jonathan. *The Fiery Holy Spirit: The Spirit's Relationship with Judgment in Luke-Acts*, edited by John Christopher Thomas. Vol. 44. Journal of Pentecostal Theology. Dorset, UK: Deo Publishing, 2015.

Kodell, Jerome. "The Word of God Grew: The Ecclesial Tendency of Logos in Acts 6:7; 12:24; 19:20." *Biblica* 55 (1974): 505–19.

Köstenberger, Andreas J., and T. Desmond Alexander. *Salvation to the Ends of the Earth: A Biblical Theology of Mission*, edited by D. A. Carson. 2nd ed. Vol. 53. New Studies in Biblical Theology. Downers Grove, IL: InterVarsity Press, 2020.

Köstenberger, Andreas J., and Peter T. O'Brien. *Salvation to the Ends of the Earth: A Biblical Theology of Mission*. 1st ed. Vol. 11. New Studies in Biblical Theology. Downers Grove, IL: InterVarsity Press, 2001.

Kruger, Michael J. *Canon Revisited: Establishing the Origins and Authority of the New Testament Books*. Wheaton, IL: Crossway, 2012.

Kung, Hans. *The Church*. Garden City, NY: Image, 1967.

Lampe, G. W. H. "Miracles in the Acts of the Apostles." In *Miracles*, edited by C. F.D. Moule. London, UK: A. R. Mowbray, 1965.

Larkin, William J. Jr. *Acts*, edited by Stuart D. Briscoe and Haddon Robinson. The IVP New Testament Commentary Series. Downers Grove, IL: InterVarsity Press, 1995.

Lewis, C. S. *The Problem of Pain*. New York, NY: HarperCollins, 1940.

Lian, Xi. *Redeemed by Fire: The Rise of Popular Christianity in Modern China*. Kindle. New Haven, CT: Yale University Press, 2010.

Liefeld, Walter L. "Women and Evangelism in the Early Church." *Missiology* 15, no. 3 (July 1987): 291–98.

Lightfoot, J. B. *The Epistle of St. Paul to the Galatians*. Grand Rapids, MI: Zondervan, 1957.

Lofland, John, and Rodney Stark. "Becoming a World-Saver: A Theory of Conversion to a Deviant Perspective." *American Sociological Review* 30 (1965): 862–75.

Long, Justin. "1% of the World: A Macroanalysis of 1,369 Movements to Christ." *Mission Frontiers*, December 2020, 37–42.

Longenecker, Richard N. *Luke-Acts*. Kindle. Vol. 10. The Expositor's Bible Commentary. Grand Rapids, MI: Zondervan, 2007.

Maddox, Robert. *The Purpose of Luke-Acts*. Edinburgh, UK: T&T Clark, 1982.

Malherbe, Abraham J. *Paul and the Thessalonians: The Philosophic Tradition of Pastoral Care*. Proclamation Commentaries. Mifflintown, PA: Sigler Press, 2000.

Manson, T. W. *The Church's Ministry*. London, UK: Hodder & Stoughton, 1948.

Marguerat, Daniel. *The First Christian Historian: Writing the "Acts of the Apostles,"* edited by Richard Bauckham. Monograph Series—Society for New Testament Studies 121. Cambridge, UK: Cambridge University Press, 2002.

Marshall, I. Howard. *The Acts of the Apostles: An Introduction and Commentary*. Tyndale New Testament Commentaries. Leicester, UK: InterVarsity Press, 1980.

———. *The Gospel of Luke*. The New International Greek Testament Commentary. Grand Rapids, MI: Eerdmans, 1978.

Marshall, I. Howard, and David G. Peterson, eds. *Witness to the Gospel: The Theology of Acts*. Grand Rapids, MI: Eerdmans, 1998.

Matson, David. *Household Conversion Narratives in Acts: Pattern and Interpretation*. Sheffield, UK: Sheffield Academic Press, 1996.

Meeks, Wayne A. *The First Urban Christians: The Social World of the Apostle Paul*. New Haven, CT: Yale University Press, 1983.

Menzies, Robert. "Acts 2:17–21: A Paradigm for Pentecostal Mission." *Journal of Pentecostal Theology* 17 (2008): 200–218. https://pentecost.asia/articles/acts-217-21-a-paradigm-for-pentecostal-mission.

Michele, C. and Joseph [surname withheld]. "Field-Governed Mission Structures: Part 1: In the New Testament." The International Journal of Frontier Missiology 18:2 (Summer 2001): 59–66.

Monnig, Matthew S. "Satan in Lukan Narrative and Theology: Human Agency in the Conflict between the Authority of Satan and the Power of God." PhD diss, Duke University, 2019.

Moo, Douglas J. *The Epistle to the Romans*, edited by Gordon D. Fee. New International Commentary on the New Testament. Grand Rapids, MI: Eerdmans, 1996.

O'Brien, Peter T. "Caesar's Household." In *Dictionary of Paul and His Letters*, edited by Ralph P. Martin Gerald F. Hawthorne, 83–84. Compendium of Contemporary Biblical Scholarship Series. Downers Grove, IL: IVP Academic, 1993.

———. *Consumed by Passion: Paul and the Dynamic of the Gospel*. Homebush West, NSW: Lancer, 1993.

———. "Mission, Witness, and the Coming of the Spirit." *Bulletin for Biblical Research* 9 (1999): 203–14.

———. "Prayer in Luke-Acts." *Tyndale Bulletin* 24 (1973): 111–27.

O'Reilly, Leo. *Word and Sign in the Acts of the Apostles: A Study in Lucan Theology*. Rome, Italy: Gregorian Biblical BookShop, 1987.

O'Toole, Robert F. "Activity of the Risen Jesus in Luke-Acts." *Biblica* 62, no. 4 (1981): 471–98.

Pao, David W. *Acts and the Isaianic New Exodus*. Biblical Studies Library. Grand Rapids, MI: Baker Academic, 2002.

Patzia, Arthur G. *The Emergence of the Church*. Downers Grove, IL: InterVarsity Press, 2001.

Penney, John Michael. *The Missionary Emphasis of Lukan Pneumatology*. Journal of Pentecostal Theology Supplement Series 12. Sheffield, UK: Sheffield Academic Press, 1997.

Peterson, David G. *The Acts of the Apostles*. Pillar New Testament Commentary. Grand Rapids, MI: Eerdmans, 2009.

Pierson, Paul. "Historical Development of the Christian Movement: Lecture Notes." Pasadena, CA: Fuller School of World Mission, 1988.

Plummer, Robert L. *Paul's Understanding of the Church's Mission: How Did the Apostle Paul Expect the Early Christian Communities to Evangelize?* Paternoster Biblical Monographs. Eugene, OR: Wipf & Stock Publishers, 2006.

Polhill, John B. *Acts: An Exegetical and Theological Exposition of Holy Scripture*. The New American Commentary 26. Nashville, TN: Broadman & Holman, 1992.

Prinz, Emanuel. *Movement Catalysts: Profile of an Apostolic Leader*. Independently published, 2022.

Prinz, Emanuel, and Dave Coles. "The Person, Not the Method: An Essential Ingredient for Catalyzing a Movement." *Mission Frontiers* 43 (August 2021): 42–45.

Rackham, Richard Belward. *The Acts of the Apostles: An Exposition*. 8th ed. Westminster Commentaries. London, UK: Methuen & Co., 1919.

Rapske, Brian. *The Book of Acts and Paul in Roman Custody*. Vol. 3. The Book of Acts in Its First Century Setting. Grand Rapids, MI: Eerdmans, 2004.

Reinhardt, Wolfgang. "The Population Size of Jerusalem and the Numerical Growth of the Jerusalem Church." In *The Book of Acts in Its Palestinian Setting*, edited by Richard Bauckham, 4:237–65. The Book of Acts in Its First Century Setting. Grand Rapids, MI: Eerdmans, 1995.

Renn, Aaron M. "The Three Worlds of Evangelicalism." *First Things*, February 2022. https://www.firstthings.com/article/2022/02/the-three-worlds-of-evangelicalism.

Rosner, Brian. "The Progress of the Word." In *Witness to the Gospel: The Theology of Acts*, edited by I. Howard Marshall and David Peterson, 215–33. Grand Rapids, MI: Eerdmans, 1998.

Saiya, Nilay, and Stuti Manchanda. "Paradoxes of Pluralism, Privilege, and Persecution: Explaining Christian Growth and Decline Worldwide." *Sociology of Religion* 83, no. 1 (Spring 2022): 60–80.

Schnabel, Eckhard J. *Acts*, edited by Clinton Arnold. Zondervan Exegetical Commentary on the New Testament. Grand Rapids, MI: Zondervan, 2012.

———. *Early Christian Mission: Jesus and the Twelve*. Vol. 1. Downers Grove, IL: IVP Academic, 2004.

———. *Early Christian Mission: Paul And The Early Church*. Vol. 2. Downers Grove, IL: IVP Academic, 2004.

———. "Evangelism and the Early Church: What Do We Know about the Disciples as Missionaries?" *Trinity Magazine*, Spring 2005, 21–23.

———. "Fads and Common Sense: Reading Acts in the First Century and Reading Acts Today." *Journal of the Evangelical Theological Society* 52, no. 2 (June 2011): 251–78.

———. *Mark: An Introduction and Commentary*. Vol. 2. Tyndale New Testament Commentaries. Downers Grove, IL: IVP Academic, 2017.

———. "Mission, Early Non-Pauline." In *Dictionary of the Later New Testament & Its Developments*, edited by Ralph P. Martin and Peter H. Davids, 752–75. Compendium of Contemporary Biblical Scholarship Series. Downers Grove, IL: IVP Academic, 1997.

———. *Paul the Missionary: Realities, Strategies and Methods*. Downers Grove, IL: IVP Academic, 2008.

Schreiner, Patrick. *The Mission of the Triune God: A Theology of Acts*. Wheaton, IL: Crossway, 2022.

Schutz, John Howard. *Paul and the Anatomy of Apostolic Authority*. Louisville, KY: Westminster John Knox, 2007.

Scott, J. Julius. "Stephen's Defense and the World Mission of the People of God." *Journal of the Evangelical Theological Society* 21, no. 2 (1978): 131–41.

Seccombe, David Peter. *Possessions and the Poor in Luke-Acts*. Linz, Austria: SNTU, 1982.

Shank, Nathan and Kari. "The Four Fields: A Manual for Church Planting Facilitation," 2015. https://www.movements.net/4fields.

Shepherd, William H. *The Narrative Function of the Holy Spirit as a Character in Luke-Acts*. The Society of Biblical Literature Dissertation Series 147. Atlanta: Scholar Press, 1994.

Snyder, Howard A. *Signs of the Spirit: How God Reshapes the Church*. Grand Rapids, MI: Academie Books, 1989.

Spencer, F. Scott. *Journeying through Acts: A Literary-Cultural Reading*. Grand Rapids, MI: Baker Academic, 2004.

Squires, John T. *The Plan of God in Luke-Acts*. Vol. 76. Society for New Testament Studies. Cambridge, UK: Cambridge University Press, 1993.

Stark, Rodney, and Xiuhua Wang. *A Star in the East: The Rise of Christianity in China*. West Conshohocken, PA: Templeton Press, 2015.

Stein, Robert H. "Baptism and Becoming a Christian in the New Testament." *Southern Baptist Journal of Theology* 2/1 (Spring 1998): 6–17.

Stronstad, Roger. *The Charismatic Theology of St. Luke*. Peabody, MA: Hendrickson, 1984.

Stott, John. *The Message of Acts: To the Ends of the Earth*. 2nd ed. Bible Speaks Today. Leicester, UK: InterVarsity Press, 1991.

Tannehill, Robert C. *The Acts of the Apostles*. Vol. 2. The Narrative Unity of Luke-Acts: A Literary Interpretation. Minneapolis, MN: Fortress Press, 1990.

———. "The Functions of Peter's Mission Speeches in the Narrative of Acts." *New Testament Studies* 37 (1991): 400–414.

———. *The Gospel According to Luke*. Vol. 1. The Narrative Unity of Luke-Acts: A Literary Interpretation. Philadelphia, PA: Fortress Press, 1991.

Taylor, Justin. "Why Were the Disciples First Called 'Christians' at Antioch? (Acts 11:26)." *Revue Biblique* 101 (1994): 75–94.

Thompson, Alan J. *The Acts of the Risen Lord Jesus: Luke's Account of God's Unfolding Plan*. Vol. 27. New Studies in Biblical Theology. Downers Grove, IL: InterVarsity Press, 2011.

Tibebe, Eshete. "The Sudan Interior Mission (SIM) in Ethiopia (1928-1970)." *Northeast African Studies* 6, no. 3 (1999): 27–57.

Twelftree, Graham H. *People of the Spirit: Exploring Luke's View of the Church*. Kindle. Grand Rapids, MI: Baker/SPCK, 2009.

Walker, Thomas. *The Acts of the Apostles*. Chicago, IL: Moody, 1910.

Walton, Steve. "The Acts – of God? What Is the 'Acts of the Apostles' All About?" *Evangelical Quarterly* 80:4 (2008): 291–306.

———. *Leadership and Lifestyle: The Portrait of Paul in the Miletus Speech and 1 Thessalonians*, vol. 108, Society for New Testament Studies (Cambridge, UK: Cambridge University Press, 2000).

Ware, James P. *Paul and the Mission of the Church: Philippians in Ancient Jewish Context*. Kindle. Grand Rapids, MI: Baker Academic, 2011.

Watson, David. "Discovering God: Field Testing Guide v2.0," 2008. https://bit.ly/3Dg2CUj.

Watson, David L., and Paul D. Watson. *Contagious Disciple Making: Leading Others on a Journey of Discovery*. Nashville, TN: Thomas Nelson, 2014.

Wesley, John. "Sermon 50: The Use of Money," 3rd ed., 6:139–51. The Works of John Wesley. Albany, OR: Books for the Ages, 1872.

Wikipedia. "Banjara." https://en.wikipedia.org/wiki/Banjara. Accessed August 30, 2022.

———. "Christianity in Iran." In *Wikipedia*. https://en.wikipedia.org/wiki/Christianity_in_Iran. Accessed November 25, 2022.

———. "Christianity in Nepal." In *Wikipedia*, December 4, 2022. https://en.wikipedia.org/wiki/Christianity_in_Nepal.

———. "Ethnic groups in London." https://en.wikipedia.org/wiki/Ethnic_groups_in_London. Accessed November 8, 2022.

Witherington III, Ben. *The Acts of the Apostles: A Socio-Rhetorical Commentary*. Grand Rapids, MI: Eerdmans, 1997.

Wright, Christopher J. H. *The Mission of God: Unlocking the Bible's Grand Narrative*. Downers Grove, IL: IVP Academic, 2006.

Wright, N. T. *Surprised by Hope: Rethinking Heaven, the Resurrection, and the Mission of the Church*. New York, NY: HarperCollins, 2008.

# NOTES

## ACTS TIMELINE

1     Adapted from: Eckhard J. Schnabel, *Acts*, ed. Clinton Arnold, Zondervan Exegetical Commentary on the New Testament (Grand Rapids: Zondervan, 2012), 43–46.

## INTRODUCTION

1     "Christianity in Nepal," in *Wikipedia*, December 4, 2022, https://en.wikipedia.org/wiki/Christianity_in_Nepal.

2     Jason Casper, "Researchers Find Christians in Iran Approaching 1 Million," *Christianity Today*, September 3, 2020, https://www.christianitytoday.com/news/2020/september/iran-christian-conversions-gamaan-religion-survey.html.

3     According to Long, a movement consistently sees four generations of disciples gathered in churches, in multiple streams. Usually that's at least one thousand new disciples, but the important measure is four generations of disciples and churches. Once a movement reaches four generations, it rarely ends. See Justin Long, "1% of the World: A Macroanalysis of 1,369 Movements to Christ," *Mission Frontiers*, December 2020, 37–42.

4     See David Garrison, *A Wind in the House of Islam: How God Is Drawing Muslims Around the World to Faith in Jesus Christ* (Monument, CO: WIGTake Resources, 2014).

5     Schnabel, *Acts*, 1084.

6     Schnabel, *Acts*, 1097. See also Graham H. Twelftree, *People of the Spirit: Exploring Luke's View of the Church* (Grand Rapids, MI: Baker, 2009).

7     Schnabel, *Acts*, 1101.

8     Acts 2:38.

9     Acts 26:18.

10    Patrick Schreiner, *The Mission of the Triune God: A Theology of Acts* (Wheaton, IL: Crossway, 2022), 18.

## 1   THE MISSION OF THE RISEN LORD (1:1–11)

1     Acts 1:1.

2     Luke 24:46–47.

3     David G. Peterson, *The Acts of the Apostles*, Pillar New Testament Commentary (Grand Rapids, MI: Eerdmans, 2009), 105.

4     See Eckhard J. Schnabel, *Early Christian Mission: Jesus and the Twelve*, Vol. 1 (Downers Grove, IL: InterVarsity Press, 2004), 402–03.

5     See Craig Keener, *Acts* (Cambridge, UK: Cambridge University Press, 2020), 104. Isa. 32:15; 42:1; 44:3; 59:21; Ezek. 36:24–28; 37:14; 39:29; Joel 2:28–3:1.

6     Isa. 49:6.

7     Matt. 24:14.

8     Acts 1:8, my emphasis.

9     Schnabel, *Acts*, 430.

10  Schnabel, *Acts*, 88.

11  "The phrase 'end of the earth', then, is geographic and ethnic in scope, inclusive of all people and locales." Darrell L. Bock, *Acts*, Baker Exegetical Commentary on the New Testament (Grand Rapids, MI: Baker, 2007), loc. 2057–58, Kindle. See also Schnabel, *Early Christian Mission*, 1:372–76.

12  Bock, *Acts*, loc. 2083–84, Kindle.

13  Schnabel, *Acts*, 79.

14  Peterson, *Acts*, 115.

15  Acts 1:11. Schreiner, *Mission*, 165.

16  Steve Walton, "The Acts—of God? What Is the 'Acts of the Apostles' All About?," *Evangelical Quarterly* 80, no. 4 (2008): 292. Schnabel, *Acts*, 1087–88.

17  Schreiner, *Mission*, 24.

18  F. Scott Spencer, *Journeying through Acts: A Literary-Cultural Reading* (Grand Rapids, MI: Baker Academic, 2004), 24.

19  John T. Squires, *The Plan of God in Luke-Acts*, Vol. 76, Society for New Testament Studies (Cambridge, UK: Cambridge University Press, 1993), 37.

20  Luke 24:45–47.

21  Squires, *Plan of God*, 2–3, 37.

## 2  FILLING JERUSALEM (1:12–5:42)

1  Luke 8:1–3.

2  Mark 3:21; John 7:5.

3  Jesus' brothers are listed in Mark 6:3. James eventually became the leader of the church in Jerusalem (Acts 15; 21:18). All the brothers and their wives served as missionaries (1 Cor. 9:5).

4  Keener, *Acts*, 113.

5  See Luke 22:32; 24:44–49.

6  Later when the apostle James is martyred, no replacement is needed.

7  At the renewal of all things, they will sit on twelve thrones judging the twelve tribes of Israel. Matt. 19:28; Luke 22:30; Rev. 21:10–14.

8  Most likely he would come from among the seventy (seventy-two) disciples Jesus sent on mission (Luke 10:1). See Schnabel, *Acts*, 99–101.

9  Polhill points out that after Pentecost, decisions were made under the direction of the Spirit. John B. Polhill, *Acts: An Exegetical and Theological Exposition of Holy Scripture*, The New American Commentary 26, (Nashville, TN: Broadman & Holman, 1992), 95.

10  Luke 3:21–22; 11:3; Matt. 7:11; Acts 4:31; 8:15; 13:2.

11  Peterson observes, "It is striking that at almost every important turning point in the narrative of God's redemptive action in Acts we find a mention of prayer (e.g., 1:24; 8:14–17; 9:11–12; 10:4, 9, 30; 13:2–3)." Peterson, *Acts*, 118.

12  Paul E. Pierson, "Historical Development of the Christian Movement," Lecture Notes (Pasadena, CA: Fuller School of World Mission, 1988).

13  Acts 1:1. See Alan J. Thompson, *The Acts of the Risen Lord Jesus: Luke's Account of God's Unfolding Plan*, Vol. 27, New Studies in Biblical Theology (Downers Grove, IL: InterVarsity Press, 2011).

14  Acts 2:38. Thompson, *Acts*, 23.

15  Schreiner, *Mission*, 53.

16  Acts 18:9–10; 23:11.

17  Acts 14:23. O'Toole, 477.

18  Peterson, *Acts*, 57. O'Toole points out that Luke intentionally blurs the distinction between "the Lord" as applied to the Father and Jesus. Robert F. O'Toole, "Activity of the Risen Jesus in Luke-Acts," *Biblica* 62, no. 4 (1981): 477–78.

19  Acts 2:42–47.

20  Acts 9:4; 22:7; 26:14.

21  Luke 21:15.

22  Schnabel, *Acts*, 113.

23  See Craig Keener, "Why Does Luke Use Tongues as a Sign of the Spirit's Empowerment?" *Journal of Pentecostal Theology* 15, no. 2 (2007): 177–84.

24  F. F. Bruce, *The Book of Acts*, ed. Gordon D. Fee, rev ed, New International Commentary on the New Testament (Grand Rapids, MI: Eerdmans, 1988), 75.

25  Keener, *Acts*, 122.

26  Schreiner, *Mission*, 117.

27  Bruce, *Acts*, 54.

28  Isa. 49:6.

29  Peterson, *Acts*, 136. See Rev. 5:9–10; 7:9.

30  Ben Witherington III, *The Acts of the Apostles: A Socio-Rhetorical Commentary* (Grand Rapids: Eerdmans, 1997), 130.

31  Jonathan Kienzler, *The Fiery Holy Spirit: The Spirit's Relationship with Judgment in Luke-Acts*, ed. John Christopher Thomas, Vol. 44, Journal of Pentecostal Theology (Dorset, UK: Deo Publishing, 2015), 207.

32  Acts 2:11; 4:8, 31; 6:10; 9:27; 11:24.

33  Acts 6:7; 12:24; 19:20. Daniel Marguerat, *The First Christian Historian: Writing the "Acts of the Apostles,"* ed. Richard Bauckham, Monograph Series—Society for New Testament Studies 121 (Cambridge, UK: Cambridge University Press, 2002), 121.

34  Schreiner points out, "The Spirit is about the mission, but the mission is to save, recreate, and reconcile a new people." Schreiner, *Mission*, 70.

35  Schnabel, *Acts*, 1093.

36  Acts 9:31.

37  Acts 5:1–11.

38  Acts 8:4–5.

39  Acts 8:14–15.

40  Acts 10.

41  Marguerat, *First Christian Historian*, 116.

42  Acts 15:28.

43  Acts 6:3; 13:1–3; 20:28.

44  Acts 16:6–10.

45  Acts 20:22.

46  Witherington, *Acts*, 12.

47  I am following Andrew Johnson's account in Andrew Johnson, *If I Give My Soul: Faith Behind Bars in Rio de Janeiro* (New York: Oxford University Press, 2017), Kindle edition.

48  See "Deeper: Peter and the Shaping of a Leader," page 54.

49  Bruce, *Acts*, 60.

50  Later in Acts, Paul was led by a vision (16:9–10), and Cornelius and Peter were each brought together by a vision (9:10; 10:3, 10, 17; 18:9).

51  Thompson, *Acts*, 132, 134.

52  Acts 11:27–28; 13:1; 21:9,11. Robert C. Tannehill, *The Acts of the Apostles*, Vol. 2, The Narrative Unity of Luke-Acts: A Literary Interpretation (Minneapolis, MN: Fortress Press, 1990), 145. See "Deeper: Prophets," page 189.

53  Spencer, *Journeying through Acts*, 48.

54  Luke 9:41; Acts 2:40. Keener, *Acts*, 157.

55  See Addison, *Movements that Change the World: Five Keys to Spreading the Gospel*, Revised (Downers Grove, IL: InterVarsity Press, 2011), 44–45.

56  Richard J. Foster, *Streams of Living Water: Essential Practices From the Six Great Traditions of Christian Faith* (Grand Rapids, MI: Zondervan, 2001), 117.

57  Foster, *Streams*, 117.

58  Frank Bartleman quoted in Allan Anderson, *An Introduction to Pentecostalism: Global Charismatic Christianity* (Cambridge, UK: Cambridge University Press, 2004), 61.

59  Seymour wrote, "The Pentecostal power, when you sum it all up, is just more of God's love." Foster, *Streams*, 120.

60  Anderson, *Pentecostalism*, 50–51.

61  Anderson, *Pentecostalism*, 54.

62  Anderson, *Pentecostalism*, 54.

63  Anderson, *Pentecostalism*, 68.

64  Philip Jenkins, *The Next Christendom: The Coming of Global Christianity* (New York: Oxford University Press, 2002), 123.

65  See Elizabeth E. Brusco, *The Reformation of Machismo: Evangelical Conversion and Gender in Colombia* (Austin, TX: University of Texas Press, 1995); and Johnson, *If I Give My Soul*.

66  The book of Acts records five evangelistic messages given by Peter: at Pentecost (2:14–40); in Solomon's portico of the Temple (3:12–26); before the Jewish authorities after his and John's arrest (4:8–12); to the Jewish council following the arrest of all the apostles (5:29–32); at Cornelius's house (10:34–48).

67  Richard N. Longenecker, *Luke-Acts*, Vol. 10, The Expositor's Bible Commentary (Grand Rapids, MI: Zondervan, 2007), loc. 22350–56, Kindle. See also Peterson, *Acts*, 70–75.

68  Eckhard J. Schnabel, *Paul the Missionary: Realities, Strategies and Methods* (Downers Grove, IL: IVP Academic, 2008), 168.

69  Schnabel, *Acts*, 712–13.

70  Witherington, *Acts*, 685–6.

71  Schnabel, *Acts*, 712.

72  Luke 24:45–49.

73  An example of a good gospel tool is the 3-Circles, https://www.movements.net/411 (accessed November 24, 2022). The 3-Thirds pattern of discipleship is a widely used method for making disciples. See Appendix: 3-Thirds Discipleship, page 224.

74  Acts 2:38.

75  Luke 3:3; 13:3–5; 24:47; 24:47–49.

76  Chris Green, "The King, His Kingdom and the Gospel: Matthew, Mark and Luke-Acts,"

in *God's Power to Save: One Gospel for a Complex World?* ed. Chris Green (Leicester, UK: Inter-Varsity Press, 2006), 104–37.

77  The original word in Greek means to "change your thinking," but behind that word is a rich tradition in the Old Testament that goes beyond a change of mind to a total transformation. See Mark J. Boda, *Return to Me: A Biblical Theology of Repentance*, ed. D. A. Carson, New Studies in Biblical Theology 35 (Downers Grove, IL: InterVarsity Press, 2015).

78  Schnabel, *Acts*, 162–63.

79  Acts 4:12.

80  See Robert H. Stein, "Baptism and Becoming a Christian in the New Testament," *Southern Baptist Journal of Theology* 2 no. 1 (Spring 1998): 6–17.

81  John 14:12. Bruce, *Acts*, 72.

82  The normal population was likely to be over one hundred thousand, and it could double during one of the great pilgrimage feasts. See Wolfgang Reinhardt, "The Population Size of Jerusalem and the Numerical Growth of the Jerusalem Church," in *The Book of Acts in Its Palestinian Setting*, ed Richard Bauckham, Vol. 4, The Book of Acts in Its First Century Setting (Grand Rapids, MI: Eerdmans, 1995), 237–65.

83  Bruce, *Acts*, 72.

84  Acts 2:47; 4:4; 5:14; 6:1, 7; 9:42; 11:24; 13:43; 14:1; 17:10–12; 21:20.

85  Luke 10:13–16.

86  Schnabel, *Early Christian Mission*, 240–42.

87  John Stott, *The Message of Acts: To the Ends of the Earth*, 2nd ed., The Bible Speaks Today (Leicester, UK: InterVarsity Press, 1991), 87.

88  Schnabel, *Acts*, 175.

89  Schnabel, *Acts* 1095.

90  Schnabel, *Early Christian Mission*, 410.

91  Acts 4:32–37; 5:1–11. "Luke describes not an early Christian 'community of goods' but the renunciation of monetary assets for the sake of the poor." Schnabel, *Early Christian Mission*, 1:413.

92  Luke 22:14–22.

93  Acts 1:24–25; 3:6; 4:23–31; 6:4; 8:15.

94  Acts 6:7; 9:31.

95  See Appendix: 3-Thirds Discipleship, page 224.

96  See Nathan Shank, "Generational Mapping: Tracking Elements of Church Formation Within CPM's," Mission Frontiers, December 2012, 26–30; and Shank and Shank, "Four Fields," 93–95. See also Addison, *Pioneering Movements*, 98–105.

97  Twelftree, *People of the Spirit*, loc. 1088, Kindle.

98  Acts 2:36–47; 4:32–35; 5:12–14.

99  Schnabel, *Acts* 1094.

100  Acts 8:1; 9:31; 11:22; 13:1; 14:23, 27; 15:22, 41; 16:5.

101  Paul identifies up to five house churches (Rom. 16: 5, 10, 11, 14, 15). See Douglas J. Moo, *The Epistle to the Romans*, ed. Gordon D. Fee, New International Commentary on the New Testament (Grand Rapids, MI: Eerdmans, 1996), 919.

102  Steve Addison, *The Rise and Fall of Movements: A Roadmap for Leaders* (Cody, WY: 100 Movements Publishing, 2019), 126–38.

103  Matt. 23:37–39.

104  See Exod. 29:38–42; Num. 28:3–8. Schnabel, *Acts*, 192.

105  Schnabel, *Acts*, 198.

106  Spencer, *Journeying Through Acts,* 57–58.

107  Isa. 52:13–53:12.

108  Schnabel, *Acts*, 2:14.

109  Schnabel, *Acts*, 71.

110  Luke 6:12–16.

111  Luke 9:1–2.

112  J. B. Lightfoot, *The Epistle of St. Paul to the Galatians* (Grand Rapids, MI: Zondervan, 1957), 95.

113  Acts 14:4, 14.

114  Gal. 1:19; 1 Cor. 4:6–9; 1 Thess. 1:1; 2:6; Rom. 16:7; Phil. 2:25. Ellis writes: "Apollos is probably included with Paul and Peter in Paul's phrase 'us apostles' (1 Cor. 4:9; cf. 3:22–4:1) and placed on a par with them." E. Earle Ellis, "Paul and His Coworkers," in *Dictionary of Paul and His Letters: A Compendium of Contemporary Biblical Scholarship*, ed. Gerald F. Hawthorne, Ralph P. Martin, and Daniel G. Reid (Grand Rapids, MI: InterVarsity Press, 2009), 185.

115  1 Cor. 15:5–7. He referred to his opponents at Corinth as "super apostles" (2 Cor. 11:5; 12:11) and once as "false apostles" (2 Cor. 11:13). His problem was not that they called themselves apostles, but that they preached a false gospel.

116  1 Cor. 12:28–29; Eph. 4:11–13.

117  Twice, Paul used the word "apostle" to refer to a third group made up of church delegates, who were not primarily missionaries (2 Cor. 8:23; Phil. 2:25).

118  Acts 1:21–22.

119  T. W. Manson, *The Church's Ministry* (London, UK: Hodder & Stoughton, 1948), 54.

120  Barnabas (1 Cor. 9:5–6; Acts 14:4, 14), Andronicus and Junia (Rom. 16:7), James, the Lord's brother (Gal. 1:19), Silas/Silvanus (1 Thess. 1:1; 2:6), Timothy (1 Thess. 1:1; 2:6), Epaphroditus (Phil. 2:25) and Apollos (1 Cor. 3:22; 4:6–9).

121  See Steve Addison, *Pioneering Movements: Leadership That Multiplies Disciples and Churches* (Downers Grove, IL: InterVarsity Press, 2015), 44–45.

122  Acts 12: 1–5, 17.

123  Schnabel, *Early Christian Mission*, 1:913.

124  Acts 13–14.

125  Luke 8:1–3.

126  See Ellis, "Paul and His Coworkers" and Eckhard J. Schnabel, *Early Christian Mission: Paul And The Early Church*, Vol. 2 (Downers Grove, IL: IVP Academic, 2004), 1425–45.

127  For more on these themes see "Deeper: The Difference Teams Make," page 172; and "Deeper: Local Leaders," page 184.

128  Witherington, *Acts*, 116.

129  Acts 19:10.

130  For more information, see Appendix: The 5-Levels of Leadership, pages 227–28. For more on this approach, see Addison, *Pioneering Movements*, 95–108.

131  Luke 21:14–15.

132  See Acts 2:38.

133  We're not sure if Luke is counting both men and women and whether the five thousand is in addition to the three thousand added at Pentecost.

134  According to one source, the seats in the Sanhedrin were "arranged like the half of a round threshing-floor so that they all might see one another." See Schnabel, *Acts*, 237.

135  Witherington, *Acts*, 191, n112. Also Schnabel, *Acts*, 236 and Paul Gaechter, "The Hatred of the House of Annas," *Theological Studies* 8, no. 1 (1947): 3–34.

136  Witherington, *Acts*, 191.

137  Acts 2:23.

138  See Addison, *Rise and Fall*.

139  Luke 24:47–49; Acts 1:8.

140  Witherington, *Acts*, 201.

141  Ps. 2:4.

142  Aaron M. Renn, "The Three Worlds of Evangelicalism," *First Things*, February 2022, https://www.firstthings.com/article/2022/02/the-three-worlds-of-evangelicalism.

143  See Addison, *Pioneering Movements*, 165–68.

144  See Appendix: 3-Thirds Discipleship, page 224.

145  Paul R. House, "Suffering and the Purpose of Acts," *Journal of the Evangelical Theological Society*, 33, no 3 (September, 1990), 330.

146  Geir Otto Holmas, *Prayer and Vindication in Luke-Acts: The Theme of Prayer within the Context of the Legitimating and Edifying Objective of the Lukan Narrative*, ed. Mark Goodacre, Library of New Testament Studies 433 (London, UK: T&T Clark, 2011), 263.

147  Luke 1:13.

148  Holmas, *Prayer*, 168.

149  See Luke 1:10, 13; 3:21; 5:16; 6:12; 9:18, 28; 11:1–13; 18:1–8, 9–14; 22:32, 39–46; 23:34, 46.

150  Acts 7:60.

151  Acts 2:21; 7:59; 9:14, 21; 22:16.

152  Acts 3:1–12; 9:40; 14:8; 28:8.

153  Luke 6:12–16; Acts 1:24–25; 6:6; 13:1–3; 14:23.

154  Acts 9:11.

155  Acts 13:1–3; 14:23.

156  Acts 4:23–31.

157  Acts 16:25.

158  Deut. 15:4.

159  Longenecker, *Luke-Acts*, loc. 23496–97, Kindle.

160  Ten years later, Mary, the mother of John Mark, still owns a substantial home with an outer gate that can contain a large gathering (Acts 12:12). See Schnabel, *Acts*, 539.

161  Acts 11:24.

162  I have relied on David Peter Seccombe, *Possessions and the Poor in Luke-Acts* (Linz, Austria: Studien zum Neuen Testament und seiner Umwelt, 1982), 225–28.

163  Luke 4:18–19.

164  Twelftree, loc 6312, Kindle.

165  In the Old Testament the poor include true Israel oppressed by conquest and foreign domination at the hand of God. See Peter T. O'Brien, "Mission, Witness, and the Coming of the Spirit," *Bulletin for Biblical Research*, 9 (1999): 206.

166  Luke 13:16; Acts 10:38.

167  Joel B. Green, *The Gospel of Luke*, ed. Gordon D. Fee, New International Commentary on the New Testament (Grand Rapids, MI: Eerdmans, 1997), 211.

168  Luke 18:18–30.

169  Luke 19:1–10.

170  Acts 2:42–47; 4:32–5:16.

171  Acts 12:12–13. John Mark's mother continued to own a large house, and she employed a servant called Rhoda. In Jerusalem, some of the disciples are poor and some are not (Rom. 15:26; Gal. 2:10).

172  Acts 11:27–30; Acts 20:1–5; 24:17; Rom. 15:26; 2 Cor. 8–9.

173  Luke 22:5; Acts 1:18; 5:3.

174  Acts 19:23–31.

175  Acts 24:24–27.

176  Acts 8:20.

177  Acts 20:33–34.

178  John Wesley, "Sermon 50: The Use of Money," 3rd ed., vol. 6, *The Works of John Wesley* (Albany, OR: Books for the Ages, 1872), 139–51.

179  Acts 8:7–12; 17:4, 12, 34; 19:31. See David Matson, *Household Conversion Narratives in Acts: Pattern and Interpretation* (Sheffield, UK: Sheffield Academic Press, 1996), 42, n 69 and n70. See also Martin Hengel, *Poverty and Riches in the Early Church: Aspects of a Social History of Early Christianity* (Minneapolis, MN: Fortress Press, 1974), loc. 742–43, Kindle.

180  See Johannes C. Hoekendijk, *The Church Inside Out*, eds., L.A. Hoedemaker and Pieter Tijmes, trans. Isaac C. Rottenberg (London, UK: SCM, 1966). See also Addison, *The Rise and Fall of Movements*, 126–31.

181  Polhill, *Acts*, 157.

182  Luke 22:3, 31.

183  1 Pet. 4:17.

184  Polhill, *Acts*, 159–60.

185  Bock, *Acts*, loc. 5916, Kindle.

186  Polhill, *Acts*, 161.

187  1 Cor. 5:5; 11:29–30.

188  1 Cor. 5:5; 11:29–30; 1 Tim. 1:20; James 5:20; 1 Pet. 4:17; 1 John 5:16–17; Rev. 2–3. See Schnabel, *Acts*, 296.

189  Peterson, *Acts*, 213.

190  Steve Addison with Terry and Amy Ruff, "194–Multiplying Movements in West Africa," *Movements*, June 27, 2019, https://www.movements.net/blog/blog/2019/6/18/194-multiplying-movements-in-west-africa.

191  Luke 11:18–26; 13:16; Acts 10:38; 26:17–18.

192  Luke 4:1–13; 22:3, 31.

193  Luke 8:11–12.

194  Luke 4:13; 22:3.

195  Matthew S. Monnig, "Satan in Lukan Narrative and Theology: Human Agency in the Conflict between the Authority of Satan and the Power of God" (PhD diss, Duke University, 2019), 308. Luke 9:1–2; 10:1, 17.

196  Luke 10:18; 11:17–22.

197   Luke 22:53.

198   Luke 22:3.

199   Acts 26:18.

200   Monigg, "Satan in Lukan Narrative," 273–74.

201   Luke 22:31–32.

202   Acts 5:3. Monigg, "Satan in Lukan Narrative," 210.

203   Acts 5:11–14.

204   Acts 4:29–31.

205   Acts 26:18. Tannehill, *Acts*, 323. Monigg, "Satan in Lukan Narrative," 267.

206   Acts 13:6–12.

207   See Kienzle, *The Fiery Holy Spirit*, 182.

208   Monigg, "Satan in Lukan Narrative," 308. Luke 8:12; 22:31–32; Acts 13:8–10.

209   Addison and Ruff, "194–Multiplying Movements in West Africa."

210   Acts 10:38; 26:18.

211   Polhill, *Acts*, 164.

212   Acts 5:16.

213   Polhill, *Acts*, 166.

214   Schnabel, *Acts*, 307.

215   Schnabel, *Acts*, 303.

216   Polhill, *Acts*, 170.

217   Deut. 25:3; 2 Cor. 11:24. See Marshall, *Acts*, 124 and Polhill, *Acts*, 174.

218   Acts 4:24–31.

219   Luke 5:1–11.

220   Schnabel, *Acts*, 544.

221   Acts 5:42.

222   Acts 6:4.

223   Acts 6:1–7.

224   Gal. 2:11–14.

225   Acts 15:7–10.

226   Acts 12:17.

227   Paul knows of the pioneering ministry of Peter and his wife. See 1 Cor. 9:5; Gal. 2:11–14.

228   1 Pet. 1:1.

229   See J. Robert Clinton, *The Making of a Leader: Recognizing the Lessons and Stages of Leadership Development*, Revised (Colorado Springs, CO: NavPress, 2014).

## 3   OUT OF JERUSALEM (6:1–12:25)

1     Acts 4:34; 5:14.

2     Luke does not give them the title "deacons"; both the *ministry* of waiting on tables and the *ministry* of prayer and the Word are described as *diakonia*, or service.

3     See Schnabel, *Acts*, 338–39.

4     See Acts 4:24–31; 12:5–17; 13:1–3; 20:28–36.

5     Acts 6:7; 12:24; 19:20.

6     Peterson, *Acts*, 229. Also House, "Suffering," 317–30.

7     Schnabel, *Acts*, 336.

8     Rosner states, "To trace the activity of the Spirit in Acts is to observe the progress of the

word." Brian Rosner, "The Progress of the Word," in *Witness to the Gospel: The Theology of Acts*, eds. I. Howard Marshall and David Peterson (Grand Rapids, MI: Eerdmans, 1998), 224. See Acts 1:8; 2:3, 38; 5:32; 6:1–3; 7:51; 8:16–17, 39–40; 9:17; 10:45; 11:12,15–16; 15:8; 11:24; 13:1–2.

9    Luke 8:15. See David W. Pao, *Acts and the Isaianic New Exodus*, Biblical Studies Library (Grand Rapids, MI: Baker Academic, 2002), 150. See also Jerome Kodell, "The Word of God Grew: The Ecclesial Tendency of Logos in Acts 6:7; 12:24; 19:20," *Biblica* 55 (1974): 517.

10   Kodell, "The Word of God," 508.

11   Pao, *Acts*, 150.

12   The summary statements are: Acts 6:7; 9:31; 12:24; 16:5; 19:20; 28:30–31.

13   Rosner, "The Progress," 223.

14   For a description and a critique see, Michael J. Kruger, *Canon Revisited: Establishing the Origins and Authority of the New Testament Books* (Wheaton, IL: Crossway, 2012), 65–71.

15   Chris Galanos says, "Movements don't happen unless people are reading, obeying, and sharing the Word of God." Chris Galanos, *From Megachurch to Multiplication: A Church's Journey Toward Movement* (Lubbock, TX: Experience Life Church, 2018), 52.

16   To find out more, visit https://www.movements.net/3-disciples (accessed February 27, 2023).

17   Acts 28:31.

18   According to Schnabel, it's called the synagogue of the Freedmen as they were freed slaves or their descendants. Some may have been enslaved by the Roman general Pompey when he conquered Jerusalem in 63 BC and subsequently freed before returning to Jerusalem. See Schnabel, *Acts*, 345–6.

19   See J. Julius Scott, "Stephen's Defense and the World Mission of the People of God," *Journal of the Evangelical Theological Society*, 21, no. 2 (1978): 133.

20   Polhill, *Acts*, 188.

21   Thompson, *Acts,* 168.

22   Dan. 7:13–14.

23   Peterson, *Acts*, 266–67.

24   Bruce, *Acts*, 166.

25   Schnabel, *Acts*, 397.

26   Acts 8:1–3; 11:19.

27   Polhill, *Acts*, 212.

28   Schnabel, *Acts*, 395.

29   Acts 22:4; 26:10.

30   Peterson, *Acts*, 268.

31   Sources for the story of Brother Haik: Felix Corley, "Obituary: Haik Hovsepian Mehr," *The Independent*, February 1, 1994, https://www.independent.co.uk/news/people/obituary-haik-hovsepian-mehr-1391238.html); Karen Hartley, "Biography of Haik Hovsepian-Mehr," *Truett Journal of Church and Mission 2*, no. 1 (2004): 43–57. See also Steve Addison, *What Jesus Started: Joining the Movement, Changing the World* (Downers Grove, IL: InterVarsity Press, 2012), 189–91.

32   The estimates of Christians in Iran vary from 380,000 to 1.5 million. "Christianity in Iran,"

in *Wikipedia*, https://en.wikipedia.org/wiki/Christianity_in_Iran (accessed November 25, 2022).

33   Marshall comments, "The shadow of rejection hangs over the ministry of Jesus from the outset." I. Howard Marshall, *The Gospel of Luke*, New International Greek Commentary (Grand Rapids, MI: Eerdmans, 1978), 190.

34   Luke 2:34–35.

35   Scott Cunningham, "'Through Many Tribulations' The Theology of Persecution in Luke-Acts," *Journal for the Study of the New Testament Supplement Series* 142 (Sheffield, England: Sheffield Academic Press, 1997): 47.

36   Luke 21:12–19. Cunningham, "Through Many Tribulations," 133.

37   Luke 6:22–23.

38   Luke 23:53.

39   Tannehill, *Acts*, 70.

40   Luke 12:4–12; 21:12–19.

41   See Cunningham, "Through Many Tribulations," 194–95.

42   Schnabel, *Acts*, 298.

43   Cunningham, "Through Many Tribulations," 319.

44   Acts 5:42.

45   Acts 4:18; 5:28.

46   Schnabel, *Acts*, 1086.

47   Acts 2:43–47; 4:23-31; 4:32–37; 5:14.

48   Cunningham, "Through Many Tribulations," 224.

49   Acts 9:23–25, 29–30; 13:50–51; 14:6, 19–20; 16:40; 17:10, 14; 22:18.

50   Cunningham, "Through Many Tribulations," 253.

51   Acts 14:22.

52   Acts 9:5.

53   Acts 23:11.

54   Nilay Saiya and Stuti Manchanda, "Paradoxes of Pluralism, Privilege, and Persecution: Explaining Christian Growth and Decline Worldwide," *Sociology of Religion* 83, no. 1 (Spring 2022): 60–80.

55   Samaritans were not strictly Jews, nor were they Gentiles. They lived in what had been the northern kingdom of Israel. When the Assyrians invaded in 722 BC, thousands of Jews went into exile. Those who remained intermarried, both with the local Canaanites as well as with the peoples the Assyrians resettled there. Their descendants became the Samaritans. They built their own temple on Mount Gerizim, accepted the first five books of the Old Testament, and looked for the coming of a Messiah who would be a prophet like Moses. Polhill, *Acts*, 214.

56   Acts 1:8.

57   Acts 9:31.

58   Acts 11:19.

59   Acts 2:38.

60   Acts 10–11, 15.

61   Acts 2:38.

62   See Polhill, *Acts*, 217–18 and Stein, "Baptism," 6–17.

63  Roger Stronstad, *The Charismatic Theology of St. Luke* (Peabody, MA: Hendrickson, 1984), 65.

64  Kienzler, *The Fiery Holy Spirit*, 163.

65  Schnabel, *Acts*, 415.

66  Acts 6:4.

67  Acts 9:31–32.

68  Acts 9:31.

69  Polhill, *Acts*, 129.

70  Deut. 23:1.

71  The Lord promised that, "To them I will give within my temple and its walls a memorial and a name better than sons and daughters; I will give them an everlasting name that will endure forever." Isa. 56:4–5.

72  In the forty days between his resurrection and ascension, Jesus had taken his disciples through the Hebrew Scriptures, explaining how they pointed forward to the Messiah's victory through suffering. See Luke 24:44–47.

73  Bruce, *Acts*, 179.

74  Schnabel, *Acts*, 433.

75  It would make no sense for the eunuch to ask for baptism if Philip had not explained it to him.

76  See Polhill, *Acts*, 227.

77  Schnabel writes that as a result of Philip and Peter, churches are established in the coastal plain in Lydda, Joppa, Caesarea and Ptolemais and perhaps Ashdod. Schnabel, *Early Christian Mission*, 2:687.

78  Schnabel, *Early Christian Mission*, 2:686–87.

79  Witherington, *Acts*, 301.

80  Polhill, *Acts*, 228.

81  Eshete Tibebe, "The Sudan Interior Mission (SIM) in Ethiopia (1928–1970)," *Northeast African Studies* 6, no. 3 (1999): 45.

82  Quoted in Ato Getachew, "The Genesis and Growth of the Kale Heywet Church," 2003, http://www.ekhc.org.et/history.htm (accessed February 24, 2006).

83  Raymond J. Davis, *Fire on the Mountains: The Story of a Miracle—the Church in Ethiopia* (Grand Rapids, MI: Zondervan, 1966), 244.

84  Eshet, "The Sudan Interior Mission," 40.

85  "There are no soaring church steeples and chimes of bells, no uncomfortable pews, no hymnals or organs, no vestments, no liturgy. The pastor if there is one, is dressed like everyone else and enjoys no special privileges." Peter F. Cotterell, *Born at Midnight* (Chicago, IL: Moody, 1973), 166.

86  Cotterall, *Born at Midnight*, 168.

87  Schnabel contends the Greek word for "baptism" always means "to immerse" and can describe the sinking of a ship or the drowning of a person. Schnabel, *Paul the Missionary*, 230.

88  Matt. 28:18–20.

89  See Stein, "Baptism," 6–17. Luke doesn't repeat the whole list every time he records a conversion. When one or more of the five are not mentioned, they are assumed. For example, in Acts 2:38 Peter does not mention the need for faith; elsewhere he does. Faith

is assumed from the other accounts of conversion, just as baptism is assumed, even if it is not always mentioned.

90  Acts 10: 44–48; 11:14; 16:31–34; 18:8; 1 Cor. 1:16; 16:15. See Thompson, *Acts*, 142–43, n60.

91  Luke 23:39–43.

92  In Acts, repentance and faith are expressed in immediate baptism: Acts 2:36–41; 8:36–38; 9:10–18; 10:24, 44–48; 16:13–15, 31–34; 18:8; 19:1–7.

93  Acts 10:45–48.

94  Acts 9:10–18.

95  1 Cor. 1:13–17.

96  See Addison, *Pioneering Movements*, 87–89.

97  See Appendix: 3-Thirds Discipleship, page 224.

98  Acts 8:1–4.

99  Peterson, *Acts*, 302.

100  See Matt. 25:35–46. On the interpretation of this passage, see Steve Addison, *Your Part in God's Story: 40 Days from Genesis to Revelation* (Cody, WY: 100 Movements Publishing, 2021), 115–117.

101  Acts 26:14. A goad was a wooden stick with metal spikes used to prod and drive livestock. Kicking against it would only cause the beast harm.

102  Acts 9:14–16.

103  Acts 7:60.

104  2 Cor. 4:7.

105  Gal. 1:15–17.

106  See Wayne A. Meeks, *The First Urban Christians: The Social World of the Apostle Paul* (New Haven, CT: Yale University Press, 1983), 9–11; Martin Hengel, "Paul in Arabia," *Bulletin of Biblical Research* 12 (2002): 47–66; Schnabel, *Early Christian Mission*, 2:1035–45; F. F. Bruce, *Paul: Apostle of the Free Spirit*, Revised. (Exeter, UK: Paternoster Press, 1980), 81–82; Paul Barnett, *Paul: Missionary of Jesus* Vol. 2 After Jesus (Grand Rapids, MI: Eerdmans, 2008), 80–82.

107  Saul related his Arabian mission closely with his call to preach Christ among the Gentiles. He told the Galatians he began to discharge this call before he went up to Jerusalem to see the apostles. Therefore, none could say that any human authority, including the Twelve, commissioned him as an apostle to the Gentiles.

108  See 2 Cor. 11:32–33.

109  See Marshall, *Acts*, 174.

110  In Acts 23:16, Paul's sister and family are living in Jerusalem.

111  In AD 42 when Barnabas goes looking for Paul's help in Antioch, he finds him based in Tarsus (11:25). See Schnabel, *Early Christian Mission*, 2:1422.

112  2 Cor. 11:23–27. Longenecker, *Luke-Acts*, loc. 25862, Kindle.

113  Acts 26:17–18.

114  Schnabel, *Acts*, 466.

115  Acts 5:16; 8:4–25.

116  See Addison, *The Rise and Fall of Movements*.

117  Acts 8:25.

118  Acts 8:1, 40.

119  Her Aramaic name is Tabitha. Her Greek name is Dorcas.

120  Acts 6:2–4.

121  Luke 10:1–11.

122  Acts 1:1.

123  Acts 10:44–48; 15:12. See Witherington, *Acts*, 221.

124  Leo O'Reilly, *Word and Sign in the Acts of the Apostles: A Study in Lucan Theology* (Rome, Italy: Gregorian Biblical BookShop, 1987), 200.

125  Matt. 11:23; Luke 10:15.

126  Acts 14:8–14. Schnabel, *Acts*, 617.

127  Acts 6:8; 8:6–7,13; 9:12,17–18; 14:3; 15:12. See also Luke 10:17.

128  Acts 4:29–31.

129  William J. Jr. Larkin, *Acts*, ed. Stuart D. Briscoe and Haddon Robinson, The IVP New Testament Commentary Series (Downers Grove, IL: InterVarsity Press, 1995),151.

130  Peter H. Davids, "Miracles in Acts," in *Dictionary of the Later New Testament & Its Developments*, eds. Ralph P. Martin and Peter H. Davids, Compendium of Contemporary Biblical Scholarship Series (Downers Grove, IL: IVP Academic, 1997), 1085–92.

131  John Michael Penney, *The Missionary Emphasis of Lukan Pneumatology*, Journal of Pentecostal Theology Supplement Series 12 (Sheffield, England: Sheffield Academic Press, 1997), 66–67.

132  O'Reilly, *Word and Sign*, 194.

133  Davids, "Miracles," 602.

134  Davids, "Miracles," 1092.

135  Schnabel, *Acts*, 1098.

136  See Robert Menzies, "Acts 2:17–21: A Paradigm for Pentecostal Mission," *Journal of Pentecostal Theology* 17 (2008): 200–18.

137  Schnabel, *Acts*, 1097.

138  Acts 16:6–10.

139  Tensions between the two groups could erupt into violence. The Jewish historian Josephus reported that in AD 66, Syrians in Caesarea massacred twenty thousand Jews in a single hour. Keener, *Acts*, 296.

140  Spencer, *Journeying through Acts*, 119.

141  See Addison, *Movements*, 71–83.

142  Witherington, *Acts*, 352.

143  Keener, *Acts*, 298. See Luke 10:5; Acts 16:15; 31–34; 18:8.

144  Especially the Synoptic Gospels of Matthew, Mark, and Luke. See Robert C. Tannehill, "The Functions of Peter's Mission Speeches in the Narrative of Acts," *New Testament Studies* 37 (1991): 400–14.

145  Luke 24:46–48.

146  Tannehill, "Speeches," 411.

147  Acts 11:14. Larkin, *Acts*, 163.

148  Keener, *Acts*, 300.

149  See Howard A. Snyder, *Signs of the Spirit: How God Reshapes the Church* (Grand Rapids, MI: Academie Books, 1989), 230.

150  Keener, *Acts*, 306.

151  Acts 1:13–2:22; 28:30.

152  Matson writes, "It is primarily by means of the house that the gospel marches steadily from Jerusalem to Rome." Matson, *Household Conversion*, 26.

153  Matson, *Household Conversion*, 195.

154  Luke 19:1–9. See Matson, *Household Conversion*, 72, n109.

155  Matson lists the parallels between Jesus' instructions to the 70 (Luke 10:1–11) and how he enters Zacchaeus's house (Luke 19:1–10). Matson, *Household Conversion*, 83.

156  Matson, *Household Conversion*, 11.

157  Acts 10:1–11:18; 16:11–15; 16:25–34; 18:1–11.

158  Acts 10:1–48; 11:1–18; 15:7–11, 13–21. See Matson, *Household Conversion*, 103.

159  Matson, *Household Conversion*, 184.

160  Matson, *Household Conversion*, 86–134.

161  Schnabel, *Paul the Missionary*, 300.

162  Matson, *Household Conversion*, 41. A peasant's house in Judea or Galilee had one room. Typical housing in a Roman city consisted of one or two rooms with no toilet or kitchen facilities.

163  In Acts 16, he identifies a number of churches that make up the church in Rome.

164  Schnabel, *Paul the Missionary*, 303.

165  See J. H. Elliot, "Temple Versus Household in Luke-Acts: A Contrast in Social Institutions," *HTS Theological Studies* 47, no. 1 (1991).

166  Elliott, "Temple Versus Household," 106.

167  Matson, *Household Conversion*, 187.

168  See Luther P. Gerlach and Virginia H. Hine, *People, Power, Change: Movements of Social Transformation* (Indianapolis, IN: Bobbs-Merrill, 1970), 97. See also John Lofland and Rodney Stark, "Becoming a World-Saver: A Theory of Conversion to a Deviant Perspective," *American Sociological Review* 30 (1965): 862–75.

169  See Movements Today: London Calling, page 120.

170  See Addison, *Pioneering Movements*, 158–60.

171  See Addison, *Movements*, 71–83.

172  See Matson, *Household Conversion*, 113.

173  Schnabel, *Acts*, 510.

174  Acts 11:16. Schnabel's translation, Schnabel, *Acts*, 511.

175  Schnabel, *Acts*, 511. Joel 2:28–32; Acts 2:17–21.

176  Schnabel, *Acts*, 512.

177  Bruce, *Acts*, 22.

178  Gen. 12:1–3; Acts 3:25–26.

179  See Steve Addison and David Bareham, "178-Becoming a Great Commission Church," *Movements*, November 29, 2018, https://www.movements.net/blog/blog/2018/11/15/178-a-local-church-takes-on-the-great-commission.

180  For an overview of the training, visit https://www.movements.net/411(accessed January 2, 2023).

181  For a copy of the Commands of Christ, visit https://www.nplsimpletools.com (accessed January 2, 2023).

182  For an outline of the 3-Thirds Approach, see Appendix: 3-Thirds Discipleship, page 224.

183  Larkin, *Acts*, 175 (Acts 21:3, 7; 27:3).

184  Stott, *Acts*, 203.

185  Bock, *Acts*, loc. 10286–87, Kindle.

186  Both Gentile converts and God-fearers were drawn to Judaism, the difference being the converts were willing to take on the full yoke of the Law and be circumcised.

187  The disciples spoke the good news about the *Lord* Jesus. The title Lord made more sense to Greeks who were not familiar with the term Messiah.

188  Acts 4:36–37; 9:27; 11:25, 30; 15:2; 15:36–39. Schnabel, *Acts*, 521.

189  Acts 9:30.

190  Gal. 1:21. Schnabel, *Early Mission*, 2: 1030–69.

191  We must not assume the teaching was exclusively for believers. In Acts, teaching can also include instruction for unbelievers. See Acts 4:2; 5:25, 28, 42; 13:12; 17:19; 18:11. Schnabel, *Acts*, 524.

192  Acts 2:36–47; 4:32–35.

193  Commonalities between the church of Jerusalem and the churches include: the presence of God resulting in numerical growth (9:31; 16:5); generosity to the poor (9:36; 11:29–30); teaching (11:25; 20:7, 18–32); prayer (12:5; 13:2–3; 14:23; 20:36–37; 21:5); the work of the Spirit resulting in witness (13:2–3); local leadership (13:2–3; 14:23; 20:17); breaking bread together (20:7); love for each other (20:36–37; 21:5, 12–13).

194  Schnabel, *Acts*, 524.

195  Acts 26:28; 1 Pet. 4:16. See Schnabel, *Acts*, 524. See also Justin Taylor, "Why Were the Disciples First Called 'Christians' at Antioch? (Acts 11:26)," *Revue Biblique* 101 (1994): 75–94.

196  See Addison, *What Jesus Started*, 92–93.

197  In addition to Agabus and his group, Luke mentions Philip's four unmarried daughters who prophesied (21:9).

198  John Stott observes, "The church of Jerusalem had sent Barnabas to Antioch; now the church of Antioch sent Barnabas, with Saul, back to Jerusalem." Stott, *Acts*, 206.

199  See Addison, *Pioneering Movements*, 98–105.

200  Luke 21:12.

201  Polhill, *Acts*, 277.

202  Acts 12:1–3.

203  Keener, *Acts*, 316.

204  Stott, *Acts*, 209.

205  It's possible the leadership transition occurred earlier. Acts 15:13–21; 21:18; Gal. 1:19.

206  Schnabel, *Acts*, 540–41. When Paul visits Jerusalem for the last time, he meets with the elders, and Peter is not mentioned (Acts 15:7–11; 21:18).

207  Schnabel, *Acts*, 541.

208  The same Greek word for "touch," *patassō*, is used in both instances (Acts 12:7, 23).

209  Acts 4:29.

210  Peterson, *Acts*, 368.

211  Exod. 1:12, 16–20. Keener, *Acts*, 326.

212  Acts 21:20.

213  Marshall, *Acts*, 207.

214  Ephesians 4:11–12.

215  Schnabel, *Acts*, 185.

216 See Richard Bauckham, "James and the Jerusalem Church," in *The Book of Acts in Its Palestinian Setting*, 415–80.

217 Acts 8:1–40.

218 Mark 6:3; 1 Cor. 9:5.

219 Acts 15:32.

220 Acts 8:1–4; 11:25.

221 Luke 21:5–38.

222 Schnabel, *Early Christian Mission* 1:407.

## 4 THE MOVEMENT INTO EUROPE (13:1–15:34)

1 See Addison, *What Jesus Started*, 150–52.

2 Estimates of the Jewish population vary from 22,000 to 65,000. John McRay, "Antioch," in Hawthorne and Martin, eds., *Dictionary of Paul*, 23.

3 Authority is not conveyed by the church or churches but by the apostolic call to spread the gospel. See Schnabel, *Early Christian Mission*, 2:1428; Harold R. Cook, "Who Really Sent the Missionaries?" *The Evangelical Missions Quarterly* 13 (October 1975): 233–39; Joseph and Michele C. [surname withheld], "Field-Governed Mission Structures, Part 1: In the New Testament," *International Journal of Frontier Missions* 18, no. 2 (Summer 2001): 59–66.

4 Peterson writes, "Luke implies that the island was evangelized, because the gospel was planted in key towns and the message could then be taken by converts in those places to other regions." Peterson, *Acts*, 379. Schnabel comments, "The return of Barnabas and John Mark in AD 49 to Cyprus (15:39) indicates, perhaps, that there were churches on Cyprus that they wanted to visit and assist in their ministry." Schnabel, *Acts*, 557.

5 Schnabel, *Paul the Missionary*, 264.

6 The diaspora or dispersion referred to Jews living outside of historic Israel. In the first century, more Jews lived outside of Israel than within it.

7 Stott, *Acts*, 220.

8 Keener, *Acts,* 347. Witherington, *Acts*, 403–4.

9 Acts 13:5, 7, 44, 46, 48, 49; 14:25.

10 Keener, *Acts*, 349. Witherington, *Acts*, 419.

11 Acts 13:13–43; 14:15–17.

12 Schnabel, *Paul the Missionary*, 163.

13 Acts 14:22–23. I'm following Holmas, *Prayer*, 225.

14 Acts 14:22.

15 Bruce writes, "It has more than once been pointed out that more recent missionary policy would have thought it dangerously idealistic to recognize converts of only a few weeks' standing as leaders in their churches; perhaps Paul and Barnabas were more conscious of the presence and power of the Holy Spirit in the believing communities." Bruce, *The Book of Acts*, 280.

16 Had the two chosen to do so, they could have continued southeast from Derbe on through the Cilician gates the 150 miles or so to Paul's hometown of Tarsus and from there back to Syrian Antioch. It would have been the easiest route home by far. See Polhill, *Acts*, 318.

17 Acts 16:1–3; 20:4.

18 Schnabel, *Acts*, 562.

19   Acts 13:49.
20   Schnabel, *Acts*, 561.
21   See Witherington, *Acts*, 398.
22   Acts 13:2.
23   Bruce, *Acts*, 280. See also Don N. Howell, Jr, "Confidence in the Spirit as the Governing Ethos of the Pauline Mission," in *The Holy Spirit and Mission Dynamics*, ed. C. Douglas McConnell, Evangelical Missiological Series Number 5 (Pasadena, CA: William Carey Library, 1997), 36–65.
24   Rom. 15:23.
25   Rom. 15:19.
26   See Addison, *What Jesus Started*, 121.
27   See Steve Addison and Lyndsey and Collin Seale, "198-Workplace Movements," *Movements*, August 7, 2019, https://www.movements.net/blog/2019/8/8/198-workplace-movements.
28   For more on 3-Thirds discipleship, see Appendix: 3-Thirds Discipleship, page 224.
29   Wikipedia, "Ethnic groups in London," https://en.wikipedia.org/wiki/Ethnic_groups_in_London (accessed November 8, 2022).
30   The Seale's resources are available here: Bit.ly/SealeTeamTraining (accessed September 12, 2022).
31   Schnabel, *Acts*, 430. Luke 24:45–49; Acts 1:8.
32   Schnabel, *Mission*, 423.
33   Twelftree, *People of the Spirit*, loc. 1581, Kindle.
34   Schnabel, *Acts*, 106–7.
35   Luke 24:47.
36   Thompson, *Acts*, 88.
37   Schnabel, *Acts*, 1085.
38   Schnabel, *Acts* 1085.
39   See Peterson, *Acts*, 338; and Witherington, *Acts*, 100.
40   Stein, "Baptism," 6–17.
41   Acts 2:36–47.
42   Schnabel, *Acts*, 1084.
43   Acts 9; 22; 26.
44   Acts 11:19.
45   Acts 9:31–32.
46   Acts 14:21–23.
47   Schnabel, *Acts*, 880.
48   Acts 11:1–18.
49   Schnabel, *Acts*, 655.
50   Schnabel, *Acts*, 654–55.
51   William H. Shepherd, *The Narrative Function of the Holy Spirit as a Character in Luke-Acts*, The Society of Biblical Literature Dissertation Series 147 (Atlanta, GA: Scholar Press, 1994), 218.
52   See Matson, *Household Conversion*, 124, n162.
53   See Steve Addison and Joey Gordy, "281-Joey's Story," *Movements*, August 25, 2022, https://www.movements.net/blog/blog/2022/8/23/281-joeys-story.

54  See "Banjara," Wikipedia, https://en.wikipedia.org/wiki/Banjara (accessed August 30, 2022).

55  See Pierson, "Historical Development."

56  Acts 11:17.

57  Acts 15:7–18.

58  Steve Addison and Stan Parks, "Multiplying Movements Among Unreached People Groups," *Movements*, May 6, 2021, https://www.movements.net/blog/blog/2021/4/27/247-multiplying-movements-among-unreached-people-groups.

## 5   THE GOSPEL GOES TO THE GREEKS (15:35–18:17)

1  Acts 15:35.

2  Paul's letters show the relationship breakdown was not permanent (1 Cor. 9:6; 2 Cor. 8:18–19; Col. 4:10; 2 Tim. 4:11; Philem. 24).

3  See Acts 9:39; 11:25–26; Gal. 1:21. Schnabel, *Acts*, 663.

4  Paul regarded Timothy and Silvanus as cofounders with him of the church in Corinth (2 Cor. 1:19). He credits both men as coauthors of some of his letters. See Paul Barnett, *Paul and His Friends in Leadership: How They Changed the World* (Abingdon, UK: Bible Reading Fellowship, 2017), loc. 549, Kindle.

5  2 Tim. 1:5; 3:15.

6  Acts 14:19.

7  Paul resisted calls for Titus, who was a Gentile, to be circumcised (Gal. 2:3–5).

8  1 Cor. 9:22.

9  Acts 2:47; 16:4–5.

10  It appears Luke stayed based in Philippi, focused on the region of Macedonia for eight years (AD 49–57). Barnett, *Paul and his Friends*, loc. 712–72, Kindle. The "we" passages: from Troas to Philippi (16:10–16); Philippi to Jerusalem (20:6–21:18); and Judea to Rome (27:1–28:16). See Keener, *Acts*, 383.

11  Later Peter writes to the believers in Bithynia (1 Pet. 1:1). Rapidly growing Christian communities are attested by Pliny, the Roman governor writing in the early second century. See Schnabel, *Acts*, 668, n25.

12  See "Deeper: The Difference Teams Make," page 172.

13  Chris tells his story in Chris Clayman, *Superplan: A Journey into God's Story* (Monument, Co.: WIGTake Resources, 2018). See also my interview with Chris, "172–Mali to New York and Back," *Movements*, September 5, 2018, https://www.movements.net/blog/blog/2018/7/18/172-mali-to-new-york-and-back.

14  Holmas, *Prayer*, 228.

15  Schnabel, *Acts*, 673.

16  Longenecker, *Luke-Acts*, loc. 27940, Kindle.

17  A synagogue required at least ten male heads of households.

18  Longenecker, *Luke-Acts*, loc. 27969, Kindle.

19  Matson, *Household Conversion*, 143.

20  According to Schnabel, "Her professional status as a merchant—evidently working on her own initiative and independently of a husband—suggests that she was widowed or divorced." Schnabel, *Acts*, 680.

21  Matson, *Household Conversion*, 147.

22   The python was the symbol of the famous Delphic oracle and represented the god Apollo, who was believed to render predictions of future events. See Polhill, *Acts*, 351.

23   Acts 16:17.

24   Luke 4:33–34; 8:32–37. Keener, *Acts*, 394.

25   This still happens today. This comment came from a missionary in Southeast Asia, "These political attacks are like the attacks on believers in Southeast Asia. The local villagers, relatives, and authorities reframe the accusations as political. There are many people in jail or without homes that I know due to this."

26   Acts 18:2. Keener, *Acts*, 405.

27   Perhaps Paul and Silas claimed citizenship but weren't heard or believed. Or Paul may have wanted to set an example of courage in the face of persecution for the Philippian believers who may not be Roman citizens.

28   Luke 21:12.

29   Acts 4:23–31; 12:5, 12. Holmas, *Prayer*, 233.

30   Acts 16:29–34.

31   Barrett observes that the "household" … could hardly have included infants, "since not only were they all baptized (v. 33), all heard the word of the Lord spoken by Paul and Silas (v. 32) and as a result the whole household rejoiced." Barrett, *Acts*, 797–98. Luke knows that "households were not always converted together, Luke 12:51–53; 14:26; 18:29." Keener, *Acts*, 412.

32   Matson, *Household Conversion*, 163.

33   Keener, *Acts*, 408.

34   Bock, *Acts*, loc. 13350–52, Kindle.

35   Schnabel, *Acts*, 697.

36   Epaphroditus (Phil. 2:25–30; 4: 18), Euodia (4:2), Syntyche (4:2), and Clement (4:3). Schnabel, *Acts*, 695.

37   Eight years later "we" appears again on the next visit to Philippi in AD 57. See Schnabel, *Acts*, 697.

38   Phil. 1:5; 4:15–16. Schnabel, *Acts*, 696.

39   Steve Addison and Don and Theresa Waybright, "288-Don and Theresa's Story," *Movements*, December 6, 2022, https://www.movements.net/blog/blog/2022/11/24/288-don-and-theresas-story. Steve Addison and Rajiv, "291-Mumbai Hilltop of Hope," *Movements*, January 13, 2023, https://www.movements.net/blog/blog/2022/12/2/291-mumbai-hilltop-of-hope.

40   They use the Church Circles tool described on page 26.

41   The women use a form of Discovery Bible Study called the 3-Thirds. For more information on 3-Thirds discipleship, see Appendix: 3-Thirds Discipleship, page 224.

42   See Gene L. Green, *The Letters to the Thessalonians*, Pillar New Testament Commentary (Grand Rapids, MI: Apollos, 2002), 189.

43   Longenecker, *Luke-Acts*, loc. 28261–62, Kindle.

44   Luke 24:31–32, 45. Marshall argues Paul drew on a common tradition going back to Jesus that would include Ps. 2, 16, 110; Isa. 53; and possibly Deut. 21:23. Marshall, *Acts*, 277.

45   Acts 17:5. Marshall, *Acts*, 278.

46   Acts 18:6–7. Matson, *Household Conversion*, 169.

47   1 Thess. 1:1. Peterson, *Acts*, 479.

48    1 Thess. 2:9; 5:12; Phil. 4:16. Schnabel suggests the mission lasted from October to December AD 49. Schnabel, *Acts*, 699.

49    Green argues that pagan Gentiles made up most of the new church as Paul does not address Jewish believers directly in his letter. Green, *Thessalonians*, 195.

50    Likely a reference to Christ. Acts 18:2.

51    1 Thess. 1:6.

52    Acts 20:4; 27:2. It's possible that is the Jason mentioned by Paul in Rom. 16:21.

53    1 Thess. 1:2–10; 3:6–10.

54    1 Thess. 1:8–9. Green, *Thessalonians*, 189.

55    Acts 13:50, 17:4, 12. See Tannehill, *Acts*, 208.

56    Acts 20:4. He could also be the Sosipater mentioned in Rom. 16:21. See Schnabel, *Acts*, 711.

57    Schnabel, *Acts*, 711.

58    Acts 18:5; 1 Thess. 3:1–6. Witherington, *Acts*, 510.

59    Schnabel, *Acts*, 722.

60    Schnabel, *Acts*, 723.

61    Xenophon quoted in Stott, *Acts*, 277.

62    Stott, *Acts*, 279.

63    Acts 26:18.

64    Schnabel, *Acts*, 724.

65    Schnabel notes, "The request to be allowed to introduce a new deity into a city would prompt the magistrates to ascertain the novelty of a cult, the desirability of allowing the cult, and the requirements of the cult, such as the need for a temple, an altar, sacrifices, festivals, priests, and processions." Schnabel, *Acts*, 727.

66    Areopagus means Hill of Ares, the Greek god of war, or Mars Hill the Roman equivalent.

67    See Schnabel, *Early Christian Mission*, 2:1392–1404.

68    Schnabel, *Early Christian Mission*, 2:1394–95.

69    Stott, *Acts*, 284.

70    "His membership in the Areopagus Council implies that he had been an Archon, one of the highest offices in Athens." Schnabel, *Acts*, 744. Regarding Damaris, "The fact that she is mentioned by name may indicate that she played an important role in the church of Athens (or in the churches of Achaia)." Schnabel, *Acts*, 743.

71    Schnabel, *Paul the Missionary*, 168.

72    Schnabel, *Paul the Missionary*, 167–68.

73    I'm following Andreas J. Köstenberger and T. Desmond Alexander, *Salvation to the Ends of the Earth: A Biblical Theology of Mission*, ed. D. A. Carson, 2nd ed., Vol. 53, New Studies in Biblical Theology (Downers Grove, IL: InterVarsity Press, 2020), 162.

74    See Addison, *The Rise and Fall of Movements*, 125–38.

75    1 Cor. 2:3.

76    There was a church planted in Cenchreae, Corinth's harbor about seven miles southeast of the city (Rom. 16:1). According to 2 Cor. 1:1 there were other churches in the province of Achaia besides Corinth. Schnabel, *Acts*, 767.

77    See Schnabel, *Acts*, 756.

78    Acts 18:18–19, 26; 1 Cor. 16:19; Rom. 16:3–5.

79   Acts 18:5; 2 Cor. 11:8–9; Phil. 4:15. See Schnabel, *Acts*, 758.

80   Acts 18:9–10.

81   2 Cor. 1:1.

82   Longenecker, *Acts*, loc. 28892–93, Kindle.

83   Schnabel, *Acts*, 762–64.

84   There is a church in the port city of Cenchreae (Rom. 16:1–2) and there are disciples throughout the province of Achaia in southern Greece (2 Cor. 1:1).

85   2 Cor. 1:1.

86   See Schnabel, *Acts*, 766.

87   Schnabel concludes, the people of "Chloe's household" (1 Cor. 1: 11) were probably slaves or perhaps freedmen; Corinthian believers who had names often attested for slaves were Achaicus, Fortunatus, and Quartus (1 Cor. 16:17; Rom. 16:23), perhaps Tertius, who was a secretary in the household of Gaius (Rom. 16:22) and other slaves (1 Cor. 7:21–22), including the members of the household of Stephanas and Crispus. Schnabel, *Acts*, 766.

88   See Acts18:4–8; Rom. 16:23; 1 Cor. 1:11, 14, 16, 26; 7:18; 16:15–17; 2 Tim. 4:20.

89   A Sosthenes is mentioned in Paul's letter to Corinth (1 Cor. 1:1).

90   1 Cor. 1:4–9. Schnabel, *Acts*, 766.

91   Steve Addison and Troy Cooper, "285-LA Update," *Movements*, October 24, 2022, https://www.movements.net/blog/blog/2022/10/19/285-la-update.

92   The events were organized by Parker and Jessi Green, after the pandemic put an end to indoor gatherings. See Carolyn Cole, "Beach Baptisms Draw Large Gatherings to the Shore," *Los Angeles Times*, August 13, 2020, https://www.latimes.com/california/story/2020-08-13/beach-baptisms-draw-large-gatherings-to-the-shoreline. See also Deepa Bharath, "Hundreds Gather in Huntington Beach to Be Baptized with Cold Dunk in the Ocean," *Orange County Register*, July 25, 2020, https://www.ocregister.com/2020/07/24/hundreds-gather-in-huntington-beach-to-be-baptized-with-cold-dunk-in-the-ocean/.

93   For an explanation of the 411 and the Commands of Christ, see https://www.nplsimpletools.com (accessed November 21, 2022).

94   For more on the Church Circle, see https://www.nplsimpletools.com (accessed November 21, 2022).

95   Troy Cooper used a tool called "The Brutal Facts". See *#NoPlaceLeft Vision*, YouTube, August 27, 2017, https://www.youtube.com/watch?v=rw4tk6xBZE4.

96   See Luke 10:1–11. For more on the person of peace, see "Deeper: Household Conversions," page 93.

97   Watch Troy Cooper unpack the 4-Fields strategy: https://www.movements.net/4fields (accessed January 2, 2023).

98   Find out more about each of these tools at https://www.nplsimpletools.com (accessed November 21, 2022).

## 6   THE WORD REACHES ASIA MINOR (18:18–20:38)

1   Rom. 16:1; 2 Cor. 1:1.

2   Acts 19:10.

3   1 Cor. 16:19.

4   The distance was 335 miles (540 km) and would have taken around three weeks. Schnabel, *Acts*, 769.

5    Tannehill, *Acts*, 230.

6    Schnabel, *Acts*, 783.

7    See Acts 13–14. This is the third time Paul has visited these cities to either plant or strengthen the churches. See Acts 14:21–28; 15:36; 16:1–6. When the work is finished in Ephesus, he will visit the churches founded during the second journey.

8    "Luke normally mentions first the dominant member of a pair, so Priscilla probably takes the lead in instructing Apollos here." Keener, *Acts*, 469. See also Schnabel, *Acts*, 786.

9    1 Cor. 1–4.

10   1 Cor. 16:19.

11   Luke 8:1–3.

12   Luke 10:1–7.

13   John 12:6; 13:29.

14   Luke 18:18–30.

15   Luke 8:14.

16   Luke 6:38; 11:1–13.

17   Acts 3:6.

18   2 Cor. 2:17.

19   Acts 20:34; 2 Cor. 11:7; 1 Cor. 4:9, 12; 9:19.

20   2 Cor. 11:8–9; Phil. 4:15–16. Schnabel, *Acts*, 851.

21   1 Cor. 9:4–12. Schnabel, *Acts*, 851.

22   1 Cor. 4:12; 9:15–18; 1 Thess. 2:9; 2 Thess. 3:6–10. Schnabel, *Acts*, 851.

23   Acts 18:3–5; 2 Cor. 11:9 and Phil. 4:14–15.

24   Acts 8:17–24; Matt. 6:24.

25   Acts 1:8; 2:1–12.

26   Acts 18:1–3; 20:34.

27   Priscilla and Aquila supported themselves (18:1–3).

28   Acts 28:10.

29   When Silas and Timothy came from the churches in Macedonia, Paul devoted himself exclusively to preaching. It's possible they brought a gift from the churches that enabled Paul to cease working his trade (18:5). See also Acts 24:23; 27:3.

30   Acts 9:43; 10:48; 12:12; 16:15, 34, 40; 20:20; 21:8, 16.

31   Luke 10:1–11.

32   See "Deeper: Household Conversions," page 93.

33   Tannehill, *Acts*, 398.

34   Acts 16:6.

35   Andreas J. Köstenberger and Peter T. O'Brien, *Salvation to the Ends of the Earth: A Biblical Theology of Mission*, Vol. 11, eds. D. A. Carson, New Studies in Biblical Theology (Downers Grove, IL: IVP Academic, 2001), 152.

36   Luke tells us the Spirit is given when Paul placed his hands on them (19:6). The Spirit was given when Peter and John placed their hands upon the Samaritans (8:17). This is not to say that the giving of the Spirit requires apostolic authority, as Paul receives the Spirit when the disciple Ananias lays his hands on him (9:17). Bruce concludes that, "if Luke held that the laying on of apostolic hands was an indispensable prerequisite for the receiving of the Spirit (as some have precariously inferred from 8:16), it is remarkable that he has nothing to say about it in this Pentecostal narrative." Bruce, *Acts*, 71.

37  Schnabel writes, "The 'kingdom of God' is the reality of the fulfillment of God's promises concerning Israel's restoration and the salvation of the world—a reality brought about by the life, death, resurrection, and exaltation of Jesus, Israel's Messiah and Savior of the world, and a reality that grows as a result of the Spirit-empowered work of the apostles and the churches." Schnabel, *Acts*, 790.

38  Later Paul identified at least one church in Ephesus that met in the home of Aquila and Priscilla. 1 Cor. 16:19.

39  Witherington, *Acts*, 574–75.

40  Enough to pay the wages of a workman (with no days off) for 137 years. Schnabel, *Acts*, 799.

41  As indicated by the value of the books burned. See Schnabel, *Acts*, 799.

42  Acts 26:17–18.

43  1 Cor. 16:8–9.

44  Acts 19:20.

45  Acts 19:10.

46  Arthur G. Patzia, *The Emergence of the Church* (Downers Grove, IL: InterVarsity Press, 2001), map 4.

47  Col. 1:3–8; 2:1; 4:13.

48  Rev. 2–3.

49  Schnabel writes, "During his mission to Ephesus his coworkers included Epaphras (Colossians 1:3–8; 4:13), Philemon (Philemon 1–2), Aristarchus from Macedonia (Acts 19:29; 20:4; 27:2; Philemon 23), Gaius from Corinth (Acts 19:29; 1 Corinthians 1:14), and Tychicus and Trophimus (Acts 20:4; Colossians 4:7). Aquila and Priscilla were with Paul from the beginning of his mission in Ephesus (1 Corinthians 16:10). Stephanas, Fortunatus and Archaicus visited him (1 Corinthians 1:17)." Schnabel, *Acts*, 794.

50  When Paul wrote 1 Corinthians, Apollos was with him in Ephesus. According to 1 Cor. 16:12 and Titus 3:13, Apollos remained associated with Paul as a coworker in his later ministry. See Polhill, *Acts*, 398.

51  Schnabel, *Acts*, 800.

52  1 Cor. 16:17.

53  Revisiting earlier churches (here in Macedonia and Achaia) fit the pattern of Paul's ministry elsewhere, both in Acts (14:21–23; 15:36; 16:4–5) and in Paul's letters (1 Cor. 4:18–21; 16:3–7; 2 Cor. 12:20–13:2; 1 Thess. 2:17–18; 3:1, 5, 10–11). Paul planned to then visit Jerusalem (Rom. 15:25; 2 Cor. 1:16) and after that Rome (Rom. 1:11, 13; 15:23–25, 31–32; 2 Cor. 10:16). See Keener, *Acts*, 478.

54  1 Cor. 15:32; 16:8.

55  Larkin, *Acts*, 282.

56  Longenecker, *Luke-Acts*, 486.

57  Barnett, *Paul*, xvi.

58  Rom. 15:18–24.

59  Bridges Church is now known as Neighbors and Nations Church. Find out more at neighborsandnations.org. See also Steve Addison and Jeff Timblin, "205-One Pastor Is Bringing Movements Home," *Movements*, November 28, 2019, https://www.movements.net/blog/blog/2019/11/21/bringing-movements-home.

60  For more on NoPlaceLeft, visit https://noplaceleft.net (accessed February 26, 2023).

61  Acts 13:1–4. For this section see Addison, *What Jesus Started*, 150–58.

62 Paul knows he has an apostolic right to be supported by the churches (1 Cor. 9:3–12) but refuses financial support when it compromises the spread of the gospel. Schutz points out "Paul refuses to invoke an authority which is rightfully his in order to submit himself to a greater authority, the demand of the gospel." John Howard Schutz, *Paul and the Anatomy of Apostolic Authority* (Louisville, KY: Westminster John Knox, 2007), 235.

63 In this section I am following Schnabel, *Early Christian Mission*, 2:1425–45. See also Ellis, "Paul and His Coworkers."

64 See Meeks, *The First Urban Christians*, 59.

65 Acts 18:18–19; 1 Cor. 16:19.

66 Rom. 16:3–5.

67 Col. 1:3–8; 4:13.

68 Acts 19:29.

69 Schnabel estimates 18 percent of Paul's fellow missionaries were women. Schnabel, *Early Christian Mission*, 2:1428.

70 Rom. 16:7. The text is disputed. The weight of evidence favors "Junia" as a woman who served as a pioneering missionary with her husband. For a discussion see Stephen B. Addison, "The Continuing Ministry of the Apostle in the Church's Mission," (D.Min. diss., Fuller Theological Seminary, 1995), 109–11.

71 Rom. 16:12.

72 Phil 4:2–3. See Schnabel, *Early Christian Mission*, 2:1428. Following Walter L. Liefeld, "Women and Evangelism in the Early Church," *Missiology* 15, no. 3 (July 1987): 291–98.

73 See Hans Kung, *The Church* (Garden City, NY: Image, 1967), 493–94.

74 Steve Addison and Jeff Bennett, "275-Church to Movement in Canada," *Movements*, June 2, 2022, https://www.movements.net/blog/blog/2022/5/31/275-church-to-movement-in-canada.

75 A church start is an attempt but still on the way. A new church is more established.

76 According to Longenecker, it was probably during this time that the gospel entered the province of Illyricum in the northwestern corner of the Balkan peninsula. See Rom. 15:19; see also 2 Tim. 4:10, where Titus is mentioned as returning to Dalmatia, the southern district of the province of Illyricum. Longenecker, *Luke-Acts*, loc. 29583–85, Kindle.

77 Longenecker, *Luke-Acts*, loc. 29583–85, Kindle.

78 Rom. 15:23.

79 Witherington, *Acts*, 628. Following Tannehill, *Acts*, 266–67.

80 Schnabel, *Acts*, 819.

81 Longenecker, *Luke-Acts*, loc. 29583–85, Kindle.

82 Keener, *Acts*, 500.

83 That could be a Saturday or Sunday night, depending on whether they were following Jewish or Roman reckoning. Schnabel, *Acts*, 835.

84 Bock, *Acts*, loc. 15139–41, Kindle.

85 Luke 22:19–20; Acts 2:42, 46; 20:11; 1 Cor. 10:16; 11:24.

86 Stott, *Acts*, 321.

87 Acts 2:42. Schnabel, *Acts*, 828.

88 Acts 20:7–12, 17–38.

89 Acts 20:7, 11.

90 Acts 20:7–12, 36; 21:5.

91 Acts 21:7.

92 Acts 20:34–35.

93   Acts 20:23; 21:4, 11.

94   Schnabel, *Acts*, 860.

95   Steve Addison and Jim McKnight, "284-NoPlaceLeft Army," *Movements*, October 6, 2022, https://www.movements.net/blog/blog/2022/9/23/284-noplaceleft-army. See also Steve Addison and John and Lauren Sweatte, "286-John and Lauren's Story," *Movements*, November 4, 2022, https://www.movements.net/blog/blog/2022/11/4/286-john-and-laurens-story.

96   For a copy of the Commands of Christ, visit https://www.nplsimpletools.com (accessed December 15, 2022).

97   Schnabel, *Acts*, 4.

98   Peterson, *Acts*, 523.

99   Schnabel, *Acts*, 838.

100  Schnabel, *Acts*, 828–29. See also Steve Walton, *Leadership and Lifestyle: The Portrait of Paul in the Miletus Speech and 1 Thessalonians*, Vol. 108, Society for New Testament Studies (Cambridge, UK: Cambridge University Press, 2000).

101  Acts 20:21.

102  Acts 20:24–25, 27.

103  Acts 20:25. The same message of the kingdom is preached and taught by Paul (Acts 19:8; 28:23, 31), Jesus (Luke 4:43; 8:1; 9:11; Acts 1:3), the Twelve (Luke 8:10), and the Jerusalem church (Acts 8:12). See Schnabel, *Acts*, 843.

104  Peterson, *Acts*, 565.

105  Acts 20:28. See Peterson, *Acts*, 568.

106  Acts 14:23. They are "elders," suggesting maturity, experience, and wisdom. "Overseer" implies managing and leading the activities of a group and guarding the group. The plural use of elders and overseers shows plural leadership. See "Deeper: Local Leaders," page 184.

107  Beverly Roberts Gaventa, "Theology and Ecclesiology in the Miletus Speech: Reflections on Content and Context," *New Testament Studies* 50 (2004): 36.

108  Acts 20:29–31.

109  Acts 20:28, 32.

110  Acts 20:4 lists Sopater, son of Pyrrhus from Berea; Aristarchus and Secundus from Thessalonica; Gaius from Derbe; Timothy, Tychicus and Trophimus from Asia Minor.

111  Beverly Roberts Gaventa, *The Acts of the Apostles*, Abingdon New Testament Commentaries (Nashville, TN: Abingdon Press, 2003), 290.

112  Acts 21:1.

113  Acts 6:1–6.

114  Acts 9:31.

115  Acts 21:8. James, the Lord's brother, was leader of the Jerusalem church from AD 41 to 62, when the Jewish historian Josephus records that the high priest had him stoned to death.

116  Acts 19:10; 1 Cor. 16:19.

117  Schnabel, *Acts*, 846.

## 7   TRIALS AND TRIUMPH (21:1–28:31)

1    Witherington, *Acts*, 629.

2    Acts 20:22–23.

3    Acts 21:4.

4    Acts 21:10–11.

5    Compare Luke 9:51 and Acts 21:13.

6    Acts 21:14.

7    Schnabel, *Acts*, 859.

8    Rom. 15:23–32.

9    Following Gaventa, "Miletus Speech," 51–52.

10   Acts 8:1–4; 11:19.

11   Schnabel observes, since Jesus had spent time in the region of Tyre, it's possible that some of these disciples had been followers of Jesus. Schnabel, *Acts*, 854. See Matt. 15:21; Mark 3:8, 7:24; Luke 6:17.

12   Acts 9:5, 15–16.

13   Tannehill, *Acts*, 266.

14   Squires, *Plan of God*, 153.

15   Acts 5:1–11.

16   Acts 9:10.

17   Acts 13:1–3.

18   Acts 15:32.

19   Acts 18:9–10.

20   Acts 19:6.

21   Acts 11:28; 21:10–14.

22   Acts 20:18–30.

23   Acts 27:21–26.

24   1 Cor. 14:29. Witherington, *Acts*, 630–31.

25   Compare Acts 21:10–11 and 22:27–36.

26   Menzies, "Acts 2:17–21," 201.

27   Menzies, "Acts 2:17–21," 217.

28   Acts 11:27; 13:1; 15:32; 21:9. See Peterson, *Acts*, 63, n35.

29   E. Earle Ellis, "The Role of the Christian Prophet in Acts," in *Apostolic History and the Gospel: Biblical and Historical Essays Presented to F. F. Bruce*, eds. W. Ward Gasque and Ralph P. Martin (Milton Keynes, UK: Paternoster, 1970), 67.

30   Acts 2:14–40; 15:13–21.

31   Ellis, "The Role of the Christian Prophet," 62.

32   Ellis, "The Role of the Christian Prophet," 63.

33   Ellis, "The Role of the Christian Prophet," 64. For instance, he doesn't define or make a clear distinction between the ministry of teacher and that of a prophet. When Peter preaches at Pentecost, is he speaking as an evangelist, a teacher, or a prophet—or all three? (Acts 2:14–41).

34   Acts 3:22. Ellis, "The Role of the Christian Prophet," 67.

35   Acts 8:18–24. Note the parallel with Paul's confrontation of Elymas on Cyprus (Acts 14:6–12).

36   Menzies, "Acts 2:17–21," 5.

37   Acts 12:16–17.

38   1 Cor. 16:1–4; 2 Cor 8:1–9:15; Rom. 15:14–32. Writing years later, Luke focuses on Paul's arrest and imprisonment rather than the collection.

39   Polhill, *Acts*, 447.

40   Schnabel, *Acts*, 877.

41   Polhill, *Acts*, 449.

42   Polhill, *Acts*, 449.

43   Marshall, *Acts*, 344.

44   Bock, *Acts*, loc. 15890–91, Kindle.

45   Luke 21:6. Bruce, *Acts*, 410.

46   Peterson, *Acts*, 591.

47   The same words they screamed at Jesus (Luke 23:18; John 19:15).

48   According to Marshall, "The revolutionary to whom Lysias was referring was described by
      Josephus as 'an Egyptian false prophet' who, about three years previously, had got together
      30,000 men (Josephus was prone to exaggeration!), led them to the Mount of Olives, and
      promised them that, when the walls of Jerusalem fell flat at his command, they would be
      able to break into the city and overpower the Romans. But the procurator Felix and his
      troops intervened, and the *sikarioi* ('dagger men', i.e. fanatical nationalist assassins) were
      killed, captured or scattered." Marshall, *Acts*, 346–47.

49   He may have spoken Hebrew or the more common, but related, language of Aramaic.

50   They weren't against Gentiles converting to Judaism and living under the law, but the
      notion that Gentiles can be saved apart from the law. Marshall, *Acts*, 348.

51   Schnabel, *Acts*, 924.

52   Bruce, *Acts*, 419.

53   "Ananias, the son of Nedebaeus, reigned as high priest from AD 48 to 58 or 59 and was
      known for his avarice and liberal use of violence. Josephus … says that he confiscated for
      himself the tithes given to the ordinary priests and gave lavish bribes to Roman and Jewish
      officials." Longenecker, *Acts*, loc. 30458–60, Kindle.

54   Acts 23:2–3.

55   Matt. 23:27; John 18:21–23. Jesus had denounced Herod as a fox and the Pharisees and
      scribes as whitewashed tombs. Luke 11:37–44; 13:32.

56   Acts 7:51–53, 60.

57   Peterson, *Acts*, 613.

58   Witherington, *Acts*, 685.

59   Peterson, *Acts*, 617.

60   See Acts 18:9–10; 22:17–21.

61   Acts 26:16–18.

62   Peterson, *Acts*, 620.

63   Schnabel, *Acts*, 933.

64   Keener, *Acts*, 549.

65   Longenecker, *Acts*, loc. 30776–77, Kindle.

66   Schnabel, *Acts*, 954–55.

67   Schnabel, *Acts*, 959. Peterson comments that by "claiming to be the Way, the earliest Jewish
      disciples were insisting that they were the true Israel, experiencing the promised blessings
      of the messianic era through faith in Jesus rather than being one of several groups within
      the people of God." Peterson, *Acts*, 635.

68   Schnabel, *Acts*, 964.

69   Acts 27:1.

70   Schnabel, *Acts*, 965.

71  This followed an incident in Caesarea where the Jews had claimed that Caesarea belonged to them, while the Greeks used the (pagan) temples that Herod had erected as proof that Caesarea was not a Jewish city. Felix ended the ensuing riots in the agora by sending in his troops, who killed many Jews, and Felix subsequently plundered their property. Both the Jewish and Greek communities of Caesarea sent their leaders to Rome. Felix was spared serious punishment by the emperor Nero only because Felix's influential brother Pallas pleaded for him. See Schnabel, *Acts*, 968.

72  According to Keener, "Before the fire of 64 CE, however, Nero was not persecuting Christians, and at the time of Paul's appeal (c. 59 CE), some positive influences on Nero remain." Keener, *Acts*, 575.

73  On Herod and his descendants see Richard Belward Rackham, *The Acts of the Apostles: An Exposition*, 8th ed., Westminster Commentaries (London, UK: Methuen & Co., 1919), 457.

74  Schnabel, *Acts*, 998.

75  Schnabel, *Acts*, 1002.

76  Witherington, *Acts*, 732.

77  Luke 21:12–13; Acts 9:15.

78  Keener, *Acts*, 581.

79  Tannehill, *Acts*, 314.

80  Acts 1:1. Schnabel, *Acts*, 1009.

81  Acts 26:16–18. See Schnabel, *Acts*, 1010–12.

82  Luke 21:12–15.

83  Acts 19:21; 23:11; 27:24.

84  Ps. 2; Acts 4:23–31.

85  Schreiner, *Mission*, 83.

86  Acts 18:14–16.

87  Acts 19:38.

88  Acts 24:27; 25:25; 26:31–32.

89  Acts 4:8–10, 18–20, 24–31; 12:1–4.

90  Acts 4:5–21; 5:17–42; 7:54–60; 25:8, 23; 26:1–29.

91  Acts 4:18–20; 12:21–24.

92  Acts 18:14–16; 19:35–41; 21:30–32; 23:23–24; 24:23; 25:12; 27:3, 42–43.

93  Acts 16:35–40; 22:24–29; 23:3; 23:23–24; 25:10–11.

94  Acts 13:12; 21:40–22:21; 24:24–25.

95  Acts 2:38; 25:8; 26:28–31.

96  Thomas Alan Harvey, *Acquainted with Grief: Wang Mingdao's Stand for the Persecuted Church in China* (Grand Rapids, MI: Brazos Press, 2002), 93. See also John Gill, "Wang Ming-Dao (1900–1991): Faithful amid Political Coercion," *The Gospel Coalition*, August 3, 2018, https://www.thegospelcoalition.org/article/wang-ming-dao-faithful-political-coercion.

97  The passage God gave him was Mic. 7:7–9a.

98  Harvey, *Acquainted with Grief*, 116.

99  Rodney Stark and Xiuhua Wang, *A Star in the East: The Rise of Christianity in China* (West Conshohocken, PA: Templeton Press, 2015), 65.

100  Xi Lian, *Redeemed by Fire: The Rise of Popular Christianity in Modern China* (New Haven CT: Yale University Press, 2010), loc. 4276, Kindle.

101  In 2010, the Pew Research Center calculated sixty-eight million Christians in China, or

approximately 5 percent of the country's population. Other independent estimates suggest somewhere between 100 and 130 million. See Eleanor Albert, "Christianity in China," *Council on Foreign Relations*, October 11, 2018, https://www.cfr.org/backgrounder/christianity-china.

102   Schnabel, *Acts*, 1022.

103   Thomas Walker, *The Acts of the Apostles* (Chicago, IL: Moody, 1910), 543, quoted in Stott, *Acts*, 385.

104   Keener, *Acts*, 593.

105   Col. 4:10; Philem. 24. Assuming Colossians and Philemon were written from Rome, which is likely.

106   Schnabel, *Acts*, 1034.

107   Schnabel, *Acts*, 993.

108   Keener, *Acts*, 610.

109   Keener, *Acts*, 610.

110   Acts 8:3–4, 11:19.

111   Schnabel observes, "The term *mare clausum* ("closed sea") denotes the closure of navigation between November 11 and March 5 because of winter storms, fog, and overcast skies, which made navigation (by the sun and stars) nearly impossible." Schnabel, *Acts*, 1036–37.

112   Schnabel, *Acts*, 1040.

113   Peterson, *Acts*, 680.

114   Steve Addison, "282-Making Disciples in Ukraine," *Movements*, September 9, 2002, https://www.movements.net/blog/blog/2022/9/9/282-making-disciples-in-ukraine.

115   For more on Discovery Bible Studies, see Appendix: Discovery Bible Study, page 225.

116   C. S. Lewis, *The Problem of Pain* (New York, NY: HarperCollins, 1940), 91.

117   House, "Suffering," 320–21.

118   Acts 9:15–16.

119   Acts 20:23.

120   House, "Suffering," 322–23.

121   Phil. 3:10.

122   House, "Suffering," 326.

123   Luke 6:43–45.

124   *Barbaros* (barbarian) originally meant someone who didn't speak Greek. It came to mean foreigners beyond Greco-Roman civilization. See Schreiner, *Mission*, 111.

125   Acts 13:7; 16:22; 17:19; 18:12; 19:31. Bock, *Acts*, loc.18043, Kindle.

126   Luke 4:38–40.

127   Schreiner, *Mission*, 112.

128   The distance was 130 miles or 209 kilometers.

129   Rom. 16:3–15.

130   Rom. 1:11–15; 15:23–29.

131   Rom. 15:25–29.

132   Brian Rapske, *The Book of Acts and Paul in Roman Custody*, Vol. 3, The Book of Acts in Its First Century Setting (Grand Rapids, MI: Eerdmans, 2004), 234.

133   Keener, *Acts*, 633.

134   Keener, *Acts*, 624.

135 Isa. 6:9–10; Luke 8:10–15.

136 Peterson, *Acts*, 716.

137 Rom. 11:25–32.

138 Luke 2:34.

139 It is most likely that Ephesians, Philippians, Philemon, and Colossians were written from Rome. They indicate Luke and Aristarchus's presence. See Phil. 1:1; Eph. 6:21; Col. 4:14; Philem. 24.

140 Rome is the traditional location for the writing of this letter. See Gerald F. Hawthorne, *Philippians*, Vol. 43, Word Biblical Commentary (Waco, TX: Word Books, 1983), xxxvi–xliv.

141 Phil. 1:13; 4:22. The soldiers of the Praetorian Guard—the emperor's personal bodyguards—had sixteen cohorts of a thousand men. Their role was to protect the emperor and his family, and to discourage and suppress plots and disturbances. They were at the very heart of the Roman Empire. Over the two years, many of these legionnaires would have heard the gospel from Paul, and some passed it on to their comrades. Paul also mentions there were believers in "the emperor's household" (Phil. 4:22). The household of a Roman aristocrat included his family, servants, slaves, and freedmen. Often their duties were specialized, such as domestic servants and professionals providing medical, commercial, and secretarial help. Caesar's household was equivalent to a modern civil service based in Rome but also in households scattered throughout the provinces. Members of Caesar's household were powerful and socially mobile, despite being slaves and former slaves. See Steve Addison, *What Jesus Started*, 130–31, 158–59.

142 Phil. 1:12–14.

143 Phil. 1:15–22.

144 Bruce, *Acts*, 511.

145 In the original Greek, the last four words of Acts are "with all boldness unhindered" (Acts 28:31). See Twelftree, *People of the Spirit,* loc. 2095, Kindle.

146 Keener, *Acts*, 634.

147 Polhill, *Acts*, 546.

148 Peterson, *Acts*, 722. References to the kingdom of God in Acts: Acts 1:3; 8:12; 14:22; 19:8; 20:25; 28:23.

149 According to Witherington, "Acts is some sort of historical work, meant to chronicle not the life and death of Paul but the rise and spread of the gospel and of the social and religious movement to which the gospel gave birth." Witherington, *Acts*, 809.

150 Two Roman governors and one Jewish king agreed: Paul was not guilty of any offense under Roman law. His accusers brought charges related to Jewish law and beliefs, not Roman law. If it wasn't for Paul's appeal to Caesar, Paul could have been released.

When Paul arrived in Rome, the leaders of the synagogues had received no communication about the matter. The authorities in Jerusalem would have enlisted the support of the leaders in Rome if they had decided to press charges before the emperor. Therefore, there are good reasons to think that Paul's case was dismissed due to lack of evidence and lack of accusers to pursue the matter.

Early Christian tradition indicates that Paul was released and had another period of public ministry—reaching "the limits of the West" (1 Clement 5:5–7)—before being re-arrested, tried, and condemned to death by beheading around AD 66. See Witherington, *Acts*, 791,

792. Schnabel concludes, "It appears that Paul was released after two years of imprisonment in Rome, engaged in missionary work in Spain, and returned to the east, spending time on Crete (Titus 1:5), in Nicopolis in the province of Epirus (Titus 3:12), in Macedonia (1 Tim. 1:3), and in Troas in the province of Asia (2 Tim. 4:13)." Schnabel, *Acts*, 845. See also Schnabel, *Early Christian Mission*, 2:1270–87. See Peterson, *Acts*, 721 and Keener, *Acts*, 630–32.

## APPENDIX

1   See Nathan and Kari Shank, "The Four Fields: A Manual for Church Planting Facilitation," 2015, https://www.movements.net/4fields (accessed February 27, 2023).

2   The 5-Levels of Leadership tool was developed by Nathan Shank. See Shank and Shank, "Four Fields," 100–120.

3   Addison, *Pioneering Movements*, 95–108.

# ACKNOWLEDGMENTS

Thanks to the readers who provided input into the early manuscript: Ryan Alberson, David Brookryk, Jared Houk, Tony Lasavath, Janet Maxim, Aaron Pribanic, Emanuel Prinz, Buck Rogers, Bill Smith, Angie Sundell, and Gretta Svendsen.

Thanks to my editor, Anna Robinson, who with input from Jonathan King helped make this a book I'm proud to put my name on.

Finally, thanks to the love of my life, Michelle, who has to put up with most conversations eventually turning to the topic of movements!

# ALSO BY STEVE ADDISON

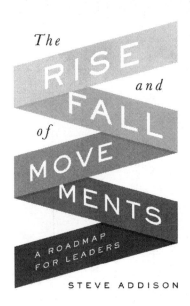

*With a sensitivity to history and an ability to extract principles from the lives of the apostolic pioneers who have gone before us, Steve gives us an inspirational peek into movements and the people who lead them.*
**ALAN HIRSCH**

# ABOUT THE AUTHOR

**STEVE ADDISON** is a catalyst for movements that multiply disciples and churches everywhere. He is a missions leader, author, speaker, podcaster and mentor to pioneers.

Steve is married to Michelle. They live in Melbourne, Australia and have four children, three grandchildren, and a dog named Jasper.

# DISCOVER MORE

Access articles, video and podcast interviews, and training resources here:
**movements.net**

Made in the USA
Columbia, SC
24 February 2024